Spirits in Spacesuits

A Manual for Everyday Mystics

Seán ÓLaoire Ph.D.

National Library of Canada Cataloguing in Publication Data

ÓLaoire, Seán, 1946-
   Spirits in spacesuits : a manual for everyday mystics / Seán ÓLaoire.

Includes index.
ISBN 1-55395-505-6

   I. Title.

BV5082.3.O26 2003   248.2'2   C2002-905981-X

 *Printed in Victoria, Canada*

This book was published *on-demand* in cooperation with Trafford Publishing.
On-demand publishing is a unique process and service of making a book available for retail sale to the public taking advantage of on-demand manufacturing and Internet marketing.
On-demand publishing includes promotions, retail sales, manufacturing, order fulfilment, accounting and collecting royalties on behalf of the author.

Suite 6E, 2333 Government St., Victoria, B.C. V8T 4P4, CANADA
Phone   250-383-6864   Toll-free   1-888-232-4444 (Canada & US)
Fax   250-383-6804   E-mail   sales@trafford.com
Web site   www.trafford.com   TRAFFORD PUBLISHING IS A DIVISION OF TRAFFORD HOLDINGS LTD.
Trafford Catalogue #02-1220   www.trafford.com/robots/02-1220.html

10   9   8   7   6   5   4

FOREWORD

The missing element in many quests is the spiritual guide. The Kingdom of Heaven lies within and without us it is true, but in most cases, only by the intervention of an enlightened spiritual guide do we seem able to translate this into actuality for ourselves.

Father Seán ÓLaoire, through his unique homilies, leads his congregation to the threshold of deeper truths that lie beneath the Hebrew Scriptures, the Gospels of Jesus, the teachings of Buddhism, Hinduism, Islam, Taoism and all other traditions that echo the way to complete alignment with God.

As the spiritual guide for The Companions on the Journey, a group of spiritual seekers in Palo Alto, California, Father Seán brings new light and understanding to all scriptures making the essence of their message come alive with clarity and honesty.

In keeping with the ancient oral traditions of the early churches, temples and synagogues, repetition of themes is used as a tool to teach as well as to aid in the enjoyment of learning. The reader will find this commonality of themes useful to better understand the essence of the scriptures. It is the essence of the scriptures that is of greatest importance.

It has been my privilege to transcribe these great homilies. I have done so in order to help spread the good news of these homilies to all spiritual seekers far and wide.

May you discover the beauty of your divine spirit within your spacesuit.

Mary Burns

INTRODUCTION

I come from a story-telling culture. My grandfather, "Daddy Jim," was a "Seanachaí" (the traditional Irish storyteller). I spent 14 years living in East Africa, among story-telling peoples. My greatest hero, Jesus of Nazareth, was a storyteller. Understandably, I wanted to become a storyteller myself.

This book is a collection of stories, fleshed out into mystical theology. It doesn't read like a book of written teachings, because it wasn't composed in written form. It is the transcripts of oral presentations to very-much-alive audiences, the members of the Companions on the Journey, a spiritual community based in Palo Alto, California.

The book retains that storyteller quality, though the more annoying mannerisms of which the ear, but not the eye is so forgiving have been edited out. There is some repetition both within and among the homilies. This is done purposefully. I believe that a good story should be at once an entertaining and a learning event. If all a person wants is entertainment, then the movies are a better choice. If all a person wants is learning, then feel free to buy an unabridged dictionary. The reason Jesus was perceived as preaching "Good News" was that his stories were both good (appealing and entertaining) and new (involved learning and discovering). For the main part, homilies and sermons tend to be neither good nor new, but simply boring and reheated leftovers. Instead of Good News we got mostly Old Hat.

An essential part of learning is repetition. Sometimes, this needs to be done formulaic-ly, using the same words or phrases exactly (like a mantra). At other times, employing new images, metaphors and stories for the same concept, idea or experience best does it. I mix these two techniques both within a particular homily and among the homilies.

My single greatest intention, however, is not to entertain, not to teach new concepts, not to moralize, but to challenge people into having their own personal encounters with the transcendent. Wisdom traditions, East and West, once their advanced-soul founders die, inevitably reduce spirituality to religion, and then, reduce religion to morality. I am not interested in trying to make people "good," but in encouraging them to become mystics.

Morality is to mysticism what the alphabet is to Shakespeare. The churches keep drumming the alphabet into us; they don't seem to experientially know anything beyond that. For the person, however, who discovers Shakespeare, the alphabet (together with grammar, vocabulary and pronunciation) will take care of itself.

May you discover the mystic within you!

Seán ÓLaoire

ACKNOWLEDGEMENTS

In Kenya, maize-planting is a four-person operation: the first person pokes holes in the soil with a stick; the second person drops two maize seeds into each hole; the third person adds a spoon of powdered fertilizer; and the fourth person covers it all up again.

This book happened in the same fashion –after many false starts! Over the last 15 years, several different people attempted to tape-record homilies which I gave three times a week. Poor equipment (little hand-held devices), in poor locations (50 or 60 feet away from the speaker on the person's lap) ensured poor quality.

Mike Choy changed all of that. With singular dedication, good equipment and lots of know-how, he has been lovingly and quietly recording all of the Sunday homilies since October 18, 1998. Mike is the "hole-poker." I am the "seed-dropper."

Then along came Mary Burns, a vital, energetic personality. With her husband, Bob, she has long been a spiritual traveler, having spent time with Thich Nhat Hahn and with Sai Baba. Mary undertook the gargantuan task of transcribing these tapes.

Mary is, easily, the single greatest reason why this book is being offered for publication. She is the "fertilizer-adder."

Margaret Park was Mary's right hand. Margaret, whom I have known since I came to Palo Alto in 1987, helped Mary with the editing. As the wife of a diplomat, she has lived all over the world – so, perhaps, neither my accent nor ideas were strange to her. Margaret is the "coverer-upper."

It's a great team.

Seán ÓLaoire

INDEX

1
Epiphany

Occasionally I'll see one on his own and it normally is a male. About two years ago when I was trekking down through the middle of Pena Creek in waist-high water, I came across 15 of them. Mothers and children splashing and bathing in the waters, and they ran when they saw me coming. Last February I had the most interesting experience. I was sitting on a log in the middle of the forest. I had taken off my backpack and was about to start writing when 40 of them passed me in a single row going along the edge of the mountain on the other side of the creek. I'm talking about the wild pigs of West Dry Creek in the mountains near Healdsburg, California.

There are two mother pigs and seven little piglets that constantly come around the cabin. We use propane gas for cooking and it's piped into the cabin from a tank beside the cabin. During the autumn the apple trees behind the cabin drop their fruit and the apples roll down the hill, underneath the cabin and around the gas pipes. The pigs disturb me at all hours of the night looking for the apples and banging against the pipes and I'm afraid they'll puncture the pipes and I will die of gas poisoning.

One night, about four months ago, I watched the same two mothers and seven little ones. They discovered a plastic gallon container of fish paste fertilizer. They sank their teeth into it squirting paste everywhere and were drinking at it like it was Christmas. All nine of them were furiously, biting, kicking and stomping in it until finally they licked up the last vestiges of fish paste fertilizer. There was a stink of fish paste around the cabin for about three weeks.

The climax came about two months ago. There's a little level area in front of the cabin and I set out little pods of daffodil bulbs, six-per-pod. I set out about 100 bulbs in these pods. About two weeks later, in the middle of the day, the pigs come back, all nine of them. They rooted up all of the daffodil bulbs by walking with their snouts down into the ground about four inches and plowed like little tractors creating waves of dirt in front of them. They must not have liked the taste because they didn't eat them. They just rooted them up as they were ferreting about for something else. I chased them off and I tried my best to cover up the bulbs but the pigs were back the next day doing the same thing. I chased them off and once again covered up the bulbs. When I returned to my cabin the next week, they had uncovered them again. This game went on for about four or five weeks. Finally, I gave up. One morning when I stepped outside the cabin to have a look I saw a tiny little sprout. One of the daffodils was beginning to sprout through the soil. I understood what Epiphany means.

Epiphany is an incarnation of God's power. I saw it. I realized that Epiphany is not just about Jesus being born 2000 years ago and three astrologers coming from the East to witness the fact. Epiphany happens over and over again. Epiphany happens with every baby born into the world. Epiphany happens when little daffodil bulbs that have been uprooted many times manage somehow to survive.

I want to talk about Epiphany. Today is the Feast of the Epiphany. I want to make three main points about it. Firstly, I want to talk about the problems of the story of Epiphany and the story of Christmas if we take it as literal fact instead of deep symbolic truth. There is a big difference between literal fact and deep symbolic truth. I want to look at what happens if we accept the Christmas story and the Epiphany story as literal truth. Secondly, I want to talk about what I consider to be the real meaning of Christmas and the real meaning of Epiphany. Thirdly, as a result of Epiphany, I want to ask myself the question: What is the greatest kind of love?

First I want to point out some of the problems. There is a beautiful story in the gospel of Matthew in Chapter 2, but there are problems with it. For one thing, none of the other writers of the New Testament has ever heard about the wise men. Paul has never heard about them. Mark has never heard about them. Luke has never heard about them and John has never heard about the wise men that came at the birth of Jesus. There are lots of problems there. Luke and Matthew are the only writers of the New Testament who actually talk about Jesus' birth, but they cannot get their stories to agree. They cannot even agree where Jesus was from. Matthew, writing about 80 A.D., was convinced that Jesus was from Bethlehem and his parents were residents of Bethlehem, but that shortly after he was born King Herod tried to kill him. This is the story we heard today. Mary and Joseph had to flee into Egypt and they remained there until Herod died. Herod died in the year 4 B.C. After he died,

2

allegedly, an angel appeared in a dream to Joseph and said, "You can go back to the land of Israel now because those who sought to kill the child are dead." And Joseph took his little family back to Bethlehem where he discovered that Herod's son, Archelaus, was ruling and he was afraid to stay there. He looked around for some other place to live and he went as far away from Bethlehem as he could while still remaining in the land of Israel. He went up north and settled in Galilee. According to Matthew, Jesus, Mary and Joseph were from Bethlehem but they had to immigrate first to Egypt and then to Galilee in order to protect the child.

Luke, writing 10 years after Matthew, has a different version. Luke believes that Jesus, Mary and Joseph were from Nazareth, and when the child was about to be born a census of the whole world was called. This is totally unhistorical. A census did not happen in this particular period of world history. Luke invented this as a reason for getting Jesus down from Nazareth to Bethlehem because the law said that a person had to be registered where his origins were. Joseph was a descendent of David who was originally from Bethlehem 1000 years before. Luke has a story about Jesus coming down in utero to Bethlehem so they could be registered, staying for eight days until Jesus was circumcised, then for 40 days until he was presented in the temple and then they go back up to Nazareth where they were from. Luke is convinced that they were from Nazareth and they just made a safari down to Bethlehem where Jesus happened to be born. Matthew is convinced that they were from Bethlehem originally, but they had to immigrate. That is the first problem.

There is a second problem with this story if we take it as literal truth instead of digging into what it really means. Judaism had been waiting over 700 years for the Messiah. Isaiah was the first one to preach the coming of the Messiah. Isaiah flourished about 750 years before Jesus. Can you imagine the consternation caused in Jerusalem when, after waiting avidly for the coming of the Messiah, three wise men appear from the East? According to Matthew's account they inquired, "Where is the Messiah of Israel? We have seen his star rising and we know he has been born." According to the story, Herod is in a terrible state, he calls in the wise men, the Pharisees and the Chief Priest and he says: "Where is the Messiah supposed to be born?" They say: "Bethlehem, it says so in scripture." He sends these wise men off to find the baby.

Bethlehem is less than one hour's walk from Jerusalem. The priests and scribes who have been waiting for 750 years for the coming of the Messiah tell the wise men, "He is going to be born in Bethlehem." Can we believe that they would just sit back and have no more interest in the Messiah? That is it? They were just there to furnish the geographical location to foreigners so they could find the Messiah and then they would ignore him. It does not make any sense when you treat it literally.

There is historical evidence that Herod was a totally paranoid character. Herod killed his favorite wife, Miriam. He killed his mother-in-law and he killed three of his own sons, because he was so paranoid about being overthrown from his kingdom. Can we believe that Herod, who was living just an hour from Bethlehem, would send the wise men off to find this person who was going to overthrow his throne and then sit back and wait for two years before he took any action, and then have all the babies under two years of age killed. It doesn't make any sense.

It does not make any sense that 30 years later, Jesus, as he was beginning his public ministry, would not have called attention to the fact and said, "Don't you guys remember thirty years ago, how three astrologers arrived from the East looking for the Messiah? I am he. Here is the gold bracelet that they gave me, look, 'To baby Jesus on your birth.' Look there it is!" That would have made things so much easier for him. So why did he not do it? Why he did not do it, of course, is because this is a story that is true at a totally different level of meaning.

This was a constant way of treating the births of all famous people. When people became famous in their own right, it was important to create a childhood for them that would adequately reflect the fact that they were "specially chosen of God." It happens in all cultures. It happened with the birth of Confucius who was born about 560 years before Jesus. According to the Chinese mythology, angels attended the birth of Confucius. The Buddha, who was born about the same time as Confucius, has the story that his mother conceived him after she had an image of a white elephant piercing her side with one of his six tusks and then she carried the baby for ten months and finally gave birth.

Extraordinary miracles and angels attended the birth of Zoroaster, who lived about 600 years before Jesus. And 600 years after Zoroaster, also in the great land of Persia, was the prophet,

Saoshyant. The story is, Saoshyant's mother walked into the lake a virgin and picked up a seed that had been spilled by Zoroaster 600 years before and she became pregnant and gave birth to the sage, Saoshyant.

Then we have the birth of Mohammed whose conception was heralded by angels and angels attended his birth. So when we talk about the angels attending the birth of Jesus and indicating and announcing the conception of Jesus, this is not a new story. This is a story that has been repeated many times before Jesus. It is a way of indicating that this is a special child - as if every child is not special!

Secondly, I want to look at what I consider to be the real meaning of Christmas and the real meaning of this beautiful story of the three wise men. What is it all about? Firstly, Matthew's account is only meaningful if you are aware of the Hebrew Scriptures. He is calling on two great parallels. There were two great exiles of the Jewish nation. The first exile into Egypt was between 1700 B.C. and 1250 B.C. At the end of that period Moses liberated the Israelites.

The Egyptian wise men tell the Pharaoh they must kill all Hebrew children because a savior is going to be born who will lead this nation into freedom. The Pharaoh gives the word that all the Hebrew midwives are to kill all male children as they are born. You know the story of how Moses survives and finally leads his people into freedom. Matthew is recreating that story with another king and he has Jesus go down to Egypt in the same way and then come back out of Egypt in order to set his people free. Except it is not a political freedom anymore, it is a spiritual freedom. So that is one of the meanings Matthew is building into it.

The second meaning is this; the second great exile of the Jewish nation took place between 587 B.C. and 529 B.C. when they were exiled into Babylon. In the year 529, the Persian Empire overthrew the Babylonians and released the Jews to go back into the land of Israel. A Persian king called Cyrus was then regarded as the savior of Judaism. He set Judaism free. Matthew is building on that with the Persian magi in this story. The Persian Cyrus, who had been the savior of Israel, now recognized that Israel was producing its own savior. So these are the hidden meanings inside Matthew's account.

The meanings are also in the players in this account. Herod has a meaning above and beyond the historical paranoid character that he was. There was no account, however, of Herod ever massacring little infants around Jerusalem as was indicated in this story. There is no historical evidence that he ever did this. Who does Herod represent? Herod represents all that is egotistical and prejudiced and violent. The part of every one of us that is so wrapped up in his own agenda that he would visit all kinds of prejudices and even violence on those who oppose his concepts. Herod represents that part in every one of us and represents that part in every culture.

Who do the wise men represent? They represent a part of us, which is honestly seeking truth, which is honestly seeking God. There is that part in every culture and there is that part in every one of us as well. Who are the angels and who are the shepherds? It is an amazing little three-part arrangement. The shepherds represent the Israelites who recognized Jesus as the Messiah. The wise men represent the gentiles who recognize Jesus. The angels represent the cosmic recognition of the role of Jesus. So you are going from a little national savior to an international character to a cosmic character. This is the build-up of these stories.

The meaning of this is about prejudice. It is about Herod who is totally wrapped up in the paranoid prejudice that might threaten his own hegemony. The wise men represent those who can go beyond prejudice. They represent the meeting of East and West, the breakdown of the prejudice between East and West. They represent this in a mythological sense more than in an historical sense. One of them is, according to tradition, black, from an African nation and that represents an end of the prejudice along the color bar. They also represent the end of the prejudice between Jew and gentile. And since Mary and Joseph are key to the whole story, they represent the end of the prejudice between male and female.

The Christmas story and the Epiphany story are about having the courage to seek the light which brings us beyond the prejudices of nationality, denominational affiliations, gender, class, creed or socio-economic status. That is, in my opinion, what they represent.

My third point is this. As a result of Epiphany, and as a result of Christmas, I want to ask myself the question, "What is the greatest kind of love? What is the greatest manifestation of love?" All of the mystics of all traditions, the Christian, Buddhist, Hindu and the Jewish traditions tell us that at the moment of death as each

6

one of us is about to breathe his last, there is an invitation from God to reach total and instant enlightenment. The question is, of course, why would we not do it? Because the price is the total letting go of all attachments to people, places, prestige, or even to the notion of separate self.

In order to merge fully with God, we have to be prepared to let go of everything including the notion of a separate self. We have to become a little drop of water in the ocean that is God, losing the ontological discrete separateness and totally merge with God.

The esoteric systems in Judaism, Hinduism and Buddhism all teach reincarnation, i.e., we get this opportunity over and over again. But obviously, we have not availed of it because we are still here today. Each one of us decided that it was a far, far better thing to be attached to an ego or to a place than it was to merge with God. Is that really true? Is that really the highest form of love?

There is a beautiful story in the Hindu scripture called the Bhagavad Gita. It is the story of Arjuna. At the end of this beautiful Hindu scripture, all of Arjuna's brothers have died and he is alone with his dog, his very faithful, loving dog that has been his companion for many years. Arjuna finally and very arduously, makes his way to heaven. He arrives at heaven and God welcomes him with open arms because he has been a good man, and God bids him to step inside. As Arjuna looks inside he cannot see his brothers, and he says to God: "Where are my brothers?" And God says: "Oh, they are not in heaven." Arjuna says: "Well, if my brothers are not in heaven, then I too will not enter." As he turns to walk away, God smiles and says: "Arjuna, this was a test. It is now obvious to me that your love for your brothers was greater than your own personal need for paradise. Look, behold your brothers," and Arjuna looks back and there are his brothers beaming at him. God says, "Come in." He steps forward joyfully to go in and God says, "Hold it. Where do you think you are going with that dog? This heaven is for human souls. This is not for dogs." Arjuna steps back and says, "Well, my dog has been even more loving and more loyal to me than my brothers. If he cannot come in, I cannot come in. I cannot spend my time in heaven thinking of his heavy heart outside. I prefer to be outside with him." Then God finally beams and says, "Arjuna, you passed the final test. Your love for all sentient beings is greater than your own personal need for paradise. Come in, you and your dog." He steps inside with his dog and as he looks down to pat his dog, the dog has turned into who he really is, an incarnation of Krishna.

Is that a greater love? Was Arjuna's love greater? What is the greatest love? Is it the bodhisattva that is prepared to come back over and over again into this vale of tears until every sentient being is saved? Is that a greater love? Or is the greater love to be the mystic that merges completely with God so no trace of her is ever heard of again. What is the greatest love? If it is to merge fully with God, why did Jesus incarnate? Saint Paul says in Philippians Chapter 2 Verses 6-11, "Although he was God, he did not cling to his divinity with God, but shuffled it off and adopted a human guise humbling himself even unto death on the cross." Why did Jesus do that? If it is a greater thing to merge than to be a bodhisattva, why did Jesus opt to be a bodhisattva? If Jesus came because of the pain, agony, and the fear on planet Earth 2000 years ago, do you really believe that he has not come again? Or that he did not come many times?

There is still pain and there is still confusion and there is still fear and there is still prejudice and there is still violence on our planet. We need Jesus as desperately today as they did then. I cannot believe for the life of me that Jesus only came once. I think Jesus was on this planet many times before he was born a carpenter's son in Galilee 2000 years ago. I also believe that Jesus has come back many times since his thorn-pricked, nail-studded body was laid in a borrowed tomb 2000 years ago. I think he has been back many times. Is he around today? Is he back in the guise of a holy man someplace else? Is he the Dalai Lama? Or is he some old wrinkled toothless white-haired grandmother loving her children in a little village somewhere in Kenya? Or is he a ruddy fisherman in a boat off the west coast of Ireland?" Wherever he is, I guarantee you he is infusing love and light into our planet. So I ask myself again in the beginning of 1999, "What is the greatest kind of love? Is it to merge totally with God or is it to come back over and over again, because you have so much love in your heart that there is no way you can agree to be in heaven while your dog or your wild pig is not in heaven." So why did <u>you</u> come back?

If you came back because you had that much love in you, why are you complaining about your fate? Why are you not embracing all facets and all circumstances of your life and saying, "Yes, yes this is why I came back. I came back to be a loving person because there is suffering and there is sin and there is fear and there

8

is confusion and there is prejudice on our planet." So, as I thought about today's homily, I was trying to make a New Year's resolution at the beginning of 1999 and this is what I came up with. I, sinner that I am, pledge to you, my companions on the journey, that I will try to love you to the best of my ability during 1999.

2
Myth

It was a theophany. I went one better than Moses. In fact, I went three better than Moses. I saw four burning bushes and it was a theophany. I almost called the Healdsburg Fire Department. I was standing on the deck of a little cabin in the middle of the forest off West Dry Creek. With the sun setting behind me on the hillside, I could see four trees down in the valley and I suddenly realized that they were on fire. A fire in that area is very dangerous. I was on the point of rushing to get my cell phone and contact the Healdsburg Fire Department when I realized a very strange thing. Although the trees were on fire, there was no smoke. Now I've heard the old proverb, "Where there's smoke there's fire," but now I was looking at a fire with no smoke, yet the trees were in flames. Then I realized what was happening. It was October and many of the leaves had fallen and those that remained were yellow, brown, orange and red. As sometimes happens in late autumn, there are these little whirlwinds that are very contained and there was a small whirlwind in the middle of the four trees and it was spinning the leaves furiously. Their colors were the colors of fire, and with the extraordinary pink glow of the setting sun, I was totally convinced that the four trees were on fire.

I think I figured out how Moses had his theophany. I want to talk about that today. I want to talk about the notion of myth. I'm going to make four main points. Firstly, I want to talk about myth understanding and I'm not lisping. Secondly, I want to talk about myth management. Thirdly, I want to talk about sin. And fourthly, I want to talk about the notion of culpability.

Let me start first with the notion of myth-understanding. We usually don't understand what myth is about. Often we think that myths are made up stories to explain in pre-scientific simplistic terminology stuff we still have not really understood. Or, on the worst face of it, a myth is a totally made up story that is a pack of lies. Myth is none of these things. A myth, in my opinion, is a symbolic articulation of some truth that is so deep and so profound that there is no philosophical system capable of articulating it. There is no theology adequate to explain it; you can only do it through some kind of mythic form. You can do it symbolically through dance, story or music, but you cannot deal with it in strict philosophical or theological parlance.

A myth goes to the core of the reality of a very profound truth. Ritual is the enactment of myth and so a ritual of Eucharist or any other great ritual is taking a myth, which is a symbolical articulation of a profoundly deep truth, and acting it out in some fashion. Is it true? Is a myth true? Once we define what we mean by true, it is profoundly true. Let me give you an example. When Jesus told the parable, the myth of the Good Samaritan, he said, "There was a certain man on his way down from Jerusalem to Jericho. He fell among robbers and they beat him up, stripped him, took all of his possessions and left him dying on the side of the road. Some hours later a priest was passing by and saw this man lying by the side of the road, naked, bleeding and dying and he passed on. Some hours later, a Levite liturgist from the temple came and saw the same man dying by the side of the road and he gave him a very wide berth. Then some hours later, a Samaritan, one of the accursed Samaritans, came by and he saw this man and his heart was moved with pity. He began to tend to him and he poured wine into his wounds and bandaged him and very gently put him on his own donkey and walked the rest of the way with him to Jericho. He went into a little inn and he said to the man in charge of the inn, 'Could you give him a bed for a few days? I'm going on a journey and I'll be back in a few days and whatever extra expenses you incur, I'll be responsible for them.' Jesus turned to his audience and he said, 'Which of these was neighbor to the one who fell among robbers?'"

Now is that a true story? If you were a reporter or a scientist listening to Jesus tell that story and you decided to check up on it and you went down to the Jerusalem Post and you said I would like to go through your files for the last few days. Is there any report of somebody being beaten up on the road to Jericho and a priest and a Levite passing by and a Samaritan looking after him? Could you get me a register of all the little hotels in Jericho and find out if anybody answering that description was admitted there in the last few days? Very possibly, you would draw a blank in every part of the inquiry. Was Jesus telling lies? Was it a myth, a meaningless simplistic little analogy? It was much more than that. It was a deep truth. The truth is that the person who is my neighbor is the person who sees me and responds to me in love. That is the truth.

The myth is a symbolic articulation of a very deep truth. Take a truth that is central to Christianity, say the virgin birth; was Jesus really born of a virgin? Is that what we mean? That someone with an intact hymen gave birth to an eight-pound baby and retained her virginity afterwards? Is that what the story is about? You read corresponding stories in Celtic, Greek, and Roman mythology and in the bible. In Chapter 6 of the Book of Genesis we read that the sons of God were infatuated with the daughters of men and they came down and they impregnated them.

Who are these sons of God? If they are not human beings, what you have is a whole bunch of virgin births recorded in Chapter 6 of the Book of Genesis. Are we talking about virgo intacta or are we talking about physiological wholeness or are we talking about a deeper truth? A charismatic character is someone who comes into this world with so much love and invites us into a whole new way of responding and relating to each other, and such a person is glorious and we make up stories to illustrate just how extraordinary he is. Is it the details of the myth that are important or is it the truth locked into it that is important?

The second point I want to make is how we "myth-manage." For instance, how we take these myths and what we do with them. When we go through the gospels, we discover very quickly that the Christian community with all its love is the dark room in which the image of Jesus is developed and computer enhanced and printed. It is from the experience of the community in its liturgies and in its togetherness that the image of Jesus begins to develop. It is not a bad thing at all, except that when we begin to try to read this mythology as factual, historical evidence we get into trouble.

In the first gospel written, the Gospel of Mark, about the year 70 A.D. in which Jesus is treated as a human being, there is no virginal conception. In this gospel, there is no account of an extraordinary birth and Jesus dies in despair, hanging on the cross. His last words are, "My God, my God why have even you abandoned me?" Mark's Jesus is a very human Jesus.

By the time we get to John's gospel, 30 years later, Jesus is not only a divine figure, he has preexisted. He is the Eternal Word who was with God in the beginning and through whom all things were made. When Jesus dies in John's gospel, he is not this despairing creature hanging on a gibbet. He doesn't hang on the cross in agony, rather he reigns from the cross and his final words are, "It is complete. I finished what I came to do."

There is the development in the laboratory of the Christian community of the image of Jesus. I want to examine it because I have the belief system that with Jesus as with many other great characters, it moves through various stages. I would suggest perhaps eight. The first stage is the person himself, his life and his teaching. Later occasionally during his life but most often after he has died comes stage two, which is the myth, which is the symbolic profound articulation and story form of who this person was and what he came to do. Stage two is beautiful.

Stage three is the organization or institution. In stage four, there is the setting of some kind of agenda. Stage five is the beginning of an ideology or the beginning of a theology. Stage six is about the paranoia and fear. Stage seven is about a sense of elitism within the group. Stage eight is about intolerance and whether we are in a position to enforce our intolerance, inquisitions and punishments. That has been the Christian story and that has been the story of many other systems.

What I would like to do at the beginning of the New Year is to invite us to become spiritual archeologists, stripping off the layers as we go back to find the original Jesus. We need to strip off the intolerance, punishment, sense of elitism, fear-based control, ideologies and theologies, agendas, and organizations, and get back to looking at the myth again. But we must look at it as a myth not as a philosophy so that we can penetrate to the core truth locked within it and really find Jesus. This is our journey.

Every generation needs to do it for itself. Jesus has been developed and computer enhanced and printed in many different kinds of laboratories. We have images of Jesus everywhere from being an anemic hermaphrodite to being a gun-toting guerilla fighter and everything in between. Different laboratories have produced a very different Jesus. The question for each spiritual traveler is, what is the laboratory that I create in my heart and what is the laboratory that we create in our community? The image of Jesus that evolves from it has a lot to do with the environment that we set up in our search for Jesus.

As my third point, I want to comment on this statement John the Baptist makes as he sees Jesus approaching, "This is the lamb of God. This is the one who takes away the sins of the world."

13

I want to look at that phrase because in my opinion it has been grievously misunderstood and grievously misapplied throughout Christian history. If Jesus was the one who came to take away the sins of the world, then if I would use "Super Bowl" lingo today, I would have to say the score stands at, sin 1999, Jesus 0.

There is as much sin in the world as there ever was. Did Jesus die for our sins? Was Jesus trying to make compensation to some vitriolic, vindictive, vengeful, distant, demanding deity who wanted blood because he was annoyed and irritated with us? Had we offended him so grievously that he was going to take this innocent victim and squeeze the last drop of blood out of him? Is this the kind of God we believe in, a God who demands that kind of retribution? Or is it not true that it was not just Jesus who died for the sins of the world; do we not all die for the sins of the world? The little girl who was discovered down in Monterey, Christina Williams, she died for the sins of the world as much as Jesus did. She died for the sins of the individuals who abducted her and killed her and she died for the sins of others of us who create the kind of environment in which this can happen. Everyone that dies violently dies for the sins of the world. What is beautiful about Jesus is that Jesus totally lived out his alignment with God.

Unfortunately, throughout Christian history what tends to happen is that the Jesus who came in total alignment with the Father and pointed as a signpost to where the Father was had become a tyrannical, megalomaniacal, self-important individual who is just pointing to himself. We created this story instead of watching where Jesus is pointing and going where Jesus would have us go instead of getting confounded with ritual, theology, ideology and organization.

Fourthly, I have traced over the years what I consider to be the development of the notion of culpability throughout the Judeo/Christian scriptures. I see it evolving in seven great stages. The first stage is what I call "passing the apple." It is Adam and Eve sinning and neither one taking responsibility. Adam, when he is caught, blames his wife. His wife blames the serpent. The serpent blames God for creating him. So no one is taking responsibility. That is stage one in the evolution of a notion of culpability.

Stage two is that God, in his law, punishes everyone. Augustine will articulate this as follows: "Because of that first sin, our will is weakened, our intellect is darkened and our bodies are subjected to sickness and ultimately to death." For this one sin, God is going to punish everyone.

Stage three is the notion of the scapegoat. When the people of Israel were in exile in the desert, once a year all of the people would come individually to Aaron who was the high priest and confess their individual sins. Then Aaron would take a goat from the herd and impose hands upon it and confess the sins of the entire group onto the goat and then run it off into the desert. Hence the origin of the word scapegoat, someone who was going to take responsibility for all the sins on a yearly basis and be punished accordingly.

Stage four was the notion that God repented of the vastness and the viciousness of his vengeance and decided to scale it back some. Henceforth, he was only going to punish the sins of the parents to the third and fourth generation. What a benign and compassionate God! He was only going to punish the great-grandchildren not the great-great-grandchildren. What a lovely, compassionate God!

Stage five came about 600 years before Jesus with two great Hebrew prophets, Jeremiah and Ezekiel who were practically contemporaries of each other. They quoted an old Hebrew proverb that said: "The fathers have eaten sour grapes and the children's teeth are set on edge." No longer will this proverb be true. No longer will the children's teeth be set on edge because the parents had eaten sour grapes. Henceforth, everyone is responsible for his own sin. It may feel to you that that was the culmination and that it didn't get any better than that.

But there are two stages beyond which are articulated by Jesus, the first one in his teaching and the second one in his life. There are two stages beyond personal culpability and they are these: Jesus would say to the religious, self-righteous of his time, "It is true that you men know all 613 precepts of Torah. It is true that you keep them scrupulously. It is true that in that technical sense you are sinless. But I tell you, you are guilty of the sins of others because you are creating theologies, and economic models, political setups, and religious institutions that are forcing other people to be sinners. You are forcing them out because of the systems you are creating and therefore you are partially responsible for their sins."

The final stage was not so much what Jesus had to say about things as what he did about things. Here was Jesus who in a very real sense was completely sinless and in total alignment with God. Never in his life had he done a personal, egocentric, selfish thing to the exclusion of others. Here was Jesus in his lifetime making a personal vow that he is going to dedicate himself to being responsible to, not responsible for, but being responsible to the sins of the world. That he would take every situation he encountered and respond with love. He will take the consequences of the sinful, selfish decisions of other people and he will respond to them with love. That is as high as it gets.

The prayer I would make for all of us as we begin this New Year is to look at Jesus, and have the courage to strip off all of those layers and discover the essential Jesus, the Jesus who operated only out of love. Unless we get to the realization that the only thing that works is love, we are doing a grave disservice to Jesus.

3
Marginalizing and Domesticating God

I wasn't a very aggressive young boy. In fact, in all my grade school years I only got into two fistfights. I'm really embarrassed to say I lost both of them. The first time I was matched against a southpaw. For those of you who don't know, when you fight you present with your left hand and come with your right. A southpaw stands very differently. I had no idea how to deal with him and I wound up with a bloody nose. The second time was even worse because I wound up with a very bruised ego. Not so much because I lost the fight, but because of the aftermath. My family had moved into a housing estate consisting of thirty-four new houses on the edge of Cork City and there were lots of kids around. It was the last year of life for my grandfather, Daddy Jim, who I regarded as a druid. He was the best storyteller I've ever known. He was a great dancer and a great musician and he loved to tell stories to children. He would take a chair outside our front door and all the kids in the neighborhood would crowd into our garden and he would tell us stories. Because I was the eldest grandson, I got to be the emcee.

This day, after the fistfight, the kids had come into the garden and I spotted my foe, the guy who had just trashed me, coming in with everyone else so I ordered him outside the gate. My grandfather intervened. He said, "Sean, let him come in." I said, "No, he's not coming in." My grandfather said, "Let him come in." I said, "No, he's not coming in." Then I did something I'm most embarrassed about. I got so mad with my grandfather that I kicked him in the shin. My grandfather said, "I need for you to go inside." In tremendous humiliation, I had to go into the house and listen through the closed door while he told stories to the other kids, including my foe.

I learned that day that you cannot control goodness. You cannot control love. And you cannot put a fence around your grandfather. Nor can you put a fence around God, and anyone who tries to domesticate God or make God his private property, is hopelessly lost. That is what I want to talk about today. I want to make five points. I want to talk firstly about killing the prophet. Then I'm going to call my second point "Jesus will come again." Thirdly, I'm going to talk about "Zen mind, beginner's mind."

Fourthly, I'm going to talk about "marginalizing God" and fifthly, "domesticating God."

The first point is killing the prophet. I just finished reading a book with an interesting title. It is called "A Catholic Priest Meets Sai Baba," written by an Italian priest, Don Mario Mazzoleni. Sai Baba, for those of you who do not know him, is an extraordinarily holy man living in India, a veritable avatar, an incarnation of divine love on our planet, and an extraordinary teacher. This Italian priest went to visit him and was totally enraptured by the love that this man was radiating and became a disciple while still being a Catholic priest. After ten years of his association with Sai Baba, Don Mario had the temerity to write a book about the merits of this holy man's teachings. For his trouble, he was excommunicated from the Catholic Church. Without a trial, without a defense, without any kind of a hearing, he was excommunicated. It would be too much to hope that the Vatican would actually embrace someone like a Sai Baba, but you would think that any follower of Jesus or any organization that claims to be open to the spirit would at least have the tolerance to investigate this person and his teachings.

But it did not happen because the truth is that meeting Jesus or meeting the Spirit of God is no guarantee of seeing Christ or seeing the Spirit of God. You just look at the evidence in the life of Jesus and the reaction of people meeting Jesus. The people in his time very often had no idea who he was. His family, we are told in Mark's gospel, were deeply embarrassed about him. In Mark Chapter 3: 21, we are told that when Jesus began his public ministry his family came to take him by force because they thought he was mad. Even growing up with Jesus was no guarantee of actually seeing Jesus. The apostles who he gathered around him didn't know Jesus. They were filled only with the self-importance of the presumed positions that they would occupy when he came into his kingdom.

The mob did not understand Jesus. They were just bored people looking for "bread and circuses." The leaders were threatened. They did not see Jesus. They just saw a threat to national security and their religious hegemony. The same thing continues right down to our present times.

I do not know of a single Christian country, or an alleged Christian country that operates either in its domestic policy or in its foreign policy with Christian principles or the teaching of Jesus. It is too dangerous. Much more important is national security or economic growth. I do not know any system that is seriously applying the teachings or the ideals of Jesus. And what of the successors to the apostles? Are they doing any better than the apostles did? Unfortunately, it does not seem like it. The successors to the apostles are still so preoccupied with self-importance and bureaucratic administration that they are afraid to leave aside the vestiges of their offices and go out with their begging bowls and look for wisdom from the little ones of other traditions. As for the rest of us, the mob, most of us are still asleep anesthetizing ourselves with a whole bunch of new breads and new circuses, not really being awake and not really allowing ourselves to be challenged by the teaching of Jesus. We still kill the prophet.

My second point is about this notion that Jesus will come again. I have no doubt, personally, that Jesus has reincarnated many times on this planet. The carpenter of Nazareth may not even have been the first one and, in my belief system, he certainly was not the last one. This extraordinary love that God has for planet Earth keeps manifesting itself and articulating itself over and over again.

Whenever the wheels of human history get stuck in intolerance, it seems to me that God sends a new avatar to try to push the chariot out of the mud. Jesus is on the planet today and we have no idea what he looks like. He may be an old toothless grandmother with her granddaughter on her knee in a little African village. He may be a young fisherman in a boat off the West Coast of Ireland or he might even be a cabby in New York City. Who knows? Who is to say what God may do and what God may not do? We need Christ consciousness as surely in our times as they did 2000 years ago.

Who is to say that in our time there is not someone like a Sai Baba or a Mahatma Gandhi or a Dalai Lama or a Thich Nhat Hanh who does not carry both Christ consciousness and Buddha nature? I had a great dream about a year and a half ago in which it seemed to me that two great religious leaders died at the same time. And in my dream it was not specified who they were but they were the leaders of two extraordinarily beautiful spiritual traditions who died at the same time and made a covenant with each other to reincarnate as a single person in order to try to bring together the two traditions. It is interesting to me that often the first people to recognize Christ consciousness or the Buddha nature are enemies who quickly set out to destroy it.

In the gospel reading today, it was the demons that recognized Jesus first. "We know who you are. You are the holy one of God. Have you come to destroy us?" Today, very often, it is still the enemy who is the first to recognize the Buddha nature or Christ consciousness and to very quickly set about destroying it before it can destroy him. That is the second point I want to make.

The third point I want to make is this; I want to talk about Zen mind and beginner's mind. About 1993, John Paul II wrote his autobiography called, "Crossing the Threshold of Hope." An extraordinarily beautiful holy man from Viet Nam, Thich Nhat Hanh, in a book called "Living Buddha, Living Christ," commented on one of the Pope's statements.. With Thich Nhat Hanh I am in full agreement. He took one statement from the John Paul II autobiography that says, "Jesus the Christ is utterly unique and utterly different. If Jesus the Christ were merely a wise man like Socrates, or if he were merely a prophet like Mohammed, or if he were merely enlightened like the Buddha, then he definitely would not be what he is, God's sole and unique voice and mediator on planet Earth." It is a tremendous pity for anyone to make that kind of statement. How anyone, even in a position like the Pope's, could be so arrogant as to circumscribe who God may be, how she may act, to whom she may reveal herself and what she may say, is the ultimate in arrogance. None of us has permission to put limits on who God is and what God may say and to whom God may reveal herself.

In the great story of Jesus' birth, we are told that several days after Jesus was born three wise men came from the East in order to pay homage and to learn from him. Maybe it is time for the shoe to be on the other foot. Maybe the wise men who are coming from the East at this time are people who are not coming merely to pay homage to us but perhaps even to be teachers for us.

At the very first World Parliament of Religions that happened in Chicago in 1893, there was a famous debate between two European theologians, one of whom claimed that in order to understand your own religion you need to study all other religions as well, otherwise you have nothing with which to compare your own system. He quoted an English proverb that says, "He knows not England who only England knows." In other words, you cannot

20

know how to be a Christian until you know what Buddhism, Hinduism, or Islam are about.

Buddhism has a beautiful teaching, the teaching of "inter-being." It says that nothing, absolutely nothing, can exist in its own right. Things are not what they appear to be. Things are not discrete, separate ontological entities existing of and for themselves. Even a flower is not just a flower. A flower is composed of many different elements: water, rain, sunshine, soil, nutrients, care and attention. It is all of these things. It is not a separate, discrete ontologically unique entity. Buddhism, says Thich Nhat Hanh, is composed totally of non-Buddhist elements. I think the same is true of Christianity. True Christianity is composed totally of non-Christian elements. Who are we to limit God and tell God how she may speak and to whom?

My fourth point is this. I want to talk about the notion of marginalizing God. There is a very powerful statement taken from the Book of Deuteronomy that is Moses' last speech to his people. Moses never actually entered the Promised Land. He sat on a mountaintop overlooking Jericho knowing that he would not be allowed to cross over, and he gave his last advice to his people, including some stuff, which, in my opinion, is now very much passé. In that speech, Moses said to his people, "God has answered your prayers. Since you are afraid to hear the voice of God, and since you are afraid to see the fire of God, God will grant you prophets as intermediaries to speak to you." I tell you, in my opinion, in these times, that is very much passé. We do not want our prophets to stand between God and us. What we need now are prophets who will encourage us, advise us and challenge us into our own direct, personal experience of God.

Enough time has gone by. We have listened to enough teachers. There have been enough mediators between God and us allegedly interpreting and channeling God's message for us. God lives as surely in the hearts of every single one of us as he lives in the heart of a Buddha or a Christ or a Thich Nhat Hanh or a Sai Baba. Every single one of us is meant to be a channel of God. The time is gone when we need to pay deference to prophets who will stand between the face of God or the fire of God and us. The time has come for every single one of us to risk the journey of seeing God's fire and hearing God's voice.

My final point is this. I want to talk about the notion of domesticating God. There is another statement in Moses' last speech to his people that I take issue with at this time. Moses says, "If any prophet speaks in the name of any other God, he shall die." My opinion is this, if any prophet does not speak in the name of any other God, he shall surely die, because every God we make up is unreal. Every theology we made up is precisely that, made up. Anyone who thinks that he can neatly package God into any theological system is wrong. The true prophets are going to be the people who invite us into direct experiences of the many faces of God, not just one unique dogmatic tradition.

But again and again we fall into the trap of wanting it pigeonholed and neatly circumscribed and delivered to us in manageable predigested packages. Judaism claimed that God stopped speaking in 400 B.C. and God only spoke in Hebrew, and therefore the only books allowed in the Hebrew canon were books allegedly written before 400 B.C. in Hebrew.

When Christianity came along, it claimed that God only spoke to the apostles and that with the death of the last of the apostles, God had nothing left to say to planet Earth. Six hundred years later, Islam came and Islam claimed that the Hebrew Scriptures and the Christian scriptures were both faulty because they were only partial and because they were written down. Islam claims that God had spoken in a voice and the Koran is not a written document, it is an oral tradition. You cannot read Koran. You can only hear the Koran declaimed. The word Koran comes from an Arabic word that means, "recite." It can only be heard as a recitation. As far as the Muslims are concerned, God only speaks Arabic. How extraordinarily arrogant of the Muslims, how extraordinarily arrogant of the Christians, how extraordinarily arrogant of the Jews to think that God is confined to a single language or a single revelation!

My appeal to us today is that we let go of our small minded tribal deities who are so insecure that they have to threaten us if we dare to follow other Gods and begin to worship the totally ineffable, unarticulateable, unexplainable, ultimate ground of our being. That we would have the courage to let go of the kind of hierarchical hegemonies that have taken control of our spiritual process and step out as individuals on our own personal safaris into the mystery which is God. Finally, that we would have the courage to let go of our fearful, narrow-minded xenophobia and to risk going out there with our begging bowls in our hands asking the little people in other traditions to drop the pennies of their wisdom into our hands.

4
Fulfilling the Law

Dante was an amateur. Dante's "Inferno" is at best a second hand account. If you really want to get the inside scoop on hell then you have to contact one of the old Irish priests of my youth. No one knows hell like Irish priests know hell. When it comes to hell, the crème-de-la-crème of Irish priests, are the Redemptorists; they have the inside scoop on hell. They can tell you precisely the exact temperature to three decimal points on either Fahrenheit or Celsius down there. They have gone down individually and pricked their fingers on the devil's pitchfork and they can tell you how it compares with the rapiers of Toledo Steel. They can describe to you the precise acrid nature of the sulphurous smoldering fires down there in great detail. They can tell you the exact precise pitch of the screams of individual sinners as they are tormented. No one does it like they do. So we flocked to listen to them.

Every two years there would be parish retreats and the shock troops, the "Marine Corps" of the Redemptorists were brought in to sort us out. Every man, woman and child would go to every sermon and every service over a period of a week. They taught us how to be suspicious of our sanctity. They taught us how to doubt our sanity. They taught us how to doubt our standing with God.

For three weeks after the end of the retreat, the pubs did almost no business. Sales plummeted precipitously. All the courting couples put their sexuality on ice. And little boys like myself went to school in fear and trembling totally convinced that the next double-decker bus was going to flatten them. I remember one particular year one of them talking about this exact text. "Anyone who calls his brother a fool is worthy of hell fire."

Going to school on a Monday morning after this, I was totally convinced that I am not going to make it. It's three and a half miles, I was on my bicycle, there was a whole line of double-decker buses taking passengers into the city for the morning, and I knew that one of them was sure to get me. I picked my way carefully because I knew I had to go to confession before I got to school. Otherwise it was the end.

The Cork Cathedral is next to the school I attended. I went in to the cathedral, and, thanks be to God, there was a priest hearing confessions. I took a deep breath, went in and waited my turn. I knew what I was going to have to tell him. The week before I had had a big fight with my brother, Séamus, and I said, "You fool." Now I knew I was in danger. One of two things was going to happen as soon as I told him. He was going to have a heart attack and die and then I would be guilty of the murder of a priest as well. Or else, he was going to rush around to my side of the box, grab me by the hand and personally deliver me down to "Old Nick" where I'd spend the rest of my life. I swallowed four- or five-times and I said, "Father, I, I, er, aaa, I called my brother a fool." There was a short silence and he said, "And is he?" At this stage I realized that this priest was no Redemptorist. He didn't have the eloquence of the Redemptorists or the erudition of the Jesuits. So taking my courage in both hands I said, "Kinda." He said to me, "How old is he?" I said, "He is nearly six." He said, "God love him, he's only a child and he doesn't know any better. Give him a break. Here is a piece of candy for you. Say three Hail Marys." I came out of the confessional with a piece of candy and three Hail Marys for a sin that should have sent me down to hell for all eternity. I couldn't believe my luck.

I want to talk about today's extraordinary text of Jesus. I want to make three main points. I want to talk about what I consider "Law" to be really about. What does Law really mean? I want to ask myself the question; "Was Jesus the great lawmaker or the great lawbreaker?" Then thirdly, I want to look at the notion of the connection between law and freedom.

Let me talk about law, as I understand it. The best definition of law I have come across is from Deepak Chopra. He says that: "Law is the process through which the unmanifest becomes manifest." It is an extraordinary pithy description. Law is the process through which the unmanifest becomes manifest. It is the process through which the invisible becomes visible. It is the process through which the potential becomes the actualization. That is the best definition of law that I know. Because law is about ultimate reality, it is about how the cosmos works. It is not about commandments. It is not about precepts. It is not about regulations. These may be secondarily related to it, but it has nothing to do with it primarily. Law is how the universe works.

I really love the Christian definition of prayer. It encapsulates this. The Christian definition of prayer says that all prayer is the Spirit talking to the Father through the Son. That is why we start all our prayers addressing the Father and we end with, "through Christ our Lord, amen." What does that mean? It is the experience of the immanence of God relating to the transcendence of God through the physicality of humanity. It means that each of us is built in the image and likeness of God; so we are at one end of the process of law. We are the actualization, or we are the manifestation of it. It is that end of the spectrum addressing the transcendence of God, the utterly ineffable creator aspect of God, through the experience of what it means to be human beings. So human beings themselves are in fact a personification of the process of law. If law is about making the unmanifest manifest, if law is about making the invisible visible, if law is about making the potential actual, then human beings through prayer are the actualization of the transcendence of God. We experience it through our humanity. That is what law really means in my opinion.

Law then is how the cosmos works. It is not that laws are precepts or regulations set up by anyone, not even God in the sky, such that if we break them we are going to be punished. Law, because it is how the universe works, has its own built-in consequences. They are not punitive retributions for making mistakes or transgressing regulation, they simply are how the universe works. If I jump from the fifth story of a high-rise, fall to the ground, and break both of my legs, it is not that God is punishing me for breaking some law. There is a law called gravity and there are equations that tell me what the consequences could be. Law is the realization that when I'm not in alignment with how the universe works, there are consequences for myself and for other people. That is the great law of Karma.

The real meaning of law, in my opinion, is getting into alignment with "Is-ness." Taoism, a beautiful system created by Lao Tzu about 600 years before the birth of Jesus, puts it best. Lao Tzu came up with the notion of "wu-wei," action-less action: being so in alignment with Is-ness that things flow effortlessly from us. He came up with a great metaphor. He said that if you could develop a thread of silk that was absolutely flawless in which there was no weakest point, you could connect it up to an anchor and you could catch a whale and the silk strand would not break because systems always break at their weakest point. If there is no weakest point, if something is in total harmony and alignment, there is no place for it to break. No matter how weak it appears to be, it is unbreakable. This is what Saint Paul says, "The foolishness of God is stronger than the wisdom of human beings," because the wisdom of human beings is predicated upon models in which there are always weaknesses. The foolishness of God is the elegance of total alignment to Is-ness. What law really means, in my opinion, is total alignment with God. Regulations, precepts and commandments are secondary considerations.

The second point I want to make is this. I want to ask myself the question, "Was Jesus the great lawmaker or the great lawbreaker?" It depends on whom you are reading. If you want to compare Matthew, Chapter 5: Verse 17, with Paul's letter to the Ephesians, Chapter 2: Verse 15, you get conflicting viewpoints. Paul says in his letter to the Ephesians, that, "Jesus came and in his own body he abolished the law." Jesus is saying in today's gospel of Matthew, "Don't think that I have come to abolish the law or the prophets. I have come not to abolish but to fulfill. Therefore I tell you, until heaven and earth pass away not a single portion of a letter of the law will pass from the law, until all is fulfilled."

Who is telling the truth? What is the real story? Did Jesus come to abolish the law or did he come to bring the law to fulfillment? The problem, of course, is what we mean by law. Jesus is talking about one meaning of law and Paul is talking about another meaning of law. There are very distinct meanings of law. For instance, you could think that the law is Torah, the first five books of the Hebrew Scriptures: Genesis, Exodus, Leviticus, Numbers and Deuteronomy. That may be regarded as the law. There are 613 precepts in it. You could think that in some sense that these 613 constitute the law of God. But you cannot legislate people into alignment. What the Torah means to do is to not give us rules for becoming holy; it is really just a reminder to mindfulness. What the Torah is doing, in my opinion, is saying every single human action is capable of becoming a sacrament. Whether you are washing potatoes or making love to your wife, everything can be a sacrament if it is done with full mindfulness. This is very Buddhist as well. That, for me, is the real meaning of Torah with its 613 precepts. That is one meaning of law.

The second meaning of law perhaps is the Decalogue, the Ten Commandments handed down by God to Moses on Mount Sinai. Except I do not think God deals in commandments or regulations. More likely, God deals with prophecies or observations. God says, when people behave so and so, these are the consequences. When people behave thus and thus, those are the consequences. So it is not so much that God is saying you have to do A, B and C otherwise I am going to punish you. It is God saying these are my observations in the universe that I created. These kinds of actions create harmony and they create alignment. These other kinds of actions create disharmony and they create misalignment. You may be interested in seeing for yourself whether or not it works. That is the meaning of Decalogue. That is the second meaning of law.

The third meaning of law was the thousands of minutia with which the Pharisees surrounded the Torah, and the thousands of minutia with which the Roman Catholic Church surrounds the law of Jesus with all of its Canon Laws. They are ridiculous, totally made-up human precepts the transgression of which merits eternal damnation. Absolute poppy cock! When Paul talks about Jesus coming and in his own body abolishing the law, in my opinion, this is the kind of mishmash he is talking about. That is the kind of craziness he is talking about.

I was only in Palo Alto less than a year when I met an old man in his nineties who told me the following story. He had been born Protestant and he fell in love with a Catholic girl. In order to marry her he had to convert to Catholicism. He went through a whole period of instruction. He became a Catholic and his marriage was to take place in Palo Alto. He lived about 10 miles away from the church. His parents were dead set against the marriage, and on the morning of the wedding they hid the horse and buggy so he couldn't get to his own wedding. He ran the 10 miles and arrived 15 minutes late. Bathed in sweat he gulped down a glass of water and the priest refused to give him communion at his own wedding because he had broken his fast. The amazing thing is the man remained a Catholic. That is the kind of craziness that Paul talks about. That is the kind of thing that Jesus came and attempted to abolish.

There are very many different meanings to law. In the famous Transfiguration scene in Matthew, Chapter 17, Jesus is on the mountaintop with Peter, James and John and suddenly there is a vision that seems to be actually manifested in such a form that all of them could see it, and Jesus talks to Moses and Elijah. I can never figure out how they recognized them. There was no photography at that time or no icons allowed. Moses was dead 1250 years and Elijah 750, but they recognized them. Here were Elijah and Moses. What did they represent? Moses represents law. Elijah represents prophecy. Jesus says today, "I did not come to abolish the law or the prophets." Jesus very definitely sees himself in continuity and in harmony with anyone who is teaching alignment with God. Jesus did not see himself as the lawbreaker. He saw himself as the lawmaker. He says, "I have come not to abolish the law, but to fulfill it." But it is very interesting to watch the way in which Jesus fulfills law. Fulfilling law does not necessarily mean obeying law. Sometimes the way to fulfill law is to obey it. Sometimes the way to fulfill law is to confront it. Sometimes the way to fulfill a law is to compensate for it, and sometimes the way to fulfill law is to complement what is missing about it. Jesus fulfilled the law in all of these four ways. Fulfilling does not "ipso facto" mean total obedience to law. There is a time when law with a small l is disharmonious with Law with a capital L and then it becomes incumbent upon us that we object to and take issue with and protest small law.

The third point I want to make is this. I want to look at the connection between law and freedom. It is very interesting that the theological definition of freedom is that a person is only truly free to the extent that he can choose the good. Freedom does not consist in doing one's thing. That is merely free will. Free will is the ability to do as one pleases. Freedom is the ability to do as God pleases. Freedom is the ability to choose the good. Socrates would say this 400 years before Jesus. He would say; "To know the good is to do the good." And 100 years after Jesus, John would say; "Love God and do as you will." When persons are in total alignment with God, every thing they do is beautiful and moral. They are truly free people, however when we think of freedom we think of freedom "from." It is the wrong perspective, in my opinion. It is not about freedom "from" it is about freedom "for." So often I have seen in the course of African history and in the course of European history and even in the history of this country that wars of independence subsequently beget civil wars. The idealism of throwing off the shackles of dependence on foreign regimes once it has been achieved brings a feeling of euphoria that everything is going to be great. What we do not realize is that the major struggle is not the freedom from the colonials; the major struggle is the freedom for the responsibility of the freedom. And most of us do not like it. Shortly after independence in many of the African countries, the voting rate for the first voter turn out is about 99 percent. After 20 or 30 years, the voting rate goes right down to about 40 percent. There are many people who are very happy to take over and to put us to sleep, sing us lullabies, and tell us, "Lie down, just elect me and I'll take care of your process." This happens in the political arena, it happens in the church, in business communities, in education, in medicine and in agriculture. Whenever human beings organize themselves there is a tendency to value only the freedom from, but not to value the freedom for. To put it in conversion language, conversion is not basically about turning from something that enslaves me. It is about turning to something that empowers me and liberates me. If my energy is focused on what I need to give up, then that is where my heart and my intellect reside. If my energy is focused on what I need to adopt and grow towards, that is a very different experience.

For me, law ultimately is not about cattle prods forcing us into a particular kind of life style or belief system. Law is ultimately about teleology. The Greek word, "Telos" from which we get the English word teleology means, "to be drawn towards an end." This is the actual word that Jesus uses or is used of Jesus in the New Testament when we talk about perfection. You must be perfect, as your heavenly father is perfect. The word perfect in Greek, telos, does not mean stainless steel sinless-ness. It means to be seduced toward an end, to be so enamored of an outcome that my entire life is focused on it. All of us have had those experiences. I guarantee that those of you who are married, once you set your marriage date, however far hence it was, whether it was six months or a year, you lived the interim of a year or a year and a half predicated upon a future event. You lived teleologically drawn towards this great event and everything you did in the present was based upon who you were going to become in the future. We are driven more by our futures than we are by our past, and rightly so. The ultimate drive to our future is our merging with God, our total union with God, a great Valentine's Day in the sky, when there is only love loving love. My prayer for all of us this morning is this: that we become people not so much of the cattle prod but of the telos.

5
Forgiveness and Healing

"Do your cattle love themselves?"

Let me back up a little bit. The Kalenjin people of East Africa are nomadic pastoralists. I had the privilege of living with them for many years. The Kenyan government had forcibly settled them into an agricultural lifestyle but basically they were cattle people. They knew cattle and they had special names for their cattle.

The Kalenjin lived very widely scattered. When they met someone on the road there was an entire ritual of greeting that had to be gone through. It went like this, "Hi, how are you?" "I'm grand." "How is the wife?" "She's fine." "How are the kids?" "They're doing great." But what they are actually saying is this; "Do you love yourself?" The answer is, "Yes, I love myself." "Do you really love yourself?" "Yes, I really love myself." "Does your wife love herself?" "Yes, my wife loves herself." "Do your children love themselves?" "Yes, my children love themselves." "Do your cattle love themselves?" "Yes, my cattle love themselves."

For the Kalenjin, a greeting wasn't just a casual encounter because it happened so infrequently, it was very important. Therefore you really had to go to the core of the existential issue, "Do you love yourself? Is everything okay in your world? Do your cattle love themselves and do your children love themselves and does your wife love herself?" The interesting thing about the Kalenjin people was that the words they had for forgiveness were, "come and greet me." Forgiveness had to do with coming to greet someone. Not saying just "Hi," but really getting into alignment and asking someone, "Are you really okay?"

I'm going to make four main points today. Firstly, I want talk about the notion of sin. Secondly, I want to talk about the notion of forgiveness. Thirdly, I want to talk about the notion of community. Then fourthly, I want to talk about the inter-penetration of the different levels of healing and illness based upon the stories of today's gospel.

Let me begin with the notion of sin. I came across this phrase attributed to God in the Book of Isaiah; "You have burdened me with your sins." I said to myself, "Rubbish!" I cannot think of anything that is less true than that. No one can burden God with sins. God is totally unburdened by our sins. It is a very pathetic anthropomorphic kind of theology to hold that little finite creatures could burden the ultimate "ground of our being." I think it is absolute rubbish.

I had dinner on Friday night with friends of mine, in their late sixties, extraordinary spiritual seekers who have gone all over the world in their search for spirituality. They have had personal meetings with Thich Nhat Hanh, and with Sai Baba and various other great teachers. This woman said at one stage, "I am God, but God is not me." I said, "What? Say that again." She said, "I am God, but God is not me." So we had a fabulous discussion and I agree totally with her.

Every single one of us is a spark of the divine. So in some sense every single one of us can say, "I am God." But it is absolutely preposterous to claim that God is me. I can claim that I am human. But to say that humanity is me is a very different kettle of fish. There are six billion different articulations of humanity. I just happen to be one of them. But I am definitely having a human experience, as are six billion other people. So I can say with this woman, I am God but God is not me.

I would like to take this phrase where allegedly God says, "You burdened me with your sins" and I want to twist it a little bit. The "who" we have burdened with our sins is the God within us, not the ultimate "ground of our being" who is totally ineffable and imperturbable, but we burden the divinity within ourselves by heaping illusion after illusion and amnesia after amnesia on top of who we really are. Thus we burden the divinity within us. Not the ultimate ground, not the ultimate transcendent creator of all, but the divinity within each one of us. That is the first thing I want to say.

So what then is sin? The old definition is, of course, that sin is a transgression of law, the breaking of precepts of God, of the country, of the community, of the church. Where we transgress, sin results. I do not believe for a moment that that is what sin is. Sin may tangentially involve the breaking of precepts or the transgression of law, but we do so only tangentially. As far as I am concerned, the basis of sin is misalignment with truth or misalignment with whom we really are. So my personal definition of sin is this, that sin is a conscious deliberate decision to not grow. When I am faced with some life event or some relationship or some possibility and I choose to do something that reinforces my ego rather than transcends my ego that is sin. Sin is that kind of misalignment. Sin, in fact, is being so overcome by the illusion that I take it for the reality. We suffer from five great illusions as human beings, the illusion of time, the illusion of motion, the illusion of change, the illusion of size and the illusion of separate identity.

If we had a movie projector and we were showing a movie up on a wall, we are engaging in four illusions straight off but for the business of enjoying the movie we buy totally into it. John Wayne, I guarantee you, is not riding across from right to left on a white charger. It is not happening. And he certainly is not 40 feet tall.

What is happening is there is a tiny little one-inch by one-inch frame that is running through a projector and having light beamed through it and it is creating the illusion. It is creating the illusion of time because the truth is everything that is going to happen in the hour and a half is already locked into the little roll of celluloid. So time is an illusion. We create time because our brains are so limited that in order to try to process the entire Gestalt of cosmic truth we have to break it into bite size pieces and process it sequentially. So we create the illusion of time and therefore we create the illusion of motion and therefore we create the illusion of change because change too, is an illusion. Change is just a snapshot of the various possibilities that are inherently present from the beginning in the plethora of possibilities that exist in the cosmic mind of God. So change, time, motion, and size are illusions.

But the most devastating illusion of all is the illusion of separateness, that there are six billion different people on the planet and that there are ten million species of life when the truth is that every one of them is just an extraordinarily creative articulation of the same extraordinary possibility of the ultimate "ground of our being."

So sin, in my opinion, is buying into those illusions. The word that is used in the Christian scriptures for sin is actually a metaphor taken from archery. It means to "miss the mark." It is not about transgressing law; it is not about breaking precepts. It is about missing the mark. But missing the mark is not all bad because if you know about archery or about darts you know that missing the mark gives you very important feedback. You know whether you are aiming too high or too low or too far to the right or to the left. The feedback we get from missing the mark is a very important part of our own evolution. So sin is not bad if we can learn from it, if it gives the feedback that allows us to perfect our aim. Building on that, perfection, in my opinion, is not about stainless steel sinlessness. It is not about that at all. The word that is used in scripture or that we translate into English as perfection is the word "telos." The Greek word telos means to be "seduced toward an end," to be so enamored of an objective that we are inevitably drawn towards it. Obviously the objective has to be God. Therefore, it is important that we be seduced by God rather than being seduced by the illusion of merely physical manifestation. That is what I want to say about sin. The invitation of sin is the feedback that allows us to seek perfection, that falling head-over-heels in love with God, so that we have no choice but to follow our hearts and our path.

Where, then, is the role of forgiveness? Or, what does forgiveness mean in this model? I talked to you about what forgiveness means for the Kalenjin. There is a great phrase in today's reading as well that says, "Who can forgive sins but God alone?" As I was reading this again this morning, I had the same reaction as I had to the first statement. This statement, in my opinion, is exactly one hundred and eighty degrees off. "Who can forgive sin but God alone?" There is only one being, in my opinion, who <u>cannot</u> forgive sin. If we want to ascribe the character of "being" to God, there is only one "being" in all of creation who is incapable of forgiving sins and that is God.

In order to forgive someone I first need to hold a grudge and then subsequently let go of the grudge. That is what forgiveness is, but since God is total unconditional love and absolutely incapable of holding grudges, God is the only being in the universe who cannot forgive. So my humble opinion is that I disagree one hundred and eighty degrees with this scriptural statement, "Who can forgive sins but God alone?" Only God <u>cannot</u> forgive sin.

There is a great insight in Jewish theology every year on Yom Kippur when it comes to Kol Nidre. The Kol Nidre is an act of contrition on behalf of Judaism for the sins of the past year. There is not a single offense mentioned in the Kol Nidre that has to do with displeasing God, not a single one. Every single offense has to do with things I have done against my brothers and my sisters because Judaism "got it" in some level that you cannot bend God out of shape or you cannot annoy God. But, you can sin against your brother and your sister and your neighbor and yourself.

34

Therefore, the Kol Nidre consists in asking for forgiveness from my brothers and sisters for my behavior in the past year.

Jesus teaches this much himself. In the only prayer Jesus taught us, "The Our Father," he explained only one line of that entire prayer. All of the other lines he took as being obvious in their meanings. This was the only line that he spread himself on. I learned this prayer as a small child in my mother tongue, Gaelic, and of course I didn't understand it, I just learned it by rote. When I went to school I learned it in English and I still did not understand it. Then I went to Kenya and I had the privilege of learning it in a few different languages. When I learned it in Swahili, it was the first time I understood it. The line that we slough off in English is, "Forgive us our sins as we forgive those who sin against us." We actually do not get what it means. In Swahili we say, "Forgive us our sins in exactly the same fashion that we forgive those who sin against us." We shrink all of this in English to a single word, "as" and it totally misses the point. Forgive us our sins "in exactly the same fashion" that we forgive those who sin against us. This is not God creating a quid pro quo situation. This is not God advocating a tit for tat mentality. It is God telling us that we cannot experience forgiveness until we give forgiveness. Not that God is withholding in order to teach us or punish us, but that I have to free the part of myself that is unavailable to receive love or forgiveness from anyone else. So the forgiveness is not a quid pro quo it is about being incapable of letting in that which I cannot let out.

When Jesus says, "I want to demonstrate to you that the Son of Man has authority on earth to forgive sins," what have we done with this? We have acted as if the phrase "Son of Man" is conferring some kind of special status on Jesus. It is almost as if we feel the phrase, "Son of Man," makes Jesus, God, when exactly the antithesis is the case. In using this phrase again and again in the gospel of Mark, Jesus is insisting on his own humanity. When he says, "I want to demonstrate to you that the Son of Man has authority on earth to forgive sins," what he is really saying is, I want to demonstrate to you that I, as a human being like you, have the ability and, in fact, the responsibility to forgive sin.

In using this phrase, Jesus is proclaiming the ability of all people to forgive sins, not putting himself on a pedestal and claiming that only he and his delegates can forgive sin. He is saying to you, I guarantee, because I am human, I have both the ability and the responsibility to forgive sin. And again at the end of the gospel of John, in a post resurrection appearance having breathed upon them he said, "Receive the Holy Spirit; whose sins you shall forgive, they are forgiven; and whose sins you shall retain, they are retained." Jesus is not conferring some kind of special privilege on some little clerical oligarchy. Jesus is giving a mandate to all that would be his followers. Every single one of us has both the ability and the responsibility to forgive. This is not what makes us priests. This is not what makes us Bishops. This is what makes us Christian. Forgiveness consists of the ability and the responsibility to forgive each other.

Forgiveness then is our duty. So who may forgive? The truth is there is no such thing as a private sin. However you define sin, there is no such thing as a private sin. When I sin, I am out of alignment with God; therefore my relationships are out of alignment as well. They will suffer. Since I am out of alignment and my relationships are out of alignment, then you are suffering because of my sin and the community is suffering because of my sin. So there is no such thing as a private sin. Every sin changes who I am. It changes how I relate and therefore changes those with whom I have a relationship. Therefore my community suffers. This is not buying into the Hebrew Old Testament notion of the corporate singularity which is: that because one person in the tribe sins, the tribe has to be wiped out. I am not talking about corporate singularity although that is a very strong model that still infuses our thinking and our international policies. On a regular basis, ethnic cleansing is the result of visiting the crime of an individual on the entire group. We in America are as guilty of it as anyone. This does not just happen in Bosnia or Northern Ireland. When I talk about the community that lives in sin, I am not talking about a corporate singularity model. I am talking about the realization that when I come out of alignment with God, I am out of alignment with "is-ness," therefore, I cannot be in alignment and so you are going to suffer because of my misalignment and the community is going to suffer because of our misalignment.

As a consequence, the community has the right to delegate some members of the group to act on its behalf. We do this in our legal system. We claim that magistrates are there to act on behalf of the group to dispense justice. Whether or not they do it is a different kettle of fish. There is another way and a much more important way and that is the delegation of healers on behalf of the community to effect reconciliation on behalf of the community and to offer healing to each other. Every community has the right and the need to commission such people.

The Catholic Church claims that this can only happen through priesthood; I disagree. I think any community would benefit from taking people who are trained psychotherapists or psychologists and give them some kind of theological and mystical training and then commissioning them as ministers to act on behalf of the community to effect healing and reconciliation for the group. Being a priest is no guarantee of being a healer. Being a psychotherapist is no guarantee of being au fait with mystical theology. If we really need to effect healing and reconciliation in our groups, then we should be creating some kind of ministry where people are trained in knowledge of the human psyche and also mystical theology so they can act on behalf of the community to effect healing for the community.

My final point is this. I want to talk very briefly about the different levels of healing and illness. I agree with Ken Wilber that our experience of living in this universe is a cycle, a devolution and evolution. The devolution is that initially there is only God. That somehow this extraordinary ultimate Ground of our Being articulated itself in various souls. That these souls create mind and through mind they manifest in a physical realm and they take ordinary matter in order to be in this realm.

The devolution consists in going from spirit to soul to mind to body to physical matter. Every one of those stages has its proper study. The study of spirit is proper to mysticism. The study of soul is proper to theology. The study of mind is proper to psychology. The study of body is proper to physiology. The study of basic matter is the property of physics. Our journey in this life is to complete that cycle, to go from being just matter to being organic organized matter, to being mindfully aware matter, to being soul and soul matter, to being spirit again.

I want to use a simple metaphor to explain what I mean by this process. What is the relation between spirit and soul and mind and body and matter? Imagine you are interested in poetry and you want to use poetry as an image or a metaphor to understand this cycle. Spirit would be the muse that informs all of poetry. That would be the spirit. What would the soul then be? Soul would be the individual poets who have manifested, i.e., Shakespeare, Rumi or Yeats. What would mind be? Mind would be the extraordinary concepts and ideas that these extraordinary individuals seem to channel. What would be the analogy of body? Body would be what they produce, maybe a "Hamlet" or "Macbeth" or a "Song of Wandering Aengus" by William Butler Yeats. That would be body. And what is the analogy of matter? the paper and the ink. So they are obviously inter-connected and you cannot intervene in any one without affecting the others.

The same thing seems to be true when we are talking about healing and illness. Therefore Jesus can say today to this young man who is physically paralyzed, "Your sins are forgiven you." Why did he say that? This man and his friends obviously wanted a physical healing. Why is Jesus addressing a spiritual phenomenon when what they want is physical healing? Because they are always inter-connected, but not in a simplistic fashion. It is simplistic to say that people get sick because of their sins. It is equally simplistic to say that all sickness is just the malfunctioning of a physical machine. It is equally simplistic to claim that all sickness is in the mind. All of these are simplifications of an extraordinarily complex phenomenon.

Illness always involves all of the others. No matter where it starts, it quickly involves the others. If it starts with basic physiology, i.e., I fall and break my leg; it does not stop there. It effects how I feel. It affects my emotions. It can make me depressed. I can rail against God. Or it can start someplace else with anxiety and the anxiety disables me physiologically and also questions my faith in God. So no matter where it starts, it affects everything else. This is what Jesus is saying today. He is not blaming this man and saying, "You sinned and that is why this happened to you." That is simplistic. Rather, it is an invitation from Jesus to look at the entire unitary nature of this phenomenon. We cannot intervene in any place without affecting every place else.

The basic message from these readings is that we have an invitation from Jesus to all of us to wake up, to let go of the illusion of separate self, to let go of the illusion of time, space, motion and change and to realize that ultimately there is only God articulating through soul into mind into body into matter and back into body, mind, soul and spirit again. We are a part of this extraordinary cycle.

6
Personification of God

If you ever go across the sea to Ireland and you really want to start one hell of a row, I'll tell you how to do it. You simply go into a pub and you stand at the bar and call for drinks for everyone in the house and when they all gather around you, you ask just one question, "Who killed Michael Collins?" You can leave after an hour and they won't even notice you've left and they will be arguing about it until three o'clock in the morning.

For those of you who don't know much about Irish history or haven't seen the movie, in the early 1920s when Ireland was wresting its freedom after 800 years of colonization, two great leaders emerged, Michael Collins and a man named De Valera. They were in some sense allies and in some sense they saw things very differently. After two years of guerilla warfare, England finally agreed to negotiations. De Valera, who knew that he wouldn't get what he wanted from the British, sent Michael Collins as the chief negotiator knowing that when Collins came back with the less than perfect solution, De Valera would be blameless. That is exactly what happened and there was a treaty between Ireland and England that partitioned the country. From then on there was a row between De Valera's forces and Michael Collins.

De Valera wanted nothing less than a whole free Ireland and Michael Collins thought at least we got 26 of the 32 counties, it's a start. De Valera became the guerilla fighter and Michael Collins became part of the new government. Then very tragically within a year, Michael Collins was assassinated. If you are in the Michael Collins' camp you are totally convinced that it was De Valera who did it. If you are in the De Valera camp you are totally convinced that De Valera was the greatest thing that ever happened to Irish politics. After 80 years of Irish politics, the divide still remains. So you can go into any Irish pub, call for a round of drinks and when everybody has clustered around you, you ask the simple question, "Who killed Michael Collins?" Bedlam will ensue.

De Valera went on subsequently to become the Prime Minister of Ireland and then in his old age he became the President of Ireland. He was a great leader in many ways but an extremely arrogant man, a kind of an Irish Charles De Gaul. On one famous occasion, De Valera is reputed to have said, "When I want to know what the people of Ireland are thinking, I go into the forest and I look into my heart." The very same notion comes through in the first reading this morning between God and Israel, God wanting to go out into the desert and look into his heart so that the people of Israel will come back into a covenant relationship with him. I want to talk about that.

I'm going to make three main points. Firstly, I want to talk about the personification of God. Secondly, I want to talk about anthropomorphizing our relationship with God. Thirdly, I want to talk about the idea of developing a personal cosmology.

I will begin with the notion of the personification of God. Almost all world religions have a desperate need to put a face on God. Theologians particularly want to put a face on God. On the other hand, the mystics of all the great religious traditions have no problem with God being faceless and nameless and totally unknown. Mystics say that it is the mystery of God that is important.

There is a great Jewish myth about the four sages all of whom enter paradise one by one. The first sage goes in and looks around and because of what he sees he dies of fright. The second one enters paradise and looks around and because of what he sees he goes completely mad and loses his sanity. The third one goes in and he looks around and because of what he sees he totally loses his faith and becomes an apostate. The fourth sage, Rabbi Akiba, goes in and he looks around and comes back out full of serenity and peace because only Rabbi Akiba understood that even the absence of God is God. The mystics know that. The mystics know that even the absence of God is God and they can be in a relationship with that reality. But theologians cannot. Theologians need God to have a face, otherwise they cannot relate. So you could put all of the great world religions, in my opinion, on a spectrum and within each religion you could create another spectrum on how each one views God. It would go from a fundamentalist literalism that will tell you what gender God is and what God had for breakfast on the Fourth of July in 1972, all the way across the spectrum to the mystical wing of any religion in which they do not even need to make images of God. They do not even need to have a name for God. They don't even need to have a face for God. So within every religion, you get that spectrum of thinking.

Buddhism is one extreme. Buddhism has been accused of being atheistic but it is not atheistic; it is simply not theistic and there is a very big difference. The other extreme would be fundamentalist Islam and fundamentalist Christianity that know exactly who is chosen and what God thinks and what God's needs are.

The first thing we do with God is to create a category of "being" for God. All the mystics of earth and Buddhism in particular, will say that you cannot ascribe any human category to God. Even to say that God is or God is not is meaningless because this is merely small human thinking. The first thing we always want to do is ascribe "being" to God.

The second thing we do is to ascribe characteristics or attributes to this "being" whom we call God. In my opinion, those attributes tend to fall into three categories. We want to talk about a God who is good, we want to talk about a God who is true and we want to talk about a god who is beautiful. The goodness of God has to do with moral issues that this God acts morally in spite of lots of evidence to the contrary. For example, the God who will say to the Israelite army in Joshua in Chapter 6:21, as they are about to attack Jericho, that every man should go straight ahead and kill every human being, man, woman or child or every ox or every sheep or donkey in front of him. Somehow this God is moral? We constantly want to attribute goodness and moral disposition to this God.

We constantly want to attribute truth to this God. This God has to accord with the known facts of science. We bend ourselves into pretzels trying to prove that the God we believe in is actually consonant with quantum mechanics.

The third attribute we want to ascribe to God is beauty, the whole esthetic realm whether it is poetry or art that somehow God lives, breathes and pulsates through beauty. First we create the "being" and then we attribute these kinds of characteristics to this "being." That is what I mean by the personification of God.

My second point is this. Having done that we then start to anthropomorphize our relationship with this being who has those attributes. Depending on how we develop the theology of our relationship with God, from that will flow our ideas of our relationships with each other and then, ultimately, our relationship with ourselves.

Unfortunately, in my experience and in my reading, so very often this theology of a relationship with a being that we have invented, to whom we have attributed all of these characteristics, is often based on fear or on arrogance. It is based on some kind of a craven attitude towards this ultimate, huge, distant, demanding deity who has total control of our future. Or it is based on the notion that somehow we are the chosen, that God has made a special covenant with us if we are Jews and we think we are the chosen people or if we are Catholics and we think that outside the Catholic Church there is no redemption.

We adduce these parables and these images and these metaphors of a covenanted relationship between God and ourselves. In particular, we want to hold up the idea of marriage as symbolic of this special relationship between God and ourselves. I think we miss the point totally.

Since the "being" of God is a totally human construct and since the attributes that we ascribe to this God are totally human constructs, I believe, there is no special relationship between God and the group, between this ultimate ground of our being and any group of us whether we are Catholic, Protestant or Jew. We miss the point completely.

The covenant and the marriage relationship are not between a being called God and a chosen group. They is between the inner divine and the outer divine or between what theologians sometimes call the transcendent aspect of God and the immanent aspect of God, the God who is somehow the ultimate ground of everything and the God whom we experience within ourselves. The covenant and the relationship, in my opinion, are between those two realizations and those two aspects of the same phenomenon.

It is not between a being and a group or a being and a human; it is not that. It is the realization that ultimately there is only God relating to God. God exists, whatever we mean by that. God knows that she exists, whatever we mean by that. Ultimately God can only experience herself through creating and then relating to what she has created. God can be, God can know she exists, but God cannot experience her own existence until she creates and then relates to what she has created. That is what the covenant is about in my opinion. The covenant is the dialogue ensuing between God's knowledge of herself and God's experience of herself. For me, this is the heart and soul of the Christian notion of trinity.

Father represents "is-ness" or being. Jesus represents God's total self-knowledge, so we call him the Word of God. The Spirit represents the love that God has for whom she knows herself to be. We are the channels and we are the vehicles of that experience of God. It is through us that God experiences who she is. God knows who she is, but God can only experience who she is through us. That is our privilege. That is the covenant. So the covenant is not between this being and this group or between this being and some prophet. This is a covenant between God and all living things. This is the very first covenant in the Book of Genesis, Chapter 9. The covenant God expressed eight different times in that one chapter is: "I make a covenant between myself and all living beings." A covenant is not between God and a group. The covenant is not between God and a chosen subgroup. The covenant is between the knowledge and the experience of God.

Therefore, in my opinion, law is only valid in so far as it enunciates the principles of this relationship. All law, whether it is the law of physics or the law of the land or the law of the church, all law is only valid in so far as it addresses and enunciates the principles of this relationship between the God who is and the God who experiences her own existence through her creation.

Now we build on that because liturgy and spiritual practice is the celebration of that fact. Spiritual practice does not allow us to find God. Spiritual practice is a celebration of the fact that we are God. We are God but God is not us. All liturgies and all spiritual practice is a celebration of the fact that God is experiencing herself through her creation. We celebrate that and we are happy to celebrate it but we are not using it as a technique to have a better relationship with God or to win God's ear or to get saved.

Our relationship with others is predicated upon that. In saying, my relationship with all others, and by others I do not just mean other human beings, I mean with buffaloes, bison, and bears, every living thing. My relationship with all living things is predicated on the realization that they too are part of God's experience of herself because that is part of what God has created in order to experience herself rather than just know herself. So if these and other expressions and other articulations of God are God experiencing herself, then there has to be harmony among them. Ultimately then, my relationship to myself is simply the individual, self reflective contemplation of this mystery happening through this

43

particular consciousness.   All relationships grow out of that realization.

The third point I want to make is developing a personal cosmology coming out of this mystery. I think it was Plato who said, "The unexamined life is not worth living." I believe that very strongly. After twenty-eight years as a priest and ten years as a psychologist, I am convinced that the unexamined life is not worth living. If we do not know why we are here and what we are doing here and what makes sense, we may as well just be automatons. What do I mean by a personal cosmology? I will draw on the scientific model.

My understanding of the scientific model is this. Step one; the scientist looks at his data. Step two; he begins to identify some kind of pattern in his data. Step three; he creates a hypothesis to try to explain the patterns in the data. Step four; he sets up an experiment to test his hypothesis. Step five; he will try to replicate his results to make sure it was not just anomalous. Step six; if it holds up under replication obviously it is a new principle. Step seven; you now can create a model of your data on the basis of this principle.

Unfortunately, once you have created a model, and you are a scientist, new anomalous data begin to come in after a while and then you have two choices. You can try to stuff those new anomalous data into the old model until it is creaking at the seams or you can create a new model that explains the new data and all of the other data. That is what I mean by creating a personal cosmology.

There are the data of your own life. No one else has the billions of experiences that are uniquely yours. All of the data of the history that is particular to you are there. The step that most of us are not prepared to make is to look at the data of our lives. Rather we just create a myth on the basis of an atypical representation of the data, we create a personal myth that makes us victims or arrogant or whatever it is and then live out the rest of our lives in an unexamined fashion on the basis of a model created from non-representative data. That is what most of us do.

Most of us live in cultures where we take in models of the universe or our cosmologies almost by osmosis. We take it in from the culture. The culture is a little bit different from society. The relationship between culture and society is that culture gives us the intuitive values that often we cannot articulate but which drive us;

44

and society is the <u>articulated</u> norms, the laws of the group. One is an externalization of the other. Most of us take in these values from our education or religion or politics or the media and we can not articulate them for you. Give us an issue and we have got viewpoints on it. But can you say here is what I believe about life and the afterlife and then put it together coherently? Almost none of us can do it for ourselves, because we have never been encouraged to do it for ourselves. Everyone is offering us predigested models. The churches are always very happy to give us models of how the universe is and even if they do not accord with our own experience of life, somehow we believe them.

The politicians give us models. The media give us models. We take these models aboard and we act as if they are the truth. The unexamined life is not worth living. It behooves every single one of us who is serious about his human journey and serious about his spiritual evolution to look at the raw data of his life and try to identify the patterns, to create a hypothesis, to test them, to lead to the principles that will give him a model of how his universe is and to always be open to the realization that new anomalous data will come in that force him to make new models.

This is exactly, in my opinion, what Jesus is saying in the gospel. He is saying that you cannot take a piece of unwashed cloth and use it to patch a hole in your cloak because when it shrinks it will tear and you will destroy the piece and you have destroyed the coat. You cannot take new wine and pour it into old skins. It is far too strong. It will burst the skins, the wine is lost and the skins are destroyed. In other words, have the courage on a regular basis to create new models of your universe, new personal cosmologies that accord with your experiences of life. Do not settle for second hand cosmologies delivered by institutions that have an agenda in having you buy in to their systems.

My prayer for all of us is this: whatever wine skins we have and whatever wine making we are into, whatever our cloaks look like and whatever our patches look like, for God's sake, for Christ's sake and for our own sake let us not try putting patches on our cloaks or new wine into our old skins.

7
Sin and Temptation

They were born about a half-millennium apart. One of them was born a prince and the other was born a pauper. One of them lived in one of the greatest civilizations planet Earth has ever seen, a civilization that was a shining jewel in the crown of human evolution throughout most of its history. The other one was born in an equally brilliant civilization that spent most of its history oppressed, beaten down and colonized. One of them was brutally murdered, probably before he reached the end of his thirtieth year. The other lived to be an old man and taught for over forty-five years. There are many differences between them and many similarities. They both set out to find enlightenment. One sat for forty-nine days under a tree fasting and meditating until finally he reached enlightenment and very quickly was tempted by Mara, the Hindu equivalent of Satan in the Judeo/Christian scriptures. And the other one went into the desert for forty days and fasted and reached enlightenment, and at the end of that period, was tempted in the very same way. They are, of course, the two shining jewels in world history: Gautama Siddhartha, born about 560 B.C. and Jesus, born about 4 B.C.

There is one temptation in the life of the Buddha to which I want to draw attention. There is a great story told that Mara, the Satan of Hinduism, appeared to the Buddha after he became enlightened and said, "If you really are an enlightened being, why don't you turn the Himalayas, the king of all mountains, into gold?" Buddha's response was, "If all of the mountains of the world were turned into gold, there would not be enough to satisfy one person's greed."

I want to talk about that today. I want to make four main points. First I want to talk about sin. Then secondly, I want to talk about original sin. Thirdly, I want to talk about temptation, and fourthly, I want to talk specifically about the temptations of Jesus as recorded in Matthew's gospel today. First let me talk about sin.

All of us good Catholics have been raised on the notion that sin is the transgression of precept. We have broken laws or trodden all over commandments of various kinds whether it is the Decalogue handed down by God to Moses on Mount Sinai or the Six

Commandments of the Church or the minutia of C
don't believe it for a moment. I do not believe t
transgression of precept. I believe that sin is tl
deliberate decision not to grow. It is only tangenti
precept or commandment. Sin is basically a conscio
decision when faced with an opportunity for growth ᵢ   ...stead
the egocentric or the selfish thing. It is not necessarily all-bad, in my
opinion. The Greek word for sin is taken from a metaphor in
archery; it means to "miss the mark." Missing the mark is very
important.

The two basic core elements of education, in my opinion, are
repetition and feedback. We learn from doing things over and over.
The great teacher is the one who can present the same material in a
different form so as to engage us. But it is the same basic message
again and again. And the second element of education, in my
opinion, is feedback. We cannot learn unless we have feedback. If I
was to put a dartboard on this wall and we were to throw darts at it,
the thing that would allow us to improve our aim, would be to watch
where the darts fall. If they are falling far to the right, I know I need
to be throwing more to the left. If they are falling on the floor, I
need to be aiming a little bit higher. If I were to put a sheet between
the dart board and myself and attempt to throw darts over the sheet
and improve my aim when I cannot see where they land, I would
never learn anything. Feedback is vital. Sin provides feedback. So
the decisions we make for selfishness are a very important part of
our spiritual journey. They allow us to readjust our sights. So sin is
not bad as long as we learn from our mistakes. It is really important
and it is really good. Sin allows us to improve who we are as
individuals. For me, sin is God's way of pulling us forward, enticing
us to do better.

What about "original" sin? There is no notion of "original"
sin in Judaism. There is a story about the first sin, but there is no
notion of "original" sin. There is no notion of "original" sin within
Islam. Islam does not believe that we suffer from a fallen nature.

In coming onto planet Earth, there is a forgetting of who we
really are, but there is not a catastrophic fall. We merely forget who
we are, what our core identity is, and then we spend our lives trying
to recover that. Christianity was the genius that invented "original
sin," maybe most particularly, Augustine. Augustine lived at a time
when the Roman Empire was crumbling. Where others of us

..apolate from our own experiences, Augustine, if I were to invent ...term, intrapolated.

He looked at the world around him and because it was falling to pieces, because Rome had been invaded and sacked in his own lifetime, he believed that anarchy and chaos were as bad as the human condition could get. Augustine considered irrationality the pits. We are most God-like, according to Augustine, when we are most rational. So reason is the highest faculty of the human. We are most God-like when we are most reasonable and most rational, and we are most un-God-like when we are most irrational.

In the sexual act, at the moment of orgasm people are totally out of control. They are completely irrational and that is the time, said Augustine, that conception takes place. So conception takes place when people are acting in the most absolutely irrational of fashions, when they are the least God-like, and therefore in the very act of creating a new child we infuse this sinful condition into it. What an extraordinary teaching! That the single most co-creative thing we do somehow becomes the greatest sin that we pass on to each other. Looking at what was happening around him, he intrapolated this and he taught it to subsequent generations. Christian theologians ran with it. They had a ball with it. The church invented limbo and purgatory, and finally in the sixteen hundreds a Parisian Catholic theologian taught that if a Catholic woman died pregnant, she could not be buried in a Christian graveyard since she carried a "pagan" within her. She would defile consecrated ground and so she needed to be eviscerated. So the little "pagan" was taken out and dumped some place so that the remaining Christian carcass could be buried in a sacred place. What an extraordinary way of twisting the teaching and the compassion of Jesus!

Psychologists have had a ball with the story of the expulsion from the garden. What really happened? Were Adam and Eve thrown out of the garden because of Adam's first sin? Some psychologists believe that this is, in fact, a metaphorical illustration of birthing. That we leave the oceanic bliss of the womb where there is total security, where all our needs are effortlessly met, into the world of harsh sounds and harsh lights where we need to breathe for ourselves and finally become independent beings. That is one explanation. Another explanation is that the expulsion from the garden means actually reaching the use of reason, that somewhere around the age of seven, children for the first time develop the hard wiring that allows them to appreciate another person's viewpoint. Before the age of seven, a child cannot really put himself in someone else's shoes. He can learn dictates. He can be told "how would you like it if I did that to you," but he cannot meaningfully comprehend what that would actually be like. It is very difficult because the hard wiring is not yet in place for a three-or four-year old child to literally walk in somebody else's shoes.

Somewhere around the age of seven we develop the ability that allows us to distinguish between good and evil. In this model, and it is a model that makes sense to me, the expulsion from the Garden of Eden was the best thing that ever happened to us. It allowed us for the first time to be self-reflective, thinking moral beings. I cannot be a moral being unless I am self-reflective. There is a great Jewish story from the Midrashim about Adam and Eve. After they were expelled from the garden, they were still so enamored with the fruit of the tree of the knowledge of good and evil, that they snuck back in one night and started eating again. They heard a noise in the tree and they suddenly realized that there was someone else eating from it as well. They looked, pulling back the branches, and there was God feeding on the same fruit, because God too, in some sense, is a being who continues to evolve and to distinguish between right and wrong. That is what original sin perhaps really is. It is our breakthrough into becoming fully self-reflective human beings with the possibility of making moral choices. We cannot do it before hand. That's my second point.

The third point I want to make is to talk about the notion of temptation. The word "temptation" has a real pejorative ring to it. But personally, I do not believe temptation is bad. I believe temptation is the thing that most challengingly invites us into alignment with our mission. It invites us to live our lives with consciousness and deliberation. It invites us to live our lives self-reflectively. If there were not such a thing as temptation, we would be one of two things. We would be robots preprogrammed to live virtuous lives or else we would be sybarites living out our lives hedonistically. There would be no possibility whatsoever of making moral choices. Temptation is the invitation by God to live with full consciousness. We typically live our lives in one of three fashions. We create reality in one of three ways. We do it through unconscious intentions, whereby we live our lives and create our

49

realities by just going with every whim or fancy or predisposition unthinkingly. Or we live our lives in the collective. We allow the collective to create our reality for us. We allow the culture to tell us what is real and what is desirable. The third way of living is to live with full consciousness, mindfulness, and with full awareness create our own reality. That is what temptation allows us to do. If there were no temptation, there would be no possibility whatsoever of distinguishing between living mindfully and living mindlessly.

The fourth point I want to make is related to this. What is the meaning of the temptations of Jesus recorded in today's scriptures? To begin with, it is very probable that the gospel writers are pulling into one crystallization all of the temptations that Jesus experienced throughout his entire life. In fact, Luke's account of this temptation says that he was tempted for forty days. Luke does not say Jesus fasted for forty days and then was tempted as Matthew does. Luke says he was tempted for forty days. It was not just three discrete temptations, according to Luke. It was forty days of it and forty is a magical number within Judaism. It is the number of completeness. It is the number of days that Moses spent on Mount Sinai in dialogue with God.

In some sense this story represents all of the temptations that Christ experienced and all of the psychic and spiritual wrestling he engaged in for the entire period of his public ministry. It is constellating and crystallizing them into these three things. In some sense, the desert just represents the wilderness of our lifetime. The beasts represent the denizens of our unconscious, the angels who come to minister at the end represent our higher consciousness, i.e., the image of God within us. That is my way of introduction.

What was the meaning of these three temptations? The first temptation, allegedly, came at the end of forty days. Satan being the great psychologist that he was, brilliant at reading body language, saw very clearly that this Jesus was hungry. After 40 days he had that kind of emaciated look one gets after 40 days without food. Satan picked up on that quickly, bright guy! You could say that the first level of this first temptation was merely, "You are hungry, go feed yourself." The second level of the meaning of this first temptation may have been that Satan was inviting Jesus to satisfy all and any of his sensual needs or all and any of his physical needs. It does not just mean bread. It could mean any physical need or any desire. Satan is inviting Jesus to go for it. Paint the town red. Do whatever you need to do. That is the second meaning, perhaps, of the first temptation.

But the most important meaning of all, in my opinion, is this: Satan was offering Jesus the same temptation that Mara was offering the Buddha. When Mara said to the Buddha: "If you are an enlightened being, why don't you turn the Himalayas, the king of all mountains, into gold?" this was not just a demonstration of power. Rather it was Mara saying to the Buddha, "If you are this being of compassion, why can't you turn these mountains into gold? Then you could feed all the hungry people of the world." I believe that this is the real meaning of the first temptation of Jesus. It was not just about satisfying his physical hunger. It was not just about giving in to his sensual needs. It was saying to him, "If you are this extraordinary, enlightened, compassionate man that you claim to be, or are attempting to be, why don't you turn all the stones of all the deserts of the world into bread and then there would be food for everyone." The knowledge of Jesus was the same as the Buddha's knowledge; "If I were to turn every single stone in every desert into bread in order to feed the hungry, there would not be enough food in the world for one person's greed." You can bet your bottom dollar that an economic model would be set up or a military regime would take over or some political process would take all the bread in the world and dish it out to the hungry only if they fulfilled the needs of the political process. It would be immediately put into huge warehouses and doled out according to a predetermined agenda. Jesus knew that just creating food is not the answer to world hunger. It is indeed a mitzvah. It is a requirement of us that we feed the hungry of the world. It is a requirement of us that we try to change the economic, political and military process so that we make food instead of guns. It is our commandment, but that alone is not enough.

If we made food out of every gun, and we turned every nuclear bomb into a feast, there would be other people with hard hearts and greedy souls who would commandeer all of that food and still dish it out to us. Jesus knew that just making bread available for everyone was not the answer. Jesus resisted it.

The devil tried a second ploy. He took him to the top of a mountain and showed him all the kingdoms of the world and he said, "If you bow down and adore me, I will give you all of this." It seemed like a ridiculous statement, like Jesus was going to bow down and adore Satan; give me a break. There is a much deeper meaning. There is a real seduction. Satan is saying to Jesus; "I will give you command over the military, political and economic processes. You can disband the armies, if that is what you choose to do. You can put people into government whom you believe are compassionate and loving people. You can create an economic model in which everyone has what he wants." It sounds really tempting. But Jesus again got it. You cannot legislate people into love. You cannot change the hearts of people by merely providing structures that work well. There is no structure that people cannot corrupt.

In 1984-85, two of my last three years in Kenya, there was a tremendous famine. I had contact with the World Bank. I managed to bring in three lorry-loads of food every month. We brought in wheat, soymilk and oil. I remember the first three lorries we took in before we got our act together. We drove these three lorries into a village in order to distribute food to the people and the villagers ransacked and ravished the lorries. It was a horrible thing to see. I realized that whether the human heart sits on top of a full belly or it sinks into the abyss of a wrinkled and emaciated stomach, it is the human heart that makes the decisions. There are people who find God both in their hunger and in their satiety. There are people who find only evil and greed in their successes and their failures. Merely bringing in lorry-loads of food was not the answer. We had to get our act together in a very different way. If the only difference between the murderer and the victim is who gets the gun first, then the cycle just continues. Something else has to happen. It is not enough to set military, economic or political structures in place, unless we as individuals, every single one of us, human being by human being, is committed to his own personal transformation.

So Jesus said "no" to the second temptation. Then Satan tried the subtlest one of all. He took him to the pinnacle of the temple in Jerusalem and he said, "If you really are the Son of God, throw yourself down." It is written in Psalm 91, "He will give his angels command over you lest you dash your foot against a stone." On the face of it, this seems ridiculous. Was he inviting Jesus to bungee jump without the bungee cord? No, it was much subtler than that. It was the final temptation. He was saying to Jesus, "You know what the world really needs is a new religion. You are going to initiate it. You, with this glorious sign, are going to start a new religion and people are going to believe. There are hundreds of people milling about at the base of the temple. You throw yourself down. They are gawking up at you at the moment and you float to earth and you announce the beginning of the reign of the kingdom of God and you set in place a whole new religion. You will have everyone eating out of your hand." Jesus knew that this too was not the answer. Jesus knew that a new religion was not the answer. I do not believe for a moment that Jesus' mission was to set up a new religion called Christianity. It happened and I am not saying it was necessarily a bad thing, but I do not believe for a moment that it was his purpose. I think Jesus realized that all world religions are merely specific cultural articulations of the same basic archetypal human search for God. They each look a little bit different. Their theologies look different. Their liturgies look different, their scriptural traditions look different, but at core is the basic human drive to "individuation" as Carl Jung called it, the basic human search for the ultimate ground of our being. Whether is comes out to be like Islam or whether it comes out looking like Christianity or whether it comes out looking like Judaism, is not that important. Jesus knew that what this world badly needed was not a new religion. Jesus realized that what this world needed was the spiritual quest of the individual soul seeking God. Then the communities that form on the basis of sharing our earthly journeys with each other become meaningful religions. But to start a religion in order to proselytize and whip people into shape has never worked, it is not working now and it never will work. Christianity has done some beautiful things in the course of its history, as have Islam and Judaism. Christianity has done some extraordinarily evil things, as have Islam and Judaism. Religions are not the answer. If religions are merely human organizations with particular agendas and specific ideologies and a particular way of doing ritual and another kind of scriptural tradition, it will get us nowhere fast and it has gotten us nowhere fast. If religion is not the community's facilitating and celebrating stories of individual human beings as they search for God in their own unique fashion, religion is meaningless and community is purposeless.

The prayer I make for all of us this morning is this: That we, too, would resist the easy fixes, in our own personal relationships, in our communities and in economic models. We certainly need to redraw our structures. We certainly need to begin dismantling the passion we have for killing. We certainly need to take seriously our need to feed, educate and house the world's population, but unless that is accompanied by the individual commitment to personal self-transformation, it is going to get us nowhere.

8
Prejudice

When I was a child growing up in Ireland in the late 40's and early 50's, most of the women baked bread. There was always fresh dough in the house. Children will occasionally swallow some foreign object, a marble, pebble or safety pin so the solution was to force-feed the child fresh dough. The fresh dough would insulate the foreign object inside the stomach and in the gastrointestinal tract so it didn't puncture something and cause serious damage. Then for the next two or three days the child wouldn't be allowed to use the toilet. He had to go to the back yard and he had to poop in the back yard. Mommy would poke through it with a stick to make sure he had passed the foreign object.

Now, prejudices are a little like that. Prejudices are the things that allow us to survive in the immediate situation but they eventually get in the way. If we don't pass the foreign object out of our system, and if we don't pass the insulating dough out of our system, the whole thing will rot and the very dough that initially protected us from the foreign object now becomes the main source of disease for us. Defense mechanisms are a little like that. Defense mechanisms are the psychic dough with which we insulate the traumatic events of childhood. They allow us to survive childhood but eventually as adults they begin to atrophy and they begin to cause disease. They get in our way. At some stage in our adult life, we have to have the courage with a friend, a spiritual director or a therapist to go out in the back yard and poop psychically, so that we can pass these defense mechanisms out of our system and learn to approach life differently.

Prejudices are a bit like that. I want to talk about prejudices today. I want to make four main points. I want to talk firstly about the nature of prejudice. Secondly, I want to talk about Jesus' prejudices. Thirdly, I want to talk about the prejudices in today's gospel story from John. Fourthly, I want to talk about the positive purpose of prejudice.

Let me begin by saying a few words about the nature of prejudice. The truth is we cannot survive an education without taking aboard a whole bunch of prejudices. We cannot survive the family. We cannot survive a denominational affiliation. We cannot survive any environment or any culture without taking aboard a whole bunch of prejudices. We take them aboard for several reasons. The first reason is this; there is a tremendous need in the human psyche for security. Therefore we have to create the prejudice that our people are the "in group." In order to feel safe, we have to surround ourselves with the prejudice of the "in group" or "our people" among whom we are safe. Whether that is a national identity or a local community identity or a religious identity we all feel the need for security and therefore we create the prejudices for the "in group."

Beside our security needs, we also have needs to feel special, not just safe but special. So we create many other prejudices of being against. There are two kinds of prejudices, in my opinion, prejudices for and prejudices against. The security needs create prejudices for our little "in group." The specialty needs create prejudices against. We have to feel superior to many people so we create prejudices that stigmatize them as the "out group." Many of us continue most of our lives with these two sets of prejudices, prejudices for and against.

Being prejudiced is not a uniquely human thing, but unlike animals we have to <u>learn</u> our prejudices. Animals are built with instinctive prejudices both for and against. There was a great incident I saw on TV a few months ago. There is a special kind of beetle in Australia that is orange colored, dimpled and has a very hard shell. Some business group in Australia started making a soft drink that they bottled in an orange, dimpled bottle. Soon the population of these sand beetles began to plummet precipitously because the male beetles mistook these discarded dimpled bottles for females, literally. All of the males were crawling over these bottles trying to impregnate them while all the females were sitting home knitting. It destroyed family life. All the males were "on the bottle" and all the females were staying home. Finally it got so bad ecologically that there was an appeal made to this group to change either the color or the texture of the bottles

That is an example of prejudice for; a prejudice for a color and for a texture that was destroying an ecosystem. It is not just human beings who suffer from prejudices for and against, even the animal kingdom does. So there are pluses and minuses to prejudices. The pluses for the prejudices are that we do not have to constantly reinvent the wheel. Prejudices allow us to build on the experiences of other people. There is a positive part to prejudices. It allows us to build on the work of others. The down side of prejudice, of course, is that all prejudices are predicated upon an unrepresentative sample. One of our ancestors a long time ago had a particular experience with a particular member of a group and that somehow became a stereotype for that entire group. And now we continue to act out of that stereotype. So there is a positive and a negative.

Secondly, I want to look at Jesus' prejudices. If Jesus was human, he had prejudices. If Jesus, at some part of his life, realized his divinity then he had to first overcome his prejudices. In my opinion, Jesus did have prejudices. In the gospels of Matthew, Mark and John, one prejudice that comes through in all three was that Jesus had a real problem with foreign women. I mean that literally. There is a story in Matthew and in Mark about an encounter between Jesus and a Phoenician woman. Jesus is on vacation in a strange country with his disciples when this Phoenician woman, who recognized him, ran after him saying, "Son of David, have pity on me. My little daughter is at home and she is seriously ill." Jesus ignored her. Finally, she ran up in front of him and grabbed his feet and said, "Please, my little daughter is dying. Please help her." Jesus in an extraordinarily abusive statement and an extremely prejudicial viewpoint said, "It is not okay to take the food belonging to the children and throw it to the dogs." But somehow this woman's love for her child was greater than her outrage at the insult and she turned the tables on him. She said, "I realize that. But you know, sometimes scraps fall from the table and the little puppies come and eat it up. That is all I want." I think that at that point, Jesus was hit in the face by the Father who said to him, "Wake up, this woman is teaching you something about who you are and what your mission is."

Previous to this incident Jesus had said to his disciples, "I was only sent to the lost sheep of the house of Israel." Here was a mere woman and a foreigner teaching Jesus that his mission was not just to the lost sheep of the house of Israel. But before he got the lesson, he was extremely rude to her. In the gospel of John, Jesus is very rude. He is sitting by the well and this woman comes along and the first thing he says to her is "Hey, give me a drink." The woman should have turned around to him like she would to a child and said, "What's the magic word?" He was really very rude. Later on in the story he says to her, "Go call your husband." And she says, "I don't have a husband." He says, "You are right; you don't have a husband. You've had five of them and the guy you're with now isn't your husband." It was none of his business. It was an extremely rude thing for him to say. Jesus had a problem with foreign women. Like all great teachers, Jesus had to learn from his own experiences. God hit him in the face with these two incidents, in my opinion, and finally Jesus got beyond his prejudices against women and against foreigners in particular. I believe, in fact, that the great teachers constantly invite us to let go of our prejudices.

This brings me to my third major point. There are four different kinds of prejudices in today's story, in my opinion. The first one is the prejudice of sexism. The woman buys into it as much as the disciples buy into it. When Jesus first asked her for a drink she says, "Are you talking to me? I'm only a woman. How can you, a man, be talking to me? I'm just a woman." When the disciples come back afterwards we are told they asked, "What is he doing talking to a woman?" Here is the sexist thing, straight off. The thing we are not getting is that the woman is the minder of the well. The woman is the one who is really in charge of the source of life. We did not get that then and we do not get that still in many ways. We have not yet recognized it in the Catholic Church even today. Many societies still have not recognized it. That is the first prejudice in today's story.

The second prejudice, I think, is literalism. We are all buying into literalism and we still do it. It is a fundamentalist exegesis of scripture and we still buy into it. And the woman bought into it. So Jesus says, "If you knew who it was who was asking you for a drink, you would ask me for a drink." Her answer is, "Really, so how are you going to do it? You don't have a bucket. It is a deep well. How are you going to do this?" So she is thinking absolutely literally. When the apostles come back and they tell Jesus, "Eat." And Jesus says, "I've already eaten." And they say, "He has? Someone came out and brought him food?" All the time there is this initial impetus to translate stuff literally. We are stuck with this in exegesis constantly, literalism in all its guises.

The third prejudice, in my opinion, is denominationalism. Here is Jesus very arrogantly saying to the woman, "You guys worship what you don't understand. We worship what we understand because, after all, salvation is from the Jews." If I were around at the time, I would have given Jesus a swift kick. It was an extraordinarily arrogant thing for him to say. It is ridiculous to believe that the ineffable God of all creation looks down at a universe that consists of over a hundred billion galaxies each of which consists of more than a hundred billion stars, and that he looks down through all of this and picks a special galaxy, and a special planet within that galaxy and then picks out a special tribe and says, "Aha, they are the ones I really love." That Jesus could have bought into the prejudice of believing that the Jews were God's chosen people or that the Samaritans were worshiping what they did not understand whereas the Jews were worshiping what they did understand, that was an extraordinary prejudice. It took Jesus time to work through that.

The fourth prejudice is related to that because they lived in a theocracy where the law of the land and the law of God were the same thing -- so there is racism involved here, i.e., the notion of a superior group and an inferior group. Here are four totally different prejudices being contended with in today's gospel.

The fourth point I want to make is this. What then is the positive purpose of prejudice? I think it comes towards the very end of this story. The people, the Samaritans, who had come out because they believed what this woman had told them about Jesus, now say to her, "Initially we believed because of what you had told us that he revealed to you your inner secrets. But now that we have seen the guy for ourselves and we have heard him for ourselves, we now believe because of our own experience." Prejudices are always based on someone else's report. That is how prejudices start. Prejudices always begin when we believe someone else's account of what happened.

Enlightenment comes when we trust our own experiences and we get into alignment with God ourselves. This is one of the great statements of the Buddha. The Buddha would say to his disciples again and again, "Be a lamp unto yourself. Do not trust any scriptural tradition. Do not trust any teacher. Test it for yourself and if it feels that it brings you into alignment with God and that it is consonant with your experience of the divine then follow it. But do not take anyone's word for anything." Prejudices are always built on the word of someone else.

So what is the purpose of prejudice? I think, as spirit beings, before we incarnate on planet Earth we do not have prejudices. As soon as we decide to incarnate, we are faced with a series of limiting choices that ipso facto create prejudices for us. I have to decide whether I am going to be born male or female, whichever I decide on there are prejudices that go with that position. Am I going to be born white, black, yellow, brown or red? All of those positions have prejudices. Am I going to be born with a genius IQ or mentally retarded? Both of those have prejudices. What socioeconomic status am I going to have? Am I going to be born into a rich family or a poor family? There will be prejudices involved there. All of the self-limiting choices that are part of being incarnate bring their prejudices with them. That is a good thing because it is only by experiencing prejudices that we can go beyond them. You take a newborn infant and an enlightened Buddha, superficially they look alike because neither of them has prejudices. But they are very different, one is pre-prejudicial and the other is post-prejudicial. They look alike because they are both non-prejudicial but they are very different. The baby is non-prejudicial simply because she has not yet met the prejudices. The Buddha figure, the enlightened figure, is non-prejudicial because she has worked through all of the prejudices and has come out at the other side. As incarnate divinity, as children of God, the limitations we experience allow us to meet our prejudices and to move beyond them, if we have the courage to do it. It is like the difference between a child who has not yet had chicken pox and one who has had chicken pox. The child who has had chicken pox is now immunized against it. The other one is not immune and is going to suffer at some stage from it. It seems to me that the spiritual journey is a question of facing our prejudices and growing beyond them.

I would like to finish up with my own personal definition of integrity. I think that it is about the age of seven that a child for the first time is cognitively wired to make moral choices because up until then a child literally cannot stand in anyone else's shoes and see the world from a viewpoint not his own. He can learn short statements like, "How would you like it if I did that to you?" But he cannot stand in someone else's moccasins. Somewhere about the age of seven, the hardwiring is in place for a child to truly appreciate what it must be like to be standing in someone else's shoes and only then can he begin to make moral choices.

I think the great teachers have come among us in order to take us far beyond that position. It is not just a question of learning as an individual person to put myself in some other individual's shoes. We must learn as communities to put ourselves in another community's shoes. We must learn as nations to put ourselves in the shoes of other nations and we finally have to learn as a species how to put ourselves perhaps not in the shoes but in the fins or the fur or the feet of another species. Until we do that we are not truly moral people; we do not have integrity. And so my personal definition of integrity is this. Integrity is the commitment to the ongoing expansion of my perspective until I finally realize that God's creation is what it really is. It is a unified, eternal context in which all moral choices must be made. As spiritual beings our purpose is to confront our prejudices one by one and grow beyond them.

9
Reality, Reactivity and Theodicy

I lived for three years in a seminary in Cork City in order to attend the National University of Ireland. Every morning, rain or shine, we set out, two by two on bicycles from the seminary to cycle the five miles to the University. We were a motley crew in ponchos, hats and roman collars. At the end of the day we would cycle back, except we were not allowed to cycle back on our own. We had to wait in the bicycle shed until one of our seminarian mates came along even if we had to wait two hours to cycle home the five miles together. God knows what might happen if we went home on our own. A girl might look at us, and then what would we do?

One day, two friends of mine, Paddy Keane and Brian Rutledge, left the university to cycle home together. They got on their bicycles wearing their ponchos and they started off. Now Paddy was a morose, moody and taciturn individual at the best of times. Brian, in order to make conversation said, "It's a nice day today, Paddy." Paddy ignored him. They cycled for about three miles and Brian tried it again, he said, "Nice day today Paddy." Paddy ignored him. Finally at the end of the five miles as they're turning into the gates of the seminary Brian tried it again saying, "Nice day today Paddy." And Paddy turned viciously to him and said, "Who the hell is arguing with you?"

I want to talk about that today. I want to make three main points. I want to talk about reality. Then I want to talk about reactivity. Then thirdly, I want to talk about a big jawbreaker and I'll explain what it is.

First I want to talk about reality. I am totally convinced that reality is an artifact of consciousness. Our senses and our cognitive abilities create reality. In fact, with tongue in cheek, I sometimes say that reality has two main criteria. In order for something to be real it must be (a) sensible and (b) sensible. In other words, it must be apprehensible to the senses and secondly it must fit in with the current belief system, it must make sense. Of course, that is totally made up. Our senses, all five of them, are extraordinarily limited. Every single one of them operates within a very narrow band. Our sight operates somewhere in between infrared and ultraviolet, between 400 and 700 nanometers. We cannot see the infrared and ultraviolet rays. We cannot see cosmic rays or TV rays or radio rays or gamma rays or any of these things that are as real as that table is. Because they are outside these particular frequencies, we cannot see them.

Snakes get a better deal. Snakes can see into the infrared rays. When a snake looks at the body he sees the hot spots and goes for that. In Africa, there is a snake called the spitting cobra. When the spitting cobra looks at you, he sees the hot spots in your body and that is where he spits. Snakes can see into the infrared rays.

Or take our hearing, we can hear between 20- and 20,000-megahertz. If we could hear below 20, we could literally hear our own muscles creak. If we were bats, we could hear up to 100,000 instead of just 20,000 megahertz. If we were bats, we might have an acoustical image of a rose instead of just a visual image or an olfactory image. Our senses absolutely limit our reality; then our belief systems do a number on our senses. By the time we define what our reality is, we have been circumscribed by our sensory apparatus and by our cognitive abilities. If we could extend any of these, not only would we perceive a different universe or a different reality, there would be a different universe and a different reality. The problem is we see things not as they are. We see things as we are. And what we see, we tend to become. This limits our reality. We become what we see and we see things as we are rather than as things are in themselves. So it seems to me, when Jesus is talking about opening the eyes of the man who was born blind he is talking not just about a sensory operation, he is talking about a perceptual reorganization of this man's belief system.

As the great scientist Einstein said at the beginning of this century, "The real object of science is to awaken the cosmic religious experience." We have a special word for that in my language; we call it a "caol áit" and it means a "thin place." By "thin places" we mean places in which the veil between the seen and the unseen, between the visible and invisible, between the material and the immaterial is so diaphanous that for a moment one can see through it. People tend to go on pilgrimages to such places that have a special kind of energy that invite us to see not with the eyes of the body, but to see with the eyes of the soul. This, it seems to me, is the real point of this story. It was not that this blind man's sensory ability was healed. It was that he saw Jesus. The others did not see Jesus. So when Jesus asks him rhetorically, "Do you believe in the son of man?" and he answers, "Who is he?" and Jesus says, "You have seen him," Jesus did not mean that his physical eyes had been opened and that the 5'9" character with black curly hair standing in front of him was Jesus. He was not talking about that. He was saying, "You have really seen to the core of it."

I want to talk about reactivity because we sometimes believe that if we could have lived in the time of Jesus and met Jesus, our lives would have been totally devoted to truth, healing and compassion. I do not believe that to be true at all. To see Jesus does not mean to "see" Jesus. To see a flesh and blood character or to hear human words emanating from someone or even to rub shoulders with him is no guarantee of insight, love or compassion. Just look at this story from today's gospel. I can pick out four different reactions. The first reaction was from the blind man's parents. Imagine their embarrassment. This man had been born blind and in the thinking of that time and in the cosmology of Judaism at that time, he was born blind because somebody had committed a sin. Therefore, his parents are deeply embarrassed about having a son who cannot see. It is a reflection on their son or on themselves.

Now to make matters worse, this man who spent his life as a beggar is bringing the authorities down on top of their heads and these very important looking people are asking them questions. The parents do what anybody would do in such circumstances, they squirm and they try to get out of it. They say, "You know, he's of age; ask him. All we know is he is our son and he was born blind. Isn't it bad enough that he was born blind? Isn't it bad enough that God is punishing us for something besides him coming back and making trouble for us? Ask him." So they are squirming and they are trying to get out of it.

Look at the reaction of the neighbors in the crowd. At first, there is denial. "This isn't the guy." "Yes it is." "Are you sure?" They go over and talk to him. They are interested in seeing a miracle. This guy used to be blind and now he can see. Their curiosity is peaked. They would love to see it happen again with somebody else. Many people followed Jesus because they were bored. They had to do something on a boring afternoon. So their curiosity was about being entertained, seeing something new. That is the only interest they had in Jesus.

The blind man is the real hero in this story. Here is an individual whose physical eyes were opened, but much more importantly, the eyes of his soul were opened. This is a man who then got to walk in a "thin place" for the rest of his life, in a place where the veil between God and humanity is diaphanous and he could see and communicate through that veil on a constant basis. This was a man who relied upon his own personal spiritual experience above all else. Religion is constantly trying to foist upon us other models, other belief systems, and other peoples' experiences of God. There is no substitute for your own individual experience of the numinous God.

The Buddha would say again and again, "Be a lamp unto yourself." This was the greatness of this blind man. He trusted his own spiritual experience. He could say to the Pharisees, to the authority figures, he who was born in sin, he could give them one of the most extraordinarily beautiful lectures on Hebrew cosmology and theology they would ever hear, except they could not hear it. They would tell him, "You are born in sin and you are going to lecture to us?" But this man stood his ground. This man said, "I just know one thing. I know my own experience. I used to be blind and now I can see. You can take all your scriptures and you can take all your teachings and all your theologies but I know that I have met my God. I know that I have had a spiritual experience and that is more important to me. That is where I want to ground my reality and not in any made up scriptural tradition or not in any theology or any fine words of philosophy." Here was a man who trusted his own experience. That is the core of the story, as I see it.

The fourth reaction comes from the Pharisees. Here are people who are grounded in a model of reality and anything that tends to shake that model of reality is deeply disconcerting. And so they set about trying to destroy the evidence. They are not people looking for evidence in order to arrive at truth. They are looking for some information that will allow them to deny or destroy or condemn. They are not seekers after truth who are looking, listening and asking questions in order to arrive at the core truth of the situation. They are only looking for information that will allow them to condemn, dismiss and deny. How often in our own lives are we standing on models of reality that do not serve us anymore? We are standing on the shoulders of other people's prejudices and we continue to view life through them. It is almost as if we create

65

models of reality that are predetermined and prejudged, and then we force all the raw data of our own experiences through these artificial categories and bludgeon them until they fit into existing paradigms. If Jesus is about anything, he is about the notion of breaking down paradigms.

There is a "Holy Trinity" in the Hindu Scriptures: Brahma, Vishnu and Shiva. Shiva is the person in the Hindu trinity who is responsible for destruction. Not the destruction in the sense of annihilation, but rather, destruction in the sense of having the courage to let go of old ways of thinking so that we can reassemble the pieces into a much more creative model that can hold our own individual experiences of God. There is no model of reality that is true for all times. All models of reality, whether scientific, Catholic, Buddhist or Hindu are all products of particular cultures. They are all relative and they will all pass. The ultimate experience is to trust your own encounters with the divine, to stand in your own truth like this blind man did. In spite of what the authorities are telling you to the contrary, and in spite of the fun that is being made of you and in spite of the fingers that are being pointed at you, there is no greater truth than to stand in your own individual experience of God.

The last point I want to make is this big jawbreaker that theologians call "theodicy." It is a big word for the problem of evil. There is an extraordinary little sideline here where the apostles and the parents and the Pharisees are all buying into a model that this man was born blind because of someone's sin. The apostles offer two possibilities. They ask Jesus, "Whose sin caused this man to be born blind? Was it his parent's sin or was it his own sin?" It is a fascinating question. How could the man be born blind for his own sin unless Judaism actually believed in some form of reincarnation? How could a little infant be born in sin because of his own fault if he had not lived before in order to build up some kind of demerit? Judaism did believe in a kind of reincarnation and certainly, esoteric Judaism, the Kabbalah, talks a lot about reincarnation. So, either this is the blind man's karma, or God is visiting the sins of the parents upon the child.

Now Judaism at this time was still struggling with the notion of life after death. Life after death came very late into Judaism. It came after the time of Alexander the Great about 330 B.C. But even at the time of Jesus there was a big controversy waging between the Pharisees and the Sadducees as to whether or not there is life after death. So if there is not life after death, and God is one and God is just, then obviously if someone is suffering it is because he has committed a sin or his parents are being punished vicariously through their child. Jesus' response was fascinating. He said, "This man was not born blind because of the parent's sin or because of his own sin but so that the works of God might be manifested through him." What did that mean? It could mean several things, in my opinion.

Maybe Jesus is saying that if there were no blind among us, if there were no sick among us, how would we appreciate sight and wellness? That could be the meaning. Or was Jesus saying that he was born blind because something extraordinary is about to happen and this man in some sense is a conduit for some great learning for a community. That may have been what he meant. Maybe the most vexatious question that we ask each other and ourselves is this question of the problem of evil. Why do bad things happen to good people or even to bad people? Why do bad things happen at all? I have a personal model that makes sense to me. I call it an equation with seven parameters in it that, to me, help to explain how there is stuff in our world that makes us squirm.

The first part I believe is DNA. Some families are predisposed to have cancers and others to have heart disease. Some ethnic groups are predisposed to sickle cell anemia or diabetes. The first factor in any illness in some way is DNA. We do not have any control over it, but perhaps with the genome project we may get a handle on it.

The second aspect, I believe, is environmental influence. All of us are raised in situations in which the quality of air we breathe, the kind of food we eat and our culture determines to some extent the kind of illnesses, whether they are psychological illnesses or physical illnesses or spiritual illnesses, that we will encounter.

A third aspect I believe is personal life style. How I choose to live my life will have an effect on the quality of health or illness I experience. If I smoke three packs of cigarettes a day, eat nothing but hotdogs all of my life, sit behind a desk and never exercise, I am determining the quality of health I can expect.

The fourth factor I believe is mindset. My belief systems about the world play some part in the illnesses or the wellness I experience. My prejudices, my viewpoints about personal control, e.g., if my health is "in the hands of a doctor," or a belief that "health is a crap shoot," all influence the kind of illnesses I experience.

The fifth one I believe is adult relationships. The people I tend to hang out with influence my mindset, my thinking and my beliefs about the world and myself.

The sixth factor I believe is Karma. I believe very strongly in reincarnation. I think we live as many times as we need until we finally understand that the only thing that works is love. God gives us as many opportunities as we need. Karma is not a punitive model of beating up on us because of past sins. It is rather further opportunities to grow until we know not just in our heads but in our hearts that the only thing that works is love. So we come back because we want to learn. We accept vicissitudes or we even accept illness because there is a part of us that can grow best through the experience of illness.

The final factor I call the Bodhisattva dimension. There is a beautiful teaching in Buddhism about the Bodhisattva. Bodhisattvas are persons who have lived sufficient lifetimes until they have become enlightened beings. They merit leaving the Earth and getting off the wheel of karma, but they take a vow that they will keep reincarnating until every sentient creature is saved. They keep coming back again and again, out of compassion and out of love not just for the human condition but also for the entire planet with all its life forms. They are Jesus figures, Buddha figures and maybe Mahatma Gandhi and maybe Mother Teresa figures. However, I believe there is a bit of the Bodhisattva in every single one of us. Whatever degree of altruism or unconditional love we are capable of, that is a bit of the Bodhisattva in each of us. So we might be accepting an illness or a situation in order to afford a wider community the opportunities to exercise compassion or to afford medical science the opportunity of studying these issues to develop some kind of a cure. All of these are factors in the question of theodicy. It is not a question of sin, in my opinion, either parent's sin or the sin of the children.

So the question I leave with you this morning is this. What do you think is your mission on planet Earth? What have you signed up to do? In what cosmic drama have you agreed to play the part you are now playing? What has been your mission and what is your role? In what areas of your life are you experiencing blindness or prejudice? In what area of your life is Jesus making mud and spreading it on your eyes and telling you to go wash. You are being sent to the pool of Siloam. Have you, and have I, the courage to follow that injunction to spread mud on our eyes? How ludicrous! How can you imagine that by putting dirt in someone's eye who cannot see, they are going to see better! Sometimes it is by going into our darkness that we really see the light. So the prayer that I would make for myself and for all of us is that we will have the courage to stand blindly in front of Jesus, allow him to make the paste, make the situation temporarily worse and then go wash so that we can really see.

10
We See Things As "We" Are

Zen Buddhism has a saying, "The water that the cow laps up becomes milk and the water that the snake licks up becomes poison." In modern psychology, you might paraphrase that and say that we don't see things as they are; we see things as we are.

All of my adult life, I have been fascinated by the fact that in his times there were so many different reactions to Jesus. As children I am sure all of us had the notion that if only we could have met Jesus or if only we had lived at the time of Jesus, there is no doubt that we would have totally accepted who he was and what he said. We find it very difficult to understand why people on meeting him and hearing him and watching him could have any reaction other than to follow him and to believe in him. But when we read through the gospels we see there is an entire spectrum of responses to Jesus. To meet Jesus was no guarantee of seeing Jesus. Even those who were close to Jesus really did not see him. The apostles saw Jesus as a meal ticket to fame. He was going to become king and they were going to become the main people in his parliament. That is what they saw when they looked at him.

Peter looked at him and puffed himself up with arrogance and pride. Peter was going to be the rock on which Jesus founded his system. Jesus' brothers and sisters, four of whom are named in the gospels while two are just mentioned without being named, thought he was crazy. In the gospel of Mark, Chapter 3: 21 we are told, "They came to take him by force because they thought he was mad." As soon as Jesus began his public ministry, his family got really embarrassed about what he was doing. Finally, in the gospel of John, Chapter 7, his brothers taunted him, "If you are such a mensch, how come you are stuck in a little place like Galilee. Why don't you go down to Jerusalem and do your schtick down there?" They didn't believe in him, even his own family did not believe in him..

Judas saw him as a ticket to a fast buck. The authorities saw Jesus in various ways as a problem that had to be dealt with very quickly. Herod saw him as a source of amusement. The soldiers taunted him. How could anyone in the presence of such beauty, power, healing and compassion see anything except healing, beauty

70

and compassion? But they did. And the question I have asked myself all my adult life is, how would I have been? In which camp would I have landed if I had been around at the time of Jesus?

So I have two main points today. Firstly, I want to share with you a dream vision I had on Easter, 1978. Secondly, I want to share a piece of creative biblical writing I did in Kenya in 1983.

In 1978, for two months, I was with a group of priests and nuns in Manressa House in Dublin, a facility run by the Jesuits to train spiritual directors. I was doing a two-month institute on spiritual direction. The first month of it consisted of a thirty-day retreat with the spiritual exercises of Saint Ignatius of Loyola. I had done this thirty-day retreat as a young man when I entered the seminary at age 18. Now at age 31 it was a totally different experience. Particularly when you get 40 or 50 people meditating in total silence for a period of thirty days, extraordinary things begin to happen. You tap into the group psyche and the group spirit. So there were many visions and many dreams for all of us during that period of time.

I remember in particular this one dream-vision. It is difficult to differentiate dreams from visions. In Hebrew, it is the same word. A dream is a vision you have when you are asleep and a vision is a dream you have when you are awake. God speaks equally powerfully through both. In this particular dream vision, I saw myself standing somewhere outside of Jerusalem. About 50 meters away there was a little post and a notice was nailed on it. People were leaving the city and they were reading this notice and then shaking their heads disappointedly and then going back to the city. Curiosity got the better of me. I went out to see what this notice was. The heading said, "Golgotha Entertainment Committee." Underneath it said, "We regret that because of a strike in the timber yards in Jerusalem, the crucifixions scheduled for the sixth hour today have had to be postponed. We regret any inconvenience this may cause our patrons and we wish you a very holy Sabbath on the morrow." As dreams will do, it shifted and it was actually Good Friday and Jesus was being crucified and there was a huge mob taunting and jeering as Jesus died in agony and despair. Finally the body was taken down and put in the tomb and everyone went home.

But on Sunday, Christ appeared in the temple preaching and people were absolutely astounded. They could not figure it out. "This was the guy we nailed and crucified. We saw him buried two days ago and here he is alive and well and preaching in our temple." The crowds began to follow him; on Sunday, Monday, Tuesday and Wednesday the crowds got bigger and bigger. He was preaching with more and more power and more and more authority. So the high priest called a meeting and said, "What are we going to do with this guy? It's worse than before." They had their meeting and they determined that there was only one thing to do. "We're going to crucify him again." He was captured for the second time and dragged off to Calvary. This second Friday there was a huge mob; word had gotten around. This guy had been crucified and buried, had risen from the dead, and he's going to be crucified again. This is something! This is super bowl to the power of eight.

The crowds came out in the thousands. They were ringed around watching this circus and some of them are convinced that this time, he is going to come down off the cross and clobber the enemies. They wait and wait until Jesus died the second time. They shook their heads rather disappointedly. He is put into the tomb for the second time. Then suddenly on the second Sunday morning word got around and someone said, "You know, this guy rose from the dead on last Sunday morning, wouldn't that be something to see it happen again?" They began to go out in droves to where he was buried. People came with blankets, six-packs and sandwiches ready to be entertained. There were semicircular rows of people around the mouth of the tomb waiting for this cataclysmic event to occur. Eight o'clock came and nothing happened. Nine o'clock came and nothing happened. One man went up and he put his eye up to the crack between the stone and the wall and as he looked in someone asked, "Is he there?" He said, "Yep, still lying down." Someone else said, "I'm going to give him a half an hour and if he's not out in a half an hour I'm out of here."

After a half an hour they began to drift away. After an hour they went off in droves. After an hour and a half there was no one left outside the tomb except myself, in my dream. I sat down disconsolately on a rock and all of a sudden there was this blast and out he came. He came over and he sat beside me. He said to me, "What do you think of that?" I said, "Pretty darn impressive." He said, "I don't mean the flash of lightning right now, I mean this whole thing that you've seen in your vision. What do you think of all that? In particular, I want to ask you a question. Who do you think disappointed me most in all of that?" I said, "I suppose it was Judas.

Judas was one of the twelve and he sold you for 30 pieces of silver. I'm sure you must have been really disappointed in Judas." Christ said, "It wasn't he. Judas did what he did with a lot of planning and a lot of cunning. It wasn't Judas. Try again." I said, "If it wasn't Judas, it was Peter. Peter was the leader. Peter was the rock on which you intended to build your church. He arrogantly boasted that even if everyone else deserted you, he would never desert you. Was it Peter?" Christ said, "It wasn't Peter. Peter did what he did because he was afraid and I know what fear feels like. It wasn't Peter. Think again." So I said, "If it wasn't Judas and it wasn't Peter then it must have been the high priest. The high priest, allegedly the scripture expert, the leader of this spirituality, should have recognized who you were. He should have facilitated your emergence instead of killing you." And Christ said, "It wasn't the high priest. He did what he did and he stuck to his guns and when I rose from the dead he nailed me the second time. It wasn't he." So I said, "I give up. If it wasn't Judas or Peter or the high priest, you tell me who it was that you were most distressed by." Christ said, "I will. It was the mob. Those bored listless people who just wanted to be entertained. They didn't particularly care whether I was being killed or rising from the dead, they just wanted to be entertained. All they saw in me was bread and circuses. They are the ones that disappointed me." Then he said to me, "When you wake up, I want you to look at the Book of Revelation, Chapter 3:15-16 and you will see what I mean." That was the only time in my dream state that I have been given a scripture passage.

So I woke up in the middle of the night and I read Revelation, Chapter 3:15-16. It is the message John was addressing to the Church in Laodicea and he says, "I wish you were either hot or cold. But because you are neither hot nor cold but only lukewarm, I will vomit you out of my mouth." In English, it is sanitized. It says, "I will spit you out of my mouth." The Greek word says vomit. "I wish you were either hot or cold but because you are neither hot nor cold but only lukewarm, I will vomit you out of my mouth." And I got it. Better to be a sinner, 100 percent passionately involved in my crime or my lust or whatever it is, or else to be a saint, but the worst state to be in is to be mediocre.

I thought of a second story in the scriptures. It is in the gospel of Luke, Chapter 7. It is the story of Jesus being invited into the house of Simon the Pharisee. He is not being brought in as an honored guest. They are trying to gauge whether he is really a prophet. They do not give him any courtesy. He is not given water to wash his feet after a dusty safari. He is not given a kiss. He is not anointed with oil. He is ushered into the dining room and they are lying around the dining room table and they are watching him and asking questions. A prostitute who had heard that he is dining there comes in because she has seen Jesus. She comes in and she does an unthinkable thing in the Jewish tradition, she lets down her hair. There are three things that should not be seen or heard in Judaism at the time regarding a woman, her hair and her feet and her voice. For this woman to come into the presence of this male group and let down her hair was the ultimate disgrace. She cried her tears on his feet and she dried his feet with her hair. Then she took an alabaster jar of precious ointment that she had probably got from one of her johns and broke it and poured it on his feet. Simon said to himself, "There's no need to ask him anymore questions. This man is no prophet. If he were a prophet, he would know the manner of woman who is touching him. She is a whore. I got my answer, he is no prophet."

Jesus is watching all of this play out and he says, "Simon, I have a question for you." "Ask it." "There was a certain rich man who had two debtors. One owed him a lot of money and the other owed him a little bit of money. But none of them could pay back. So he forgave both of them; let them off the debt. Who do you think is going to love him more?" Simon said, "Obviously, the guy to whom more is forgiven." Jesus said, "You are right. You see this woman. I came into your house and you did not give me even water to wash my feet. She has washed my feet with her tears. You did not kiss me. She has been kissing my feet. You did not anoint my head with oil. She has anointed my feet with perfume. So I tell you Simon, her sins, and she has committed many, have been forgiven her because she has loved much. From the one to whom little is forgiven, little love comes forth."

There is a huge difference between a lover and a law keeper. The law keeper is the one who walks the middle path, no passion. This is what Jesus' biggest complaint was against the Pharisees. They had no passion for God. They had no passion for life. They were obsessives compulsively involved in keeping all 613 precepts of the Torah. There was no fire in their bellies. This woman had fire in her loins and fire in her belly and when she saw Jesus that energy went into love and compassion for Jesus.

Jesus in some sense is saying, "You, Simon, are the one whom God vomits out of his mouth. You have no standing. You do not go to the right or to the left because there is no passion in you. All you have is law." It is the worst possible place to get stuck, to be stuck on the middle course where there is no passion in your life. Better to go out and paint the town red or decide to become a saint but this middle path works not at all.

I took that dream vision from 1978 and went back to Kenya and I worked quite a bit with the Jesuits doing directed retreats. In 1983, I had another vision and I wrote this down as a dialogue. I took two biblical characters from the New Testament and I just fused them together in a story that I made up. I wanted to illustrate for myself a very important teaching. It is this: that meeting Jesus was no guarantee of seeing Jesus. This is the story I wrote. I call this:

"When I Remember Zion"

He seemed somehow different. Not the normal importunate beggar thrusting a bowl in one's path and clawing with broken and dirt-encrusted fingernails at one's cloak. He seemed almost disinterested in alms as if it mattered little to him whether he ate or not. Beggars are one of the reasons I don't much fancy these trips to Jerusalem which are now much more frequent since my father's death and his bequeathing of the family's business to me. My recollection of Jerusalem has always been an impressive incense-clouded temple and a most unimpressive horde of fly-infested mendicants. Walking any of the main streets is a veritable running of the gauntlet. All manner of disfigured creatures obstructing one with mutilated and hideous limbs cursing earthly if ignored and grinning ingratiatingly if thrown a coin; a disquieting affair, really.

But this chap was different. Beneath the unkempt beard, emaciated face and pathetic attire was a deep and abiding wistfulness. Moreover, I seemed to recognize his face from long ago. I dallied a little too long in pitching my offering into his bowl and he looked up sensing that I was watching him. I knew then that I had met him before. He used to be the Synagogue leader in Capharnaum where my father took me to worship each Sabbath when I was a boy. Gathering my robes carefully about me I squatted before him and asked, "Are you by any chance Jairus once the Synagogue leader in Capharnaum?" A look of alarm dilated his gray eyes so that the white contrasted sharply with his brown weather-beaten countenance. I held his gaze relentlessly until he lowered his head in

75

shame and whispered, "I am he." A memory of two noble, dignified men greeting each other each Sabbath flashed across my mind. For my father's sake, I proffered my hand and pulled him to his feet. "Come," I said, "tonight you lodge with me." We looked a peculiar pair as we made our way towards where I normally lodged. Other beggars eyed him, some with envy, some with admiration at his having found a patron.

After the evening meal, we sat by the fire. There were no other guests and his eyes glazed over as waves of melancholy memories swept through him. Without any bidding, he turned to me and he began to tell his story. "I am Jairus and I was once the Synagogue leader of Capharnaum. I was married and my wife Veronica and I had one child, a girl." At the mention of the child, large tears rolled down his cheeks and he was unable to proceed for several minutes. "We were very happy, my wife and child and I. I was well respected in the community. I loved my wife and next to my God, I lived for my child. Then one summer our child became seriously ill. Nothing or no one could ease her pain or cool her fever. I brought doctors from Jerusalem, even from Damascus. But having first secured their fees they all professed themselves unequal to the task of curing her. I became frantic. I declare on my immortal soul that if anyone could have restored her to health I would have offered a sacrifice for him or her.

One day when she was at death's door, having been in a coma for two weeks, a friend told me that Jesus the Nazarene was in town. It was said that he had the gift of curing sickness of all kinds, and indeed, huge crowds from Galilee and Judea followed him about. Throwing caution and pride to the wind, I rushed out to try to meet him. I was told he had moved on and was headed for Cana. I set out after him and towards evening came upon him and a large group of people. I stayed the night there and early the next morning I went to meet him. I was told that he had gone out very early to be alone to pray. I tracked him down and throwing myself on my knees I begged him to come and cure my daughter."

Here the old man broke down again. Then he said a very strange thing, "I wish to God I had never met him or that he had refused to cure her. It would have been easier to have lost her the first time." There was no sound but the fire crackling for a few minutes. I thought he would not go on with the story, but finally he pulled himself together and continued. "This Jesus readily agreed to come and we started back to Capharnaum, hope and fear wrestling together in the knot that was my stomach."

"When I got to the street where we lived, the blood drained from my face. In the distance, I could hear the death dirge of the flutes and the synthetic shrieking of the professional mourners. My child, my little girl, was dead. My knees buckled and I would have collapsed in a heap were it not for the strong grip he took of my shoulder. 'Have faith,' he said. That was all. Somehow it did not sound like pious platitudes so we stumbled on. When we arrived at the house, my wife was sitting outside gazing into the distance, seeing no one. She couldn't cry. She couldn't speak.. The keeners seemed to be enjoying their work. No doubt they wanted to impress their employer and be sure of their remuneration. The Nazarene raised his voice and asked them. 'What business have you here? The child is not dead, but sleeping.' The caterwauling ceased and a torrent of abuse took its place. The stupidity of his assertion coupled with the suspicion that we were trying to cheat them out of their money lent volume and viciousness to their vitriol. He simply pointed to the front door with such power and authority that the entire group, with very subdued mutterings, packed their instruments and hurried out. An eerie silence descended on the house, so intense that it jerked my wife to attention. He said, 'Show me where the child is.' Veronica led the way. When I saw my little girl lying ashen-faced, cold, and her little pink lips frozen into immobility, I wanted to swear at God for his cruelty. Then the Nazarene walked to the bed and took the lifeless hand in his. 'Little girl,' he said, 'Arise.' I could not believe it. Her eyes fluttered and opened and they looked long and intently into his. I could see that he was smiling and she too began to smile, white pearls in an oyster-shell of red. He drew her gently to her feet and said, 'Go and greet your mommy and daddy.' Veronica fell to her knees and wrapped her arms about our child weeping uncontrollably. It was now my turn to be frozen into immobility. When I recovered, he was gone."

"But I was to meet him again twice, unfortunately." The old man kicked at a flaming ember that had fallen out of the fire, sighed deeply and then he continued. "That very week a letter arrived from Jerusalem. Apparently one was sent to all of the Synagogues in Galilee and Judea warning us about this Jesus, about his total disregard for the customs of our ancestors, his flagrant breaches of the Sabbath rest and his cures and miracles that were worked through the powers of Beelzebub. Needless to say I was shocked that I had entertained such a fellow and shocked that the demonic power of him was the reason for my little daughter's vigorous new health. The letter concluded by admonishing all officials that the man, Jesus, was under no circumstances to be invited to or even to be allowed into any Synagogue. Anyone disregarding this decree was himself to be banished from the Synagogue."

"I showed the letter to my wife. As she read it, all hell broke loose. She called the Sanhedrin a bunch of fools and the high priests blind leaders of blind followers. Her voice rose in hysteria, and clasping our bewildered child, she continued, 'that man is the anointed of God. He is everything that Isaiah prophesized he would be, and you, you the shepherds of Israel, you want to *ostracize him as you did all of the prophets. You judges of the darkness, you will sacrifice love and mercy and compassion for stifling man-made precepts. Could you not feel the power and the gentleness of him? Is your male heart and your male head so hard, so dense, that you could not bathe in the healing and the mercy that radiated from him? Is our little girl not a living proof that God is with him? Or would you prefer the self-righteous babbling of those dithering and decrepit old fogies in Jerusalem?' At length her hysteria subsided and she began to plead with me, 'Jairus, I beg of you, do not bar this holy man from the Synagogue. Let him help others as he has helped us. You owe him at least that much.'"*

"But I had made up my mind. I said, 'Veronica, remember that the enchanters and the magicians of Egypt produced signs and wonders at the side of Moses and Aaron at the bidding of their Pharaoh. Do not be deceived.' With many other passages of scripture I showed her how Satan can deceive even the elect. She made no reply. But I sensed that a rift had developed between us and I was very frightened by it. For nine whole days she never spoke a word. On the second Sabbath, Jesus appeared at the Synagogue, but we were ready for him. Tactfully and with as little fuss as possible I told him that he was no longer welcome. In fairness, he took it like a man. He turned on his heels and wordlessly walked away. Just then I caught Veronica's eye. She looked at me as if I was a stranger. When I got home that evening, she was gone. So was the child."

"For three days I was too ashamed to ask anybody if they had news of her. When I did ask, nobody knew of her whereabouts. Pride would not allow me to take it any further. When she has discovered which of us is right about this son of Satan, I thought, she'll come back and beg my forgiveness."

"With dignity and a certain haughtiness, I continued my duties ignoring the knowing looks of my neighbors. Months, silent months, soundless, never ending nighttime months passed by. I went up to Jerusalem to celebrate the Paschal feast. On the Friday before the great Sabbath, as I made my way along a small side street, I found myself on the fringe of an exultant motley mob of excited citizens and Roman soldiers. They were bringing three criminals towards Golgotha for crucifixion. One of them was the Nazarene. I almost felt pity for him. He struggled under a huge beam of wood and his face and body were a mess of gaping wounds, sweat and spittle. Suddenly, as he drew near where I stood, a woman burst out of the crowd and ran to him. The soldiers were too surprised to intervene. She held a soft, white cloth to his face and ever so gently swabbed and patted the blood, sweat and the spittle. His lips formed the words, 'Thank you.' Then the soldiers prodded him forward with their spears. She turned to follow his progress and I found myself looking into the face of Veronica, my wife. It

78

was as if she never saw me. Slowly she turned away and began to walk after him. I was rooted to the ground. When I got control of myself, I too, followed the crowd. By the time I reached Golgotha, the crosses had already been erected and he was hanging grotesquely from the center one. The soldiers kept a mocking, jeering multitude at bay, but a little group of people was standing at the foot of his cross. Veronica was among them and by her side, her little upturned face bloated with crying, was my child. I edged nearer and I found that she was speaking to the figure on the gibbet, 'Jesus, thank you for saving my life. If I were a man, I'd fight these soldiers and save your life. I love you, really I do.'"

"I would give anything to have her say those words to me. But she never will. I turned and ran from the place. I got so drunk that the feast was long since finished when I sobered up. I have never seen my wife since then. I have never seen my child since then. If she is still alive, she's thirty years old now. I have never been back to Capharnaum and I have never been in a Synagogue since. I beg alms within a stone's throw of the temple but I never go inside. I don't know if God dwells there any more and care less. I have lost my wife. I've lost my child. I lost my faith. I have lost all hope. Only one emotion survives in me, hatred. I hate the Nazarene who gave my daughter life and took away her love. I wish he had failed to revive her. I would have a tomb to visit, a loving wife to comfort me and the memory of a tousled-headed child clambering onto my lap. Now, there is nothing."

The old man got to his feet and despite all my protestations and pleadings disappeared into the night. I never laid eyes on him again.

11
Resurrection

Have you ever noticed how inspiration can come to you in the most unlikely places? Two of the most satisfying inspirations I have ever had about the notion of resurrection came in a Safeway supermarket, and in a Fresh Choice restaurant in Mountain View. I want to start by telling you these stories and then lead on. I spend every Monday, Tuesday and Wednesday in a little cabin in the forest up beyond Healdsburg and so on Sunday evenings, I do my shopping at Safeway in Healdsburg. I get my Tater Tots and my milk and my eggs. Every Sunday when I go in there, it is crowded and there are people wheeling out their carts absolutely chock-full of food. I always know exactly which aisle I'm going to. I know exactly where to find the eggs and exactly where to find the Tater Tots. The shelves are always full. I could never figure it out. People keep carrying out this stuff and it is all still there. After going through this exercise maybe 50 times over the course of the year, I finally got it. Safeway supermarket is not some huge place for stocking stuff. It's a software package. Since I first had that realization, I actually met one of the engineers who designed the software program.

I finally got it. When I go up to the counter with my eggs, Tater-tots and milk, and the cashier takes them and passes them over the little glass that goes beep, some little voice somewhere in the back room says, "One dozen, Rock Island eggs, organic, cage free, large brown, please replace." And someone somewhere comes out and replaces them. I got it that that is what resurrection is about.

The second great realization was in a little restaurant in Mountain View called Fresh Choice. I had just finished reading a book by an extraordinary Buddhist monk, Thich Nhat Hanh, in which he talked about mindful eating. Given my diet, it's not very easy to be mindfully eating, but I tried it. I went into Fresh Choice and I got a bowl of vegetable soup and I sat down at my table and I tried to eat mindfully. I fished out a piece of broccoli and suddenly I fell into a kind of a reverie. I realized that this simple piece of broccoli had at least three different kinds of intelligence. There was a time on planet Earth when broccoli didn't even exist as a life form. Somehow some kind of an information matrix was created and through this information matrix energy poured until it got a physical articulation in what we now call broccoli. I call that energy, "creative intelligence." That is the first kind of intelligence broccoli has. This little piece of broccoli on my spoon at some stage was planted in the earth. Of all the minerals in its vicinity, it knew which ones to take in and which ones to ignore. It was able to do what I can't do or you can't do. It was able to draw energy directly from sunlight through photosynthesis. I call that intelligence, "sustaining intelligence."

It has a third kind of intelligence. I believe that when this piece of broccoli was cut, even if it had been thrown aside to die, I don't believe it would have died. I don't believe death exists. I believe what happens is that a third kind of intelligence takes over. I call it "regifting intelligence." It is the intelligence of meaningfully, lovingly and compassionately redistributing its molecular structure back into the ecosystem. In the few moments, when I took it into myself, it wasn't just a bunch of gastric juices operating on a piece of dead vegetable; it was an intelligent dialogue taking place between two souls; the intelligence of this creature, me, and the intelligence of the broccoli.

So I want to use those two stories as a jumping off point to talk about the notion of resurrection. I am going to make four main points. The first point I am going to mention is, what is body? When we talk about Jesus rising bodily from the tomb, what do we mean by body? The second question I want to ask myself is, who is this Jesus who rose from the dead and who is the "you" that will rise from the dead? Thirdly, I want to look at the notion of the cross not as a symbol of death or sacrifice, but as a symbol of resurrection. Then fourthly, I want to ask myself the question and ask you the question, were you there when he rose up from the tomb?

The first question I want to examine then is the notion of body. When we talk about body, of what do we speak? When we look into the cosmos in the night sky, astronomers tell us that there are at least one hundred billion galaxies consisting of about one hundred billion stars per galaxy. They also tell us that the universe is 99.999999 percent empty space. We are also told, and we are asked to believe, that the human body is 99.999 percent empty space. How could that be? I am going to use a few metaphors to wrestle with this idea. If you take your typical atom, which consists of a nucleus and a few electrons and you scale up an atom to the size of Yankee Stadium the nucleus would be about the size of the baseball in mid-field somewhere. The few electrons twirling around would be like annoying little gnats or flies buzzing around the ball. The rest of it is empty space.

You take the number of these in the human body and you condense them and the following is scientifically accurate. If we could take all the empty space out of every single individual sitting in this room this morning we could be condensed to less than a single grain of sand. So what do we mean when we talk about body? How is it even imaginable that something as solid looking as people and chairs and buildings could be condensed in that fashion? Imagine that somebody gave you a gift of one million cardboard cartons each measuring 4' x 4' x 4' and you decided to build a mansion from these cartons so you put down your walls and your roof and you have this huge mansion of a house. It takes up a lot of space and a lot of real estate. Then you got fed up and you decided that you did not want to play house anymore and you folded them all to recycle them. You could probably put all of them into the closet of the house that you had just deconstructed. That appears to be how we are constituted. When we talk about body and we talk about resurrection, we need to have some notion about who we actually are as physical beings.

Every single great culture has wrestled with this idea of body. The Egyptians had a word for it. They called it *Ka*. *Ka* was like the esoteric slightly immaterial blueprint out of which the physical body was formed. The Persian Zoroastrians had a word for it, they called it *Fravashi*, and it was the same idea. It was like the information matrix residing within the physical body that gives it life. In my opinion, the most sophisticated model is the Hindu model of body, where they talk about the body existing at seven different vibrations of frequency. They talk about the gross body, the etheric body, the astral body, the mental body, the causal body, Atman and Brahman. It is an extraordinarily sophisticated model of body. The Greeks had a model of body like that. Aristotle said, "The soul is the form of the body." Saint Paul had to try to understand and explain and teach what the resurrection of Jesus looked like. The Greeks had three words for body. The first word was sarx, which means your flesh and blood body. The second word, soma, means a psychical body. The third word, pneuma, is a spiritual body. Saint Paul is very definite in his first letter to the Corinthians, Chapter 15. He said, "Sarx does not inherit the Kingdom of God." When Paul talks about the resurrection of Jesus, he was not talking about sarx, flesh-and- blood body. He was talking about different levels of body. We have to understand what we mean by body before we can meaningfully talk about Jesus.

I want to ask myself the question, "Who then is the Jesus who rose and who is the you who will arise when your time comes?" Maybe the most important question asked in the synoptic gospels is posed in an interesting story of Jesus on the road to Caesarea Philippi. Jesus is walking ahead of his disciples, obviously deep in thought wrestling with some kind of a conundrum. The disciples are traipsing along behind him talking about the ball game. Finally Jesus stops and allows them to catch up with him. He says, "When you listen to people talk about me, who do they say that I am?" They said, "Well, you know, some people think that you are John the Baptist come back to life. Some people say you are Elijah, some people say that you are one of the Old Testament Prophets." Then Jesus said, "What about you? You have been with me for about three years. Who do you say that I am?" Peter says, "You are the Christ, the Son of the living God." There is one question that was not asked in any of the three gospels that I think is the most important of all and the one I believe Jesus was wrestling with before he asked the other two questions. The question that Jesus was wrestling with was, "Who do I believe myself to be?" Only when he got that, when he finally figured out who he was, was he ready to die. Then he was ready for the last week of his life. This happened at the beginning of the last week of his life.

Who do you believe yourself to be? We are constantly misidentifying ourselves. We think we are our bodies. You ask somebody, who are you? They give you a name. We think we are our names. You ask someone who he is and he will tell you some relationship he is in. I am such and such a person's father, or mother, or child or whatever. Or you ask someone, who are you? and he will tell you a job he does. I am the school janitor, or I am the bus conductor. If you really sit someone down and say, I would really like for you to tell me who you are, I got fifteen minutes, tell me who you are. He will likely string together a whole bunch of memories and say that that is who he is. The truth is that we are not any of these things. We are not our names. We are not our physical bodies. We are not our emotions. We are not a string of memories. We are not the relationships we are in. We are not even the jobs we do. We are spirit beings having a human experience. Hinduism gets it right again. Hinduism says, "I have a body, but I am not my body. I have an intellect, but I am not my intellect. I have emotions, but I am not my emotions. I have a personality, but I am not even my personality. I am a spirit being having a human experience. I am incarnated divinity." Every single one of us is incarnated divinity. It helps to understand resurrection if we can understand that.

The third point I want to make is this. I want to talk about the cross as a symbol of resurrection. So often we see the cross as a symbol of death or a symbol of self-abnegation or a symbol of sacrifice. It is much more that that. The early apostles who were radically transformed by the experience of meeting the risen Jesus, had the problem of trying to explain to people who had not had that experience that it was true. They ran into two kinds of difficulty. The first difficulty was persuading people that it was not hallucination or illusion. They were not on "mushrooms." They were not doing "pot." This was a real experience they had. So how do they explain it? How is this illustrated in the scriptures? They prove that the Jesus they met after the resurrection was exactly the Jesus they had known before the resurrection by saying, "He ate with us. He asked us, 'Do you have any food?' We had some fish and we gave it to him and he ate it." Thomas, who was not there for the first appearance and would not believe it, thought the apostles were high on something. Finally, when Jesus came back again he said, "Thomas, come here. You could not believe I was risen unless you put your finger into the nail holes in my hands and your fist into the hole in my side. Come and do it." Thomas said, "I do not need to." Jesus said, "Go on." And Thomas came up and he stuck his fingers in there. Jesus pulled aside his garments and said, "Okay, there is where the spear went in. Put your fist into it." And Thomas did. Jesus finally said, "Blessed are those who know without ever seeing."

The apostles tried to persuade the unbelievers or those who had not experienced Jesus for themselves, that it really was he. Theologians call these metaphors, the before and after images, that the Jesus after resurrection is exactly the same Jesus as before resurrection.

Then they ran into more problems of course, "Well, if he is just back from the dead, what is the big deal? So he is just a human being. Lazarus came back from the dead. What's the big deal?" So they had a second problem, to show that Jesus had not just come back from the dead, he had gone through death. He would never die again and he was glorified. He was transformed in some way. Theologians call these images the below/above images; that Jesus had ascended in some fashion. They would point out that although he ate fish with us and although we actually touched his body, he seemed to be able to materialize and dematerialize at will. He could walk through closed doors. He could disguise his identity. Even the ones who loved him most and were closest to him did not recognize him if he chose not to be recognized by them. He had been glorified. He was radically different.

When you put those two sets of images together, the before and after images, they give you the horizontal arm of the cross. When you put the below and above images together you get the vertical arm of the cross. The cross is a beautiful symbol of resurrection. Since the before is the past and the after is the future then the horizontal arm symbolizes that Jesus is the "Lord of Time." There is no time in Jesus' dispensation. Since the below represents earth and the above represents heaven it represents also that Jesus is master of space. You put the two pieces together and the intersection is the realization that Jesus has mastered both time and space. In some fashion, the resurrected Jesus totally blows all of our scientific paradigms. So the cross becomes an extraordinary image not just of death and destruction but also of resurrection.

My final point is this; I ask you the question, "Were you there when he rose up from the tomb?" All of the other questions in some sense are meaningless. All of the how he did it or what happened is meaningless if the final question is not answered. The final question is "What was the effect on the people who experienced the post-resurrection Jesus." Certainly if you know anything about Christian teaching or Christian scriptures, they were utterly, radically and permanently transformed. These bumbling, cowardly people who hid themselves in an upper room because they were afraid of being associated with Jesus, even the person who denied him three times, those were the same people who gave their lives because they believed so powerfully. Whatever it was that happened, whatever the scientific explanation for what happened, it was the most powerfully transformative experience of these people's lives.

There is a great question to ask yourself today on this Easter Sunday. If you had to look for one incident in your life that was the most utterly and radically transforming experience you have ever had, what would it be? Probably you will come to the conclusion that the only way to facilitate those experiences, the only way to conceive and receive and to perceive the resurrected Jesus is not through scientific curiosity. It is not even through faith and it is not even through hope. The only adequate container in which such experiences can be had is love, total love. Since God is utterly ineffable, the only adequate container for a post-resurrected experience of Jesus is to be filled with love. Then it happens. In my opinion, that is why Jesus appeared first not to Peter, not even to his own mother, not to the beloved disciple John, but to Mary Magdalene, because there was no one who had the kind of love for Jesus that Mary Magdalene had. She may not have had faith that he would rise. She may not have even hoped that he would come back. But this woman had so much love in her heart that this was the reason she was the first person to whom Jesus appeared. She was the very first evangelist. She was the one whom Jesus told, "Go tell the rest of my brothers and sisters that I have risen and I will go ahead of them into Galilee."

It was Mary's extraordinary ability to love that facilitated her having the experience of Jesus. Then she could really run to the apostles and say, "I have seen the lord." She saw him, because she had seen Jesus long, long before in her heart and in her soul. The only space in which Jesus can be seen is not mind-space, it is soul-space. It is the space of love. And that is why, in my opinion, the real heroine of the Easter Story is Mary Magdalene.

12
Life is an Elephant's Belly

I'm going to say something very briefly and very profoundly so listen carefully because you might miss it. Life is an elephant's belly. Now if I were a Zen master I'd bow to you and go away. I'm not that advanced and moreover I'm Irish. I have a captive audience and I will never say in one phrase what I can say in a hundred. So I'm going to tell you what I mean by that. Life is an elephant's belly.

The last mission where I lived in Kenya was a small place called Kipsaraman. It is in the highlands that sweep down into a large valley right on the equator with regular temperatures of 115 and 120 degrees Fahrenheit. Part of it was on forested slopes. Herds of elephants lived there. A particular kind of tree grew in the area with a fruit so hard that when the nut fell on the ground even if it lay there for many years and even if you were to cover it over, it could never germinate. The shell was so hard it would never germinate. So the trees had made an agreement with the elephants. The elephants would eat this nut and the gastric juices in the belly of the elephant were so corrosive that they would crack open the shell and then the elephant would poop and bingo, you had a new tree. Life is an elephant's belly. We're just waiting for the elephant to come along to crack us.

I want to talk about that today. I want to make three main points. I want to talk firstly about movie making and then secondly, I want to talk about deep devolution and evolution. Then thirdly, I want to examine the notion of afterlife because it's mentioned in the readings today.

Let me talk firstly about movie making. I don't think we give ourselves credit for just how consummate we are at movie making. Every single one of us deserves academy awards for best picture of the year, because every single one of us has created this extraordinary movie that is just as illusory as the stuff coming out of Hollywood. We create these extraordinarily extravagant movies of our lives and of the illusions that we believe in and then we step into them and we become the directors and the costume makers and the main actors and we deliver our lines with consummate skill. We get so involved in it we call it life. We think it is real.

I want to examine just three aspects of that in my first point. I am convinced that in this movie of life, we create God. We create the notion of covenant. We create the notion of afterlife. Depending on where we are in our own evolution as individuals or our own evolution as cultures or civilizations, the movie we make about God is going to look very different. The movie we make about covenant is going to look very different. The movie we make about the afterlife is going to look very different. When you live in a culture experiencing chaotic times or you are an individual who is living in times that are totally unpredictable, then very often that culture or that individual creates a God or an image of God who is equally unpredictable, equally chaotic and totally capricious. These are the gods that come down and devastate and the survivors are left wondering why in hell did he kill those and leave us. There is no order to it. There's no predictability to it. There is no pattern to it. It is just "guess as guess can." These are the kinds of gods to which people who are violent and chaotic subscribe.

Those kinds of cultures and those kinds of people have no notion of covenant between God and us because there is absolutely no pattern to the relationship between God and the civilization or God and the individual. So covenant does not exist. This God is far too unpredictable. All order, all information has been washed out. There is ultimate entropy. There is no sense of theme or motif wending its way through the relationship. There is just total unpredictability. As you might guess, such cultures or such individuals do not believe in a life after death. They are so concerned with merely surviving the wrath of this totally unpredictable God and these totally unpredictable circumstances they do not have time to think about whether or not there might be something afterwards. They are just dodging lightning bolts.

At some stage of civilization, an individual moves beyond that phase into a place of law and order. He begins to identify patterns in nature, cycles in nature perhaps. He begins to identify scientific patterns in his examinations of the phenomena of life and then a whole other kind of movie begins to emerge. Such a culture or such an individual will make the following kind of movie. His movie about God will be that of a distant, demanding, unsmiling deity but at least one who is just and regular and predictable. This God will always give laws and commandments so that you will have some idea what the rules are. Gone is the unpredictability of not knowing how to behave or who is going to be rewarded or punished. Now there is some kind of regularity. You are still afraid of this God because this God never smiles. But at least you can predict how he is going to behave.

For the first time ever the notion of covenant becomes possible. Now there is a possibility of some kind of regularization of relationship between that God and this group or between that God and this individual. So what does covenant look like? Covenant begins to look in this stage like the choosing of an elect band. Whether it is the Jews in the Old Testament or whether it is the Christian belief in the New Testament, some group believes that it is chosen and that this God of law and order and justice has taken a shine to this group and loves it especially. What is the notion of life after death that comes at this stage? It is always the notion of a heaven and a hell. One group is going to be rewarded with some kind of ongoing love whether it is on this planet or someplace else and the other group is going to get the thumbs down. There are many religions and many civilizations and many individuals who continue to live in that kind of a movie, sometimes with occasional throwbacks to movie number one.

Then there are cultures that occasionally make a breakthrough into a third kind of movie. Or sometimes, there are individuals within the first two kinds of civilizations who make their own breakthrough into a third kind of movie. In this third kind of movie, what kind of God emerges? The God that emerges in the third kind of movie is a God of ultimate love and peace and tolerance. There is no judgment from this God. There is just unconditional love and the extraordinary patience of a parent waiting for a child to learn the lessons the child needs to learn until he comes back home as a mature individual.

What is the notion of covenant that emerges? The covenant in such thinking is not between God and an elite group. The covenant is not even between God and anyone. The covenant is an understanding and an agreement between the spirit and the spacesuit. Between the physicality of me, my material composition, my emotional nature, my intellectual part and my ability to be in relationships and have personality between that part of me, all of which are artifacts of the spacesuit on the one hand, and on the other the inhabiting spirit that Hinduism calls the Atman. Covenant in this third kind of movie does not involve God at all. At least it does not involve the transcendent creator of it all. It involves recognition between the indwelling spirit of God in whose image we are made and the spacesuit that this spirit inhabits.

When a person makes this kind of movie, what does the afterlife look like? It does not look like a heaven or a hell. It does not look like a reward or punishment. It looks like the total merging of all manifestations with the ultimate ineffable source. It means heaven for everyone. Not in the sense that people are sitting around in concentric circles playing harps or accordions or whatever. It means everyone merging back to the origin from which everyone originally came.

I ask myself today and I ask you, what kind of movie are you making? In what kind of movie are you making, directing and taking the starring role? Are you still making a stage one movie with an angry God with no covenants and nothing but survival? Are you making a movie in which God is a distant, demanding, unsmiling deity but at least you have been chosen and there is the possibility that you might get a "thumbs up"? Are you making a movie in which there is only a God of love? And is there a covenant between you and your spirit that recognizes your source and your ultimate destiny so that all of your brothers and sisters and all life forms ultimately find their origin as you are finding your origin?

Today's readings give us a glimpse of different moviemakers at different stages of human evolution. The first moviemaker today is Jeremiah. Jeremiah lived about 600 years before Jesus. If you look at Jeremiah's movie, it is quite an advanced one. Jeremiah is making a movie in which he is inviting people to go from a stage two understanding of God to a stage three understanding of God. He is trying to make the law and order God who writes the decrees on stone into a God who writes them in our hearts. He is really moving from stage two to stage three in his understanding of God. However, he is still stuck at a stage two covenant. He is still stuck in the notion that there is a chosen group and it is the Jews and God has made a special kind of agreement with them. So he is still stuck there. As far as life after death is concerned, he is stuck in stage one. He is very advanced in his understanding of God. He is a little advanced in the study of covenant. But he is fairly unsophisticated in his understanding of life after death, because in the time of Jeremiah, in Judaism, there was no belief in the afterlife. That came into the Jewish tradition 300 years after Jeremiah. So there was Jeremiah making his movie. He made a stage three God, a stage two covenant and a stage one life after death.

Here is Jesus in the third reading making his movie. What kind of a movie is Jesus making? Very much a stage three God, a God who is accessed by the inner journey. The God who would allow Jesus to say, "I and the father are one." This was not the ultimate in megalomania. This was Jesus accessing the core of his own being and inviting every one of us to do the same. Very shortly after he made that statement in the gospel of John, he would go on to say, "The same things that I do, you will do because I will go up to the father and I will send you the spirit." In other words, I want you to have the same recognition of the spirit that I have so that every single one of you can say, "I am the light of the world. I and the father are one." In so far as I access my inner divinity that is true. But the same Jesus will say, "The father is greater than me." What does that mean? It means, as long as I identify with my spacesuit then I am limited. If I identify with my physicality, emotionality, intellectuality or my personality, all of these are limited and then the father is greater than me. So the two statements stand side by side in the gospel of John, "I and the father are one," and "the father is greater than me."

We can only make sense of them by differentiating between the spacesuit and the spirit. Jesus is talking today about the stage three covenant. He is not talking about a special group of people. He is talking about the patrimony of all God's people. When Jesus talks about a life after death, he is not talking about a reward or punishment after we die. He will say again and again, "The kingdom of heaven is within you," or "the kingdom of God is among you." It has already happened. It is not something that is going to happen down the road for the elect band. Jesus is definitely a stage three moviemaker.

The second point I want to make is this. I want to talk about the notion of devolution and evolution. I am convinced that in scientific terminology, the moment of the Big Bang, 13-billion years ago, represented in some way the devolution of God into material reality, that from this extraordinary Big Bang, the creator through eons manifested flowers, dinosaurs, poetry and you. The Big Bang was the beginning of the devolution. The Big Bang proceeds in five stages. Initially, there is just pure spirit. There is God. From the spirit emerges soul and the soul is an individual articulation of spirit.

The soul is to the spirit as Hamlet is to Shakespeare. The soul is to the spirit as the ceiling of the Sistine Chapel is to Michelangelo. A soul is a particular articulation of the genius of spirit. Spirit begets soul. Soul creates mind. Mind manifests as body and the body is composed of matter. Each of these has its own area of study. The study of matter is proper to physics. The study of body and life is proper to biology. The study of mind is proper to psychology. The study of soul is proper to theology. The study of spirit is proper to mysticism. That is what happened with the Big Bang. Devolution proceeded from spirit to soul to mind to body to matter.

Then the return journey begins. We call it life. Life is the beginning of the realization that the journey away from God is only one leg of the trip and that we have a lifetime to make the return journey from being mere matter to understanding life to understanding mind to understanding individual soul to re-merging with God.

That process can only happen with full mindfulness and full awareness. It is not going to happen through any magical rites. It is not going to happen through any special blessings. It only happens with the mindfulness and the wakefulness of participating in the journey.

So Jesus will make two extraordinary statements in today's gospel, very difficult things to understand. He will say, "Anyone who loves his life will lose it." What is he talking about? Being the great storyteller he is, he will exaggerate wildly in order to get our attention. "Anyone who loves his life will lose it." By life here, he means, the illusion that physicality is all there is. Anyone who is stuck at that stage will lose everything because ultimately it will not sustain him. Then Jesus goes on to make the opposite statement, "Anyone who hates his life, will save it." What does he mean by hating life? He means, literally, a commitment to evolution because evolution proceeds by breaking down all of the old paradigms. It is the Hindu God, Shiva, the destroyer God, who overturns all our preexisting anthropomorphic ideas of God and life so that we can begin to evolve to higher and more advanced ones. So the one who loves life is the person who is addicted to the illusion. The one who hates his life, in Jesus' terminology, is the one who is committed to evolution.

The third point I want to make is this. I want to look at the notion of life after death particularly in this context of movie

92

making.   We call people who do not believe in life before conception, Catholics. We have a special name for people who do not believe in life after death; we call them atheists. We have a special name for people who do not belief in life; we call them pessimists. I do not believe in life before conception. I do not believe in life after death because I believe there is only one life.

This life happens in three recurring stages again and again and again. But there is only one life. This life has a pre-incarnate stage before conception. It has an incarnated stage where we are physical beings with intellects and personalities and it has a post-incarnate phase after we "die." I believe that this cycle continues again and again. Our experience on earth is not all of life, it is merely an incarnated stage of life that is continued from forever and will continue forever.

What is the most difficult traumatic moment in that process? Some people would say that death is the most traumatic moment in that process. I would disagree and I have had the privilege of being with a lot of people as they die. I do not believe that death is the most traumatic stage or event in that process. From my own prayer, meditation and visions, I believe that the most traumatic stage of the process is conception. You have heard about near death experiences where someone is declared clinically dead and what happens. Typically they go from the darkness and the density of this body through a tunnel and see a light.   There is then some kind of life review and then they are told, "Your time is not yet up. You need to go back." We call that a near death experience.

I have a belief system in what I call a "near birth" experience. I think it is more traumatic. I think there are beings or entities or spirits that leave the light and come down through the tunnel and are faced with the darkness and density of being incarnated and they change their minds and go back. Real death is where we actually make the transition to this earth plane. Real conception is where we actually make the transition.

There are near birth experiences and near death experiences and I have a theory about miscarriages. When a woman has a miscarriage, it is for a reason. The parents only create the spacesuit. The spacesuit has an intellect, emotions, personality and materiality, but is does not have a spirit. It is merely a spacesuit. I believe that a miscarriage is the result of an unoccupied spacesuit being finally shed by the mother's body, because as my mother said to me one time, who the hell wants to be carrying around an empty suitcase? It does not make a whole lot of sense. Miscarriages are evidence that the spacesuit is empty. Since no spirit has taken up occupation, the spacesuit is shed.

I want to talk about the transition from stage two (incarnation) to stage three (post-incarnation). What about the afterlife? What happens in the afterlife? I am totally convinced that we create the kind of afterlife we believe in. That people who believe in an afterlife of heaven and hell will create an afterlife of heaven and hell. There is an old statement that says, "As a man lives so shall he die." I believe it is true. People, who live their lives violently and with mean-spirited intolerance, often die mean-spirited and violently intolerant. The way in which we transition from stage two (incarnated) into stage three (post-incarnated) creates our experience in the afterlife.

If I transition in anger, confusion and intolerance then I create a scenario for myself in which intolerance, violence and confusion are my experience afterwards. If I have lived with love, compassion and tolerance for everyone, very probably that is how I will transition. And if I transition with that mind set that is the kind of afterlife I will create for myself.

In my belief system, the good news is that since we have a God who is ultimate love, every single one of us gets as many opportunities as we need, and as many transitions as we require until finally even the most mean-spirited among us, even the most violent among us, even the most intolerant among us finally gets it through trial and error that the only thing that works is love. Then we begin living in love and then we begin dying in love and then we begin creating an afterlife of love.

Finally, as we move through different phases of the afterlife, there is only one place left to go and that is total union with God. It may not happen the first or second or the third time around. And remember, Jesus said that the grain of seed falling on the ground is useless unless it dies and cracks open. Sometimes the seeds do not crack open. Sometimes they lie there for the entire season and never germinate and never give birth. My prayer this morning is that life would manifest for each one of us an elephant.

13
Transformation

There is an apple tree outside my office in Los Altos. It is an extraordinarily beautiful tree. My office is on the second story and when I go out onto the balcony I am on a level with the branches of this beautiful tree. I have been in this office about ten years and the apple tree has been there probably 60 or 70 years. During the course of the year, I watch it in fascination. Two months ago it was a gnarled stump, leafless and apparently lifeless. About five weeks ago the most beautiful semi-diaphanous little pink flowers began to appear on it. Over the course of the last two weeks these petals have begun to fall off and carpet the whole area with a pink sheen. In their place are beautiful bright green leaf-lettes. I know that in two or three months time they will turn brown and eventually fall off and once again I will be looking at an old gnarled apple tree. I have watched this cycle for ten years.

Three years ago it really got my attention because in the winter and spring of that year I was doing house calls from my office to a man whom I will call Richard who was dying of a brain tumor. As he was dying over the course of three months, his face was becoming terribly disfigured and gnarled like the old apple tree. His brain function was deteriorating and he was beginning to hallucinate and talk strangely and was unable to remember his words. I watched his progress as I watched the tree.

I remember one day in March 1997, I had a visit with him in the morning, and then in the afternoon I was meeting a friend whose daughter is an ice skater, a beautiful little girl. She reminded me of the pink apple blossoms that were the texture of her skin and I loved the elegance of the way she walked. I began to think of the cycle of the apple tree. It seemed as if Richard represented the winter apple tree, with its gnarled, lifeless and disfigured bark and it seemed as if this little girl was the pink apple blossom.

I came to the realization, in some sense, that they are just roles. All of them are artifacts of these spacesuits that we wear. Deep down hidden in the core of Richard as is hidden inside this little girl is pure spirit, the presence of God. We cycle through these different aspects sometimes looking young and beautiful and sometimes looking old, wrinkled and dying. But that is just an artifact of the spacesuit. At the core there is only God and the image of God.

I want to start with that story and I want to talk about the notion of resurrection. I am going to make four main points. Firstly, I am going to ask myself the question, "Who in God's name do you really think you are?" Secondly, I am going to ask the question, "What do you mean he rose from the dead?" Thirdly, I am going to ask the question, "How quick is a flash?" Then fourthly, I'm going to talk about what I call, "Falling in love and rising in love."

Firstly, I ask myself the question, "Who in God's name do you really think you are?" I am going back to my ubiquitous apple tree. I am going to talk about apples. To quote a very beautiful Buddhist teacher, Thich Nhat Hanh, "There is no such thing as an apple or an apple tree. Everything 'inter-is' with every thing else. There is no such thing as an apple existing in its own right. An apple is the sum of fire, earth, air, and water." An apple does not exist without the fire of the sun and the photosynthesis of the leaves. An apple does not exist without the water that falls on it in the form of rain. An apple cannot exist without the oxygen and the carbon dioxide that are part of its cycle. An apple does not exist without the earth and the nutrients in which its root system is sunk. There is no such thing as an apple. There is no such thing as me and there is no such thing as you. There is just this extraordinary interplay and inter-is-ness of all physical manifestations. So, when you eat an apple, eat it very carefully. The truth is, when you eat anything, even as simple a thing as an apple, what is happening is not some kind of gastric mechanism operating on a dead piece of fruit. What is happening is this extraordinary dialogue between two intelligences, the intelligence that went into the manifestation of an apple and the intelligence that went into the manifestation of you. So it is not just that you are <u>what</u> you eat. I believe you are <u>how</u> you eat. Eat mindfully because all eating in some sense is cannibalism. It is even worse than cannibalism; all eating is self-eating.

Everything exists in and through everything else. So the apple, in some sense, is this metaphor for this cycle of life. When you think about it, an apple seed has an extraordinary ability. An apple seed gives birth to its own grandmother. I think that must be why there is a kind of apple called Granny Smith! When you think about it, when an apple seed falls to the ground and dies, it does not just die, it gives birth. But it does not just give birth to another seed that looks just exactly like itself. It does not even give birth to an apple that would have been its own mother; it gives birth to an apple tree that is its own grandmother. Every seed gives birth to its own grandmother.

When I think about Jesus' resurrection and I think about Eucharist that is exactly what happens. Jesus is like the seed dying on Good Friday. What did Jesus give birth to? He did not just give birth to another Jesus. He gave birth to a church that holds the Eucharist that again births Jesus. So Jesus gave birth to his own grandmother, the community. Jesus says, "Where two or three are gathered in my name, there am I in their midst." Jesus, in his dying and his rising, gave birth to his own grandmother and you and I are the grandmothers of Jesus. As Jesus' grandmothers, we give birth to the Eucharist that gives birth to Christ who feeds us. So the thing that the grandmother gives birth to winds up feeding the grandmother. So who are you really? Who, in God's name, do you really think you are?

Do you really think you are this stuff, flesh and bones? Is that it? The Western model of personality and the Western model of body are so limited. I much prefer the Hindu notion of body. Hindus believe that the body exists at seven totally different levels each vibrating at higher frequencies only one of which can be seen because it is vibrating within 700 to 400 nanometers within the infrared to ultraviolet range. But the other bodies are just as real. Hinduism says we do indeed have a physical body: the gross body. When it dies, it is just recycled molecularly back into the ecosystem. Vibrating at a slightly higher level is the subtle body: the aura body. When the first body dies, this second one is recycled as free energy back into the universe, as intelligence back into the universe. There is a third level of body that they call the astral body and it is the body you use when you dream. That is the body you are using when you have out of body experiences and that is the body you use during near death experiences and that is the body you use as a place for your emotions.

There is a fourth level of the body that is called the mental body. It is like Plato's ideal realm: the place where all ideas already exist, the place of ratiocination, reason, concept and inspiration. This is called the mental body.

There is a fifth level of body that is called the causal body. The causal body is, in Hinduism, the repository of all of the experiences you have had in all of the life times in which you have lived. It is the first truly transpersonal dimension to the human being. It is at this level that clairvoyance and telepathy and precognition are possible because at this level there is only one mind. There are not ontologically discrete brains each gestating their own ideas, there is only one super-mind giving birth to the ideas that flow through all of us.

There is a sixth level of body. It is called atman or individual soul. This is the tiny little articulation of God. This totally separate essence that is as far back as you can go and be separated from God. Then there is a seventh level of body that is called Brahman. Brahman is unity consciousness. At this stage, we merge back into the source whence we originally came where there is only God loving God. So who do you think you are in that model? Do you think you are just the meat, blood, veins, and the tendons? Or do you think you are just your ideas? Or do you think you are just your emotions? Where do you put yourself on that scale?

I remember going down to Anaheim for the first time ever in 1984 and walking through Disneyland. I loved all of the rides. I was excited by everything, but what fascinated me most was Mickey Mouse. I am serious. I followed Mickey Mouse around for about an hour and a half because it was near the close of the day and I wanted to see who came out of the suit at the end of the day. I was fascinated. There was this extraordinary creature, not allowed to speak, walking around greeting children, interacting with people and I had no idea who was inside. Was it an old man in his 90's? Was it a high-school student earning a bit of money? Was it a little girl? Was it a mother of a family? I had no idea. I followed that Mickey Mouse for an hour and a half but unfortunately he disappeared into some kind of changing room and I have no idea who was in the costume.

So who steps out of your spacesuit? Who steps out of this Mickey Mouse costume that you inhabit and call your body? At the end, when the show is over and Disneyland closes down for the night, who steps out of your Mickey Mouse suit? So my first question is, who in God's name do you really think you are?

My second question then is this. What do you mean, "He rose from the dead?" A few weeks ago, I was reading a book by

Deepak Chopra and I came across this interesting fact. Snails, your little common garden snails, take three seconds to process something visually. So if something happens in less than three seconds, they cannot register it. If you had a snail walking towards an apple and you reached in and took the apple at that speed, the snail would not see your hand. In the snail's perception, the apple would have just disappeared; the snail could not process it. If something happens in less than $1/20^{th}$ of a second, humans cannot process it visually, so if you are sitting at the breakfast table with an apple in front of you and someone reached in and pulled away the apple in less than $1/20^{th}$ of a second, you would not see it happen. As far as you are concerned, your apple just went poof.

Now it gets much more frightening because, in truth, when we get down to the quantum mechanical level, a photon winks in and out of existence a million times per second. At the quantum mechanical level we are not able to process anything. We do not see anything. But if you could get down to that level, you would realize that all motion is an illusion. Things do not move at the quantum mechanical level. Simply different photons wink into existence and wink out of existence in different locations giving the idea of motion. It is like your Christmas tree and the Christmas lights. You put a row of Christmas lights around your house and you get them to wink on in sequence and from a distance it looks like there is a single light running around your house. The truth is there is no motion happening. Just individual lights are winking in and out of existence in different positions to give the impression of something moving. That is the kind of body you have. Your body at the quantum mechanical level is made up of photons that are winking in and out of existence millions of times per second. So no matter how fast you think you are, you are a lot faster.

Is that the body? Is that what we mean by Jesus rising from the dead? What do we mean he rose from the dead? Are we talking about the meat and the flesh resurrecting? Or are we talking about something happening beginning at the quantum mechanical level and somehow being made visible to the chosen ones? Jesus, it seems, could, after his resurrection, materialize and dematerialize. He was able to appear in rooms and then suddenly he was gone. Locked doors? No problem! They could not recognize him. It is very hard to recognize a photon. Is that what we are talking about?

Paul, for instance, is very definite when he writes in the First Letter to the Corinthians, Chapter 15, about the resurrection of Jesus. He uses two different words for body. The Greek actually has three different words for body and Paul is using two of them in that letter "sarx" and "soma." "Sarx" is flesh. "Soma" is a different notion of body. Paul says, "Flesh and blood cannot inherit the Kingdom of God." So when Paul is talking about the resurrection of Jesus he is saying, "Flesh and blood cannot inherit the Kingdom of God." He is not talking about "sarx," resurrecting but perhaps about "soma." Paul says, "What you set in the ground and what blooms consequently, are totally unrecognizable from each other." The apple seed and an apple tree look very different. So often when we think about the resurrection of Jesus we are asking ourselves the wrong kind of questions.

How quick is a flash? We have been brought up with the belief system that life proceeds in sequences: you are conceived and you are born and you live and you die and if you are lucky, you will rise from the dead. That happens sequentially. When you listen to Jesus, it is not like that at all. It does not spin itself out over 60, 70 or 80 years nor do we have to wait until the end of the world and the general resurrection and a general judgment for all of us to get to heaven. Here is what Jesus had to say. As he is dying on the cross, one of the thieves turned to him and said, "Lord, remember me when you come into your Kingdom." Jesus' response was not, "Okay, wait until the end of the world, go to Purgatory, suffer for your sins, then we will talk about it again." He did not say that. What he said to him was, "This day you will be with me in paradise." Because time is a human construct, the big illusion under which we labor is that life is what happens between birth and death. The truth is life is what happens between incarnation and enlightenment, not between birth and death.

Therefore, resurrection is not about the rising of the physicality of a personality. Using a Zen koan, resurrection is about recognizing the face you had before your parents were born. But you cannot recognize that in your head. It only happens in the secret place of the human heart. Resurrection can only be understood at the soul level and at the heart level. So how do you know it is true? I believe you know something is true if it transforms you. And you know something is utterly true if it radically transforms you. That is the acid test of truth and that is the acid test of reality. So how do we know resurrection is true? How are we absolutely sure resurrection happens? Because it was a radically transforming experience for those who participated, as it is still a radically transforming experience 2000 years later to those who understand it not in the head but in the heart.

Exactly 20 years ago today, on Easter Sunday, 1980, I had a vision of someone encountering resurrection, Mary Magdalene, and I wrote it down and I am going to finish by reading that story to you. I call it:

"Falling in Love, Rising in Love."

"She emptied the big earthen pitcher into a wooden basin and splashed the cool water on her face. Her deep brown eyes were swollen and bloodshot. She tied back her long shiny black tresses with a piece of cloth and bundled them into a veil. Her face was pale and gaunt after her 50-hour fast. Hastily she threw a cloak over her shoulders, carefully picked up the alabaster jar, took the wooden bar from the inside of the door and stepped into the half-night. The morning chill stung her throat as she turned swiftly and sped along the silent streets.

Yellow-white ribbons of light infiltrated feebly from the East erasing the fainter stars. She hadn't expected that it would end like this. She didn't know what she had expected except that this had never occurred to her. It was still difficult to believe it had really happened. But like everything else about him she accepted it completely with a total love only a woman is capable of offering a man. Life had never been the same since she met him. The searching gentleness of his eyes and the soothing healing touch of his hands had melted the bitterness within her and had banished the despair and depression that until then had frequently enveloped her like a thick, choking, claustrophobic fog. Sin and guilt and suicidal remorse had given way to a deep, tranquil peace.

In the darkness of a doorway, a mongrel dog stood up, arched his back, yawned and then stealthily watched her. My god, she thought, is all the blackness and the nauseating despondency to return now that he is gone? Gone? He is gone. Is there nothing more for me now except to remain faithful to a memory? She skirted the hill and her sandals kicked up fluffy cloudlets of red dust. As she opened the gate of the garden, she suddenly remembered that there would be a very large stone at the entrance of the burial chamber. Frustrated, she ran the last few yards and stopped abruptly looking at the gaping mouth of the empty tomb. Terror wrapped itself around her heart. Even in death, is he to find no peace from the relentless pursuit of his enemies? she thought. Hysterically she raced back to the city and told Peter and John what had happened. In utter bewilderment, they ran to the graveyard to see for themselves while she followed breathlessly far behind.

Peter and John saw and began to dare to believe. They headed back to the still slumbering city rushing past her without a word. Again she was left alone with an empty grave. Her pent-up grief exploded and she fell to her knees, body shaking convulsively, hair spilling around her face and tears trickling through her fingers. My God, let all of this be just a bad dream. Let me wake up and find it is only a phantom of the night. She raised her head and looked into the tomb again. Two young men were seated there. They asked her, "Woman, why are you weeping?" "They have taken my lord away," she sobbingly replied, "and I don't know where they have put him." As she said this, she was conscious of a movement behind her and looking around she saw another man standing there. He asked her the same question. Shimmering tears refracted her vision, stray locks of hair stuck to her face and a newborn sun was silhouetting his form so she did not recognize him.

Thinking him to be the keeper of the graveyard, she bowed and clasped his feet and pleaded, "Sir, if you have taken him away, tell me where you have put him and I will go and remove him." Jesus smiled and said, "Mary." It was enough. The intonation, the accent, the sensitivity and the love all intertwined in that last word could only be his. She struggled to her feet and fired herself at him smothering him in an embrace. He stroked her hair and gently brushed the tears from her face with his fingertips, smiling all the while. Then he said to her, "Mary, do not cling to me. Go and tell my brothers and sisters that I'm alive." "No, Jesus, let me stay with you. I don't ever want you to go away again," she protested. He smiled again and said, "I also want to remain with you always and I will, but how you do not understand. Do you believe me?" "Yes, oh, yes I believe. And my love gives me understanding. I know that you will keep this promise also." He kissed her gently on the forehead and said, "Go then and tell them what you have seen." She pressed his fingers to her lips and then left him, lightly dancing her way back to the city.

Early groups of workers were beginning to wake sluggishly. A wizened old man in a white flowing beard stumbled out of a doorway, as she was about to pass. "Shalom," she smiled at him. "Shalom, daughter of Zion," he replied wondering how swollen, bloodshot eyes could laugh as hers did. "Did you have a pleasant Sabbath yesterday?" he asked. Her bottom lip quivered involuntarily, "No ancient one," she said. "Not yesterday, today is my Sabbath." He looked quizzically after her departing form. "Strange," he thought. "Strange eyes, strange face, strange words, very strange words."

14
Symbols, Sacraments and Disguising Christ

Kitty Ahearn was a widow in her late 70's who lived about a quarter of a mile from us in Mayfield when I was a child growing up. Kitty had a tribe of cats that lived with her, all sizes, shapes, ages and sexes. These cats lived, ate, slept, mated, and littered (in every sense of the word) on her table, on her sofas and on her bed. The place was a total mess. It looked like it hadn't been cleaned since before Jesus was Bar Mitzvahed. Everyone was afraid to visit her because Irish hospitality demands that wherever you go you have to accept food. The idea of taking food in Kitty's house was too much for most people, so most people give her a very wide berth.

Then one time there was a new pastor appointed to the parish church and duty demanded of him that he visit all of his charges and inquire after their eternal well-being. So he was briefed on Kitty. He knew what to expect. He kept putting it off for months and months and finally when it couldn't be put off any longer, he decided to take the bit between his teeth and go for it.

He came up to Kitty's door and he knocked on the door and said, "Bail ó Dhia anseo isteach," (the blessing of God precede me in here.) That's the normal Irish way of entering a house. In the case of the pastor it was also a disconsolate plea for divine protection. Kitty said, "Fáilte 'gus fiche romhat, athair" (A welcome and twenty welcomes to you father.) So he went in and he looked around and his worst fears were realized. She took a whole bunch of cats off the armchair and she sat him down and when he sat down, clouds of dander lifted up and he knew that his black suit was never going to be the same again. Immediately he started to sneeze one violent sneeze after the other and every time he sneezed he shook more dander out of the armchair. Kitty was sitting on her little couch perched up looking over at him and every time he sneezed she would say, "Dia linn, Dia linn, Dia linn," (God be with us, God be with us, God be with us.) Certainly God needed to be with the pastor at this stage.

It was just one violent sneeze after the other. In and out between sneezes, he managed to inquire after her eternal well-being. She assured him she was ready to meet her maker at any time. It looked to the pastor as if he was much more likely to be meeting his maker before Kitty did. He tried to make small talk in and out between the sneezes and then finally when he thought things couldn't get any worse, she invited him to have a mug of tea.

She went over to her range where there was a big black kettle of water boiling. On her way to the range, she pushed a whole bunch of cats off the table. There was one big tomcat licking furiously with his head inside a jug of milk. She threw him onto the floor and said, "My God, are you going to leave us a drop of milk at all for our tea?"

She took a mug off the table and she threw the slop out the half door. She took a glass jar and put it on the table. Then she took a fist-full of tealeaves and put them into the mug and the jar and put boiling water on top. She took milk from the jug recently vacated by the tomcat's head and poured it into the mug and jar and stirred it with a spoon that she first cleaned on her skirt. Then she handed the mug to the pastor. He knew very well that this was <u>her</u> mug. He knew that in the kindness of her heart she was using a jar for herself and she was giving him her own favorite mug. He didn't know what he was going to do. There was no way he could refuse it. He sat in the chair with perspiration streaming down his face fearing he was going to get cholera and typhoid and yellow fever. It was only a matter of which one was going to strike first. There was only one tiny glimmer of hope and finally he realized what that was. He took the cup in his left hand thinking that he would drink out of the opposite side of the mug and at least that may lessen the danger minutely. He put it to his mouth, closed his eyes and prayed to God to protect him. He took one slug and Kitty, sitting on her chair watching him started clapping her hands and said, "Praise be to God, Father, I see you're a lefty like myself."

I want to talk about that today. I want to make four main points. I want to talk about signs, symbols and sacraments. That is the first thing I want to talk about. Then secondly, I want to talk about the Liturgy of the Word. Thirdly, I want to talk about the Liturgy of the Act. Then fourthly, I want to talk about, "Now you see me now you don't," recognizing and disguising Jesus in the scriptures.

Let me talk first about signs, symbols and sacraments. There are subtle but very important differences between them in my opinion. A sign is merely one physical reality standing for another physical reality, such as a road sign. A road sign is a piece of metal with yellow and black paint on it which indicates that if you proceed on for another 100 meters you will meet a piece of road going off to your left or to your right. So a sign is just one physical thing standing for another physical thing.

A symbol is different. A symbol has one foot in physicality and the other foot in the non-physical, the immaterial or the unseen. For instance, the idea of men tipping their hats to a woman is a symbol not a sign. It comes from the time when men wore suits of armor including headgear. When someone rode up on his horse in battle armor and you could not see whether he was a friend or an enemy, he would tip his visor so you could see his face. That is the origin of the idea of tipping your hat to a lady. That is a symbol. It has one foot in physicality. It is about physically touching a cap. The other thing is that it is a sign of respect and a declaration of friendship. So that is a symbol.

A sacrament is a particular category of symbol. A sacrament is a symbol that accomplishes exactly what it says. The problem with signs is that they can tell lies. The problem with symbols is that they can be made to lie. For instance, a kiss is a symbol of love and friendship, but in a great story in the Christian scriptures it was used to betray Jesus. So a symbol can tell lies. Or even handshakes can tell lies. That is the point of Kitty's story. The origin of shaking hands is that the right hand is the weapon hand, the place you hold your sword or your dagger. So in ancient times when two people met in order to demonstrate to each other that they came in peace they would show each other their weapon hand and they would grasp each other's weapon hand and shake. That was a sign saying, look I do not have any hidden weapon. I come as a friend.

The problem with a lefty is that a lefty can give you what purports to be his weapon hand and he may be holding a dagger in his real weapon hand. So symbols can be made to tell lies, but sacraments do not lie. Sacraments are that group, that subset, of symbols that accomplish exactly what they set out to do. In different churches we use different symbols and different sacraments.

I think the Catholic Church got it right with their seven sacraments. I think it is beautiful because sacraments are about ritualizing transitions or initiations. That is what they are about. We have one for the initiation into life when a baby is baptized. That is the first transition and initiation and it is ritualized through Baptism.

The second one comes at age seven in the Catholic Church and it is First Holy Communion. It represents that the child has reached the use of reason and now can meaningfully participate in the ritual of the community. So we give him First Holy Communion.

About the age of 12, depending on what country you come from, as children transition into puberty and into adolescence, we symbolize it through Confirmation. This is the recognition that you are now looking at someone who is growing into adulthood.

The next two sacraments initiate us either into marriage or into priesthood through Ordination or through Matrimony. The sixth one is initiation into transition between this world and the next. We talk about Anointing the Sick. It is ritualizing the transition between this world and the next. The seventh one is a kind of a floating one, the sacrament of Reconciliation. It ritualizes symbolically the constant transition between life and death, spiritual life and spiritual death: the death of making the wrong kind of choices that creates disharmony within us, interpersonally or within communities. Reconciliation is the resurrection to newness, harmony and resonance.

The seven sacraments are beautifully done. Except that there are many more than seven sacraments, in my opinion. I believe that every meaningful, fully mindful encounter between human beings is a sacrament. Every time I encounter a human being with full mindfulness and full awareness of the fact, as they say in Hindi, "Namasté, the divine in me recognizes and honors the divine in you," that in my opinion is a sacrament. That is the first point I want to make: the difference between signs, symbols and sacraments.

The second point I want to make is I want to look at what we do here on Sundays. I want to look at the Liturgy of the Word. It was interesting that in this beautiful story from the gospel of Luke, Chapter 24, as the two disciples are walking along the road and they finally meet up with Jesus, whom they have not recognized, and he begins explaining the scriptures to them. Their hearts are on fire. They say later, "Weren't our hearts burning on the way?" Now we are not talking about acid reflux. We are talking about being on fire with the realization of the presence of God. That is all that is happening for them. That is what Liturgy of the Word is supposed to be about on a Sunday. It is about somehow hearing the word of God together so that our hearts literally are on fire. But it does not stop on a Sunday when we leave church. The word of God must continue to burn in our hearts throughout the week. How does that happen?

The Buddha, Gautama Siddhartha, had a fabulous insight into this, 500 years before Jesus was born. The Buddha said one time, and I am paraphrasing it into a kind of psychobabble, he said, "Language is at once the greatest diagnostic tool and the greatest psycho-therapeutic intervention known." It is a diagnostic tool in so far as it tells you who you are. Listen to the way you speak. Do you speak words of meanness? Do you exaggerate? Do you tell lies? Do you criticize? Or do you speak words of encouragement and affirmation and truth and love? That is who you are. Do you want to change who you are? Speak differently, said the Buddha. Instead of exaggerating and telling lies and being mean-spirited, speak words of love and affirmation and confirmation and compassion and that is who you become. So the word of God needs to continue throughout our week

We need to be so on fire with the word of God that we build community and we build love and we build bridges between each other, because as one person said very effectively one time, words are either walls or they are bridges. They connect us or else they remove us from each other. That is the word of God. That is hearing the word. It fascinates me to think, why was Jesus acting as a joker in today's gospel? Why did he come up to them, make himself in some sense unrecognizable to them and then while listening to their conversation, ask them, "What are you talking about?" When they told him what had been happening for the last three days in Jerusalem, he said, "What's happening? Nobody told me about it." Why did he do that? Why was he joking? Why was he pulling their leg? And when he finally got to Emmaus and they were going into an inn for the night, why did he pretend he was going on further when he knew very well he was not going to go on any further? Why was he joking?

I think that in some sense he really wanted to find out where they were in their thinking. A great teacher always starts where his pupils are in their thinking. He wanted to find out what their hit was on what had happened. He wanted to hear if the story had been mangled in just three days. Had it been misinterpreted or had it really been understood? He wanted to hear it from them. However, if they recognized him first, then their ability to listen to the scriptures would have been totally permeated and filtered through their expectations and their personality issues and their own fears. Listening as a stranger was a very different experience. They were projecting nothing of Jesus on to the listening or on to the telling.

It is really hard for us, 2000 years later, having heard this story many times not to put up many projections, expectations and preconceptions before the word of God comes into it. Jesus was trying to create Zen mind in his hearers. Zen mind, beginner's mind, is the ability to hear a story for itself without having to bring it through a series of filters.

The third point I want to talk about is the Liturgy of the Act. They still had not recognized him in the Liturgy of the Word. At the end of the journey, when they had reached Emmaus, they still did not know that it was Jesus. They knew that he was someone special and they wanted to hear more of what he had to say, but they had no idea it was Jesus. They invited him in to have the evening meal with them and they sat down and then, and only then, in the breaking of bread did they suddenly recognize who he was. What was it about the Eucharist that made them recognize Jesus? It was only in the breaking of the bread. There is a beautiful formula every time Eucharist is spoken of in the Christian scriptures. You can recognize it even if the word Eucharist is never mentioned. "He takes bread, he blesses it, he breaks it and he distributes it." That is the essence of Eucharist. Every single time in the New Testament when you talk about Eucharist there will be that formula, those four elements; take it, bless it, break it and distribute it. Taking it means being open to what God wants to do. Blessing it is not that we are blessing something and making it sacred as a result, the blessing consists in recognizing its internal sanctity. Blessing is not about calling forth some kind of a benediction on a secular object. Blessing is recognizing the presence of God in all things when we have that kind of mindfulness. Then he breaks it because everybody needs something and then he distributes it to show the unity. Even in the breaking, there is unity. That is what Eucharist means.

How do we bring Eucharist into the week? We bring Eucharist into the week by sharing bread with each other not just with our families, not just with the people next door, but with the people in Iraq, the people in Africa and the people in India. As long as there is still war in our world, we are not breaking bread together and we are still not recognizing Jesus. Anyone, who can make war has not recognized Jesus. He still does not know what Eucharist is about, in my opinion.

The final point I want to make is this. I want to talk about, "Now you see me now you don't," recognizing Jesus in the scriptures. It was fascinating that Jesus' very physicality confounded them. Many of them did not recognize Jesus. Somehow his very physicality became an obstacle. It was the symbolic gestures that allowed them to recognize him. Sometimes it seems as if symbols are more important than even physical presence, because physical presence confounded them and confabulated what they were about. It was Jesus' symbolic acts that made them aware of who he was.

Why did Jesus disguise himself? Why did he want to disguise himself? Again I come to the same conclusion. By taking his physicality out of the picture he was withdrawing any projections, taking them away, projections and filters and preconceptions and allowing the symbols to speak for themselves and allowing the word of God to speak for itself.

How did Jesus disguise himself? How could it be that people with whom he lived for three years, who ate with him and slept with him and walked with him and talked with him, how could they not recognize him three days after he had died? I remember how I very facetiously answered this question one time. I was living in a little mission in Kenya, and we had just finished a seven-day seminar with catechists and one of the catechists was an African nun. We had been talking about the resurrection. It was the end of the week, I was very tired and just wanted to go home and get a cup of tea. She asked me one last question, "Why was it that the disciples of Jesus didn't recognize him after he rose from the dead?" And very flippantly from over my shoulder as I was going out the door, I said, "Because while he was still in the tomb, he shaved off his beard." I don't believe that that is why they did not recognize him.

So how did Jesus disguise himself? I think Einstein got it right. I think Einstein's formula is the response, $E = mc^2$, energy and matter are convertible into each other. Except, Einstein did not quite get it exactly right. I only figured it out this morning in my meditation after 52 years. E does not stand for energy. M does not stand for mass in the sense of matter. C does not stand for the speed of light. E stands for enlightenment. M stands for mass as in Eucharist. C stands for communication and it is c^2, a double-sided communication. It is we receiving the word of God and it is we speaking to God. Enlightenment consists in recognizing the presence of God in the Liturgy of the Act and in listening to God and in speaking to God. That is enlightenment in my opinion.

Finally then, I leave myself with these questions. Why was it that Mary Magdalene did not recognize him initially? Why did the two disciples on the road to Emmaus think he was a total stranger? Why is it that we, 2000 years later, continue to act as if Jesus was a blond, blue-eyed Arian? Why do we see the pictures of Jesus in Africa as if he were Negro? Jesus, historically, was Jewish. But much more importantly than that, Jesus essentially was everyone. He was every person. Therefore, to the extent that we still discriminate against body type, color or ethnicity, we still have not recognized Jesus. We are still not seeing who is there. We look at someone and see an Iraqi. We look at someone and see a Protestant. We look at someone and see an African. We do not see Jesus in them. Jesus is still disguised because of our inability to see.

Finally, the church in its infinite wisdom compounded the error further. The disciples were making the big breakthrough in Eucharist when they broke bread together. They recognized Jesus, but then the church took that away. It took the priest away from the people, placed him with his back to the congregation, celebrated the mass in Latin and insisted that only celibate males could encounter Christ. Whatever happened to the biblical teaching that where two or three are gathered together, there am I in their midst?

I spoke to you before about how the church had hijacked the sacrament of Reconciliation and created it as if it were an institutional prerogative when, in fact, it is a community obligation. Forgiveness is not an institutional prerogative. It is a community obligation. This week, it seems to me, we are remembering the fact that the church hijacked the Eucharist and made it a ministerial prerogative; it is not about male celibates with their back to us talking in strange words. Eucharist is about two or three people gathered in the name of Jesus. We are still disguising and we are still failing to recognize who Jesus really is.

15
Reincarnation

Ian Stevenson, a professor of psychiatry at the University of Virginia, spent the last 35 years of his life investigating medical evidence for the possibility of reincarnation. He has written several books and many medical monographs. He has worked a great deal in four particular geographical areas where he now has many informants who continue to bring cases to his attention. These communities all believe in reincarnation. They are a Buddhist community in Burma, a Hindu community in northern India, the Shiite people in Turkey and a group of Native American people from Alaska. All together he has personally investigated more that 2,600 cases.

These communities have different belief systems about reincarnation. Many believe that reincarnation is preceded by an announcing dream in which either the mother, who is about to become pregnant, or one of the family members has a dream in which she is told that a certain person wants to be born into that particular family. They take these dreams very seriously. A second source of information is an elder, who is about to die, predicting that he or she is going to come back into a particular family. Often they will point to particular marks on their own body and say to look out for these as birthmarks on the child. Often these societies have children who begin talking about previous lives, giving themselves previous names and talking about previous families in other areas.

Some of these communities actually put experimental marks on dying bodies so that when a person is reborn they will look very closely for marks at those places. In these communities, when a baby is born, they go through the child's body in absolute detail looking for birthmarks or birth defects which will correspond to wounds or the manner in which someone else may have died in the village around them.

I'll give you a typical case. The British defeated the Japanese forces in Burma in the spring of 1945. Many Japanese soldiers committed suicide rather than give up. Stevenson has had several cases of Burmese children claiming that they were Japanese. They would refuse Burmese food, wanted raw fish and sweet teas and seemed to be much more Japanese in their behavior than they were

Burmese. The Burmese are a much more relaxed community than the Japanese. Stevenson investigated children exhibiting Japanese characteristics and asked the parents about marks present at birth. A typical case was the one in which there was a child with two birthmarks, one at the crown of its head and the other under its chin. He examined them and the one under the chin was found to be much bigger than the one on the crown on the head. The child claimed that in a previous life he was a Japanese soldier who was shot in the head and killed by British aircraft. We know from medical evidence that the entry wound of a bullet is always much smaller than the exit wound because as the bullet goes through it begins to pitch and yaw and push tissue and bone fragments in front of it.

I want to talk a little bit about that today. I want to make four main points. Firstly, I want to make a few introductory remarks about today's reading in the gospel of John. Secondly, I want to take this phrase of Jesus; "In my father's house there are many mansions." Thirdly, I want to look at the statement from Jesus, "I am the way and the truth and the life." Finally, I want to look at Jesus' statement where he says, "I and the Father are one."

I will start with few introductory remarks about reading the gospel of John. Of the four gospels, John is the most difficult to read. The other gospels tend to be more anecdotal and more a telling of stories and parables. John is very densely packed mysticism. You cannot read the gospel of John with a simplistic fundamentalist, literalistic mindset. You can only read John as mystical literature. If we insist on listening to the gospel of John as a truly historical recording of facts, we miss the whole point. John's is the last of the four gospels written. It was probably written somewhere between 70 or 80 years after Jesus had died. It is the distillation of the experience of the Christian community over two or three generations, the extraordinarily transformative experience of the following of Jesus. They are viewing Jesus' ministry, Jesus' works, and Jesus' words through the prism and in the hothouse of 80 years of personal, Eucharistic and community experience. They are articulating the experiences of the early church in extraordinarily mystical language. The difficulty for us is that we miss the mysticism and the mystery and only see the literalistic and fundamentalist understandings of it.

Between the gospel of Mark, written probably about 40 years after Jesus died, and the gospel of John, written between 70 or 80

112

years after Jesus died, there is a huge shift in the community's understanding of Jesus. In Mark, there is no mention of a miraculous conception of Jesus. There is no mention of Jesus' birth. In Mark, Jesus dies on the cross saying just one thing, "My God, my God, why have you forsaken me." It is a very human account of an extraordinary human being. By the time you get to the gospel of John, although John has no birth account or miraculous conception, there is no need because John is talking about Jesus as the preexisting logos, the Word of God that has existed long before time began. In John, Jesus does not die in despair on the cross; Jesus exits as a king whose mission is finished. His last words in John are, "It is complete. I've done what I came here to do." When we read the gospel of John it becomes very important for us that we try to read it through the eyes of mystical understanding. If you pick up your daily newspaper you see the national news on the front page, you look at the comic strip section, you look at the financial market and you look at the sports accounts. You cannot read all four sections with the same mindset. You bring a very definite and different mindset to each section of your morning newspaper. The same thing is true as we read the scriptures.

It is very important for us, in order to get an understanding of what the authors in the community were trying to communicate, to try to read the particular genre of literature with the particular mindset that is necessary. We can only read the gospel of John, in my opinion, in a mystical fashion. I want to go on to examine three statements of Jesus and try to look at them through the prism of a kind of mystical understanding rather than a literal interpretation.

The first one is, "In my father's house there are many mansions." Jesus said this at the Last Supper, according to the gospel of John, the day before he died. He is leaving and says to them, "In my father's house there are many mansions. If it were not so, I would not have said this to you. I go to prepare a place for you and I will come back to take you with me." What do you think the "many mansions in my father's house" means? Is Jesus talking about eggs in the super market, where there are small, medium, large and jumbo size eggs and that you are going to be arranged by stature in the Kingdom of Heaven, or, are there going to be different places for different belief systems? Is that what Jesus meant by saying my father's house has many mansions, the Protestants one place, the Catholics another place, and the Jews someplace else? Or is Jesus talking about levels of spiritual evolution? Is he saying that the really advanced people are going to be in one place and the lesser advanced someplace else? Is this what he is talking about? Or is Jesus talking about belief systems? Do we create in the afterlife what we believe to be the truth? Certainly our belief systems in this life radically affect our sense of reality. Our mindset has a huge impact on the reality we perceive. Is that true in the afterlife? Is that what Jesus is saying, that in my father's house there are many mansions because the belief system that you bring into the afterlife with you determines your experience? Is that what he is saying? Or is he saying that there is some kind of progress to it? Do we get into the afterlife still concerned with sensory experience and therefore want to experience a heaven that addresses our sensory needs? Then after a few million years of addressing those needs, do we then move on to identifying what our emotional needs are and satisfying those in different layers of heaven? Do we move on beyond merely our emotional needs to satisfying our intellectual needs? For example, are there huge libraries there when we get to a certain stage? Will we finally get to a place where we move beyond purely sensory satisfaction, emotional satisfaction and intellectual satisfaction into spiritual satisfaction? Is that what it is about?

Is Abraham Maslow there with his "hierarchy of needs" as we move from mansion to mansion to satisfy different needs? Or has it to do with our understanding of love? Is the heaven we reach the place where we are reunited with all our loved ones? Do we create a heaven where we get to meet all the people who have been important in our lives and we get to be with them forever and ever? At some stage, do we grow beyond that? When Jesus says, "In heaven there is neither marriage nor giving in marriage," is that a frightening possibility or is that about spiritual evolution? Is that about reaching a place where we realize that there is no place for special relationships? That if we really know what love is about no one can be more important to us than anyone else, not because everyone is equally valued but because everyone is capable of receiving our total love. Is that what the evolution in heaven is about?

I had a sister, Eithne, with whom I was very close. She died very suddenly four years ago of a brain aneurysm. Her husband was an oil engineer and they lived in the Middle East for many years in Abu Dhabi, Dubai and Saudi Arabia at a time when I was living in

East Africa and occasionally we would get together. We had a young sister, Dearbhla, living in Ireland, who was a little child at the time. She was 17 years younger than Eithne and 22 years younger than me. Both of us loved Dearbhla very much and we would write to her occasionally and we always used aerogrammes. About two months after Eithne died, Dearbhla had a dream in which she was going into her own house in Ireland that has a frosted glass front door and as she looked through the door she could see an acrogramme on the floor. The postman had put it through the mail slot; she thought in her dream, "Oh, this is a letter from Seán or from Eithne." As she opened the door the aerogramme got caught in the underside of the door which opened it a little. The first line of the aerogramme said, "Hi Dearbhla, this is Eithne. I'm at the university and I'm really happy." Now, the university originally was the place for studying the cosmos, literally. It was a place for studying the entire universe. Is that what happens afterward? Do we progress through stages of our university career to some kind of enlightenment? Is that what Jesus is saying today when he talks about "in my father's house there are many mansions?"

My third point is to look at Jesus' statement, "I am the way and the truth and the life." He says to Thomas, "I go and you can follow me because you know the way." And Thomas says, "Know the way? We don't even know where you are going. If we don't know where you're going, how can we know the way?" Jesus replies, "I am the way and the truth and the life." How do we understand this statement of Jesus mystically rather than fundamentally? In 1996, I was giving a series of Lenten talks in the First Presbyterian Church in Palo Alto on the historical Jesus. I entitled the entire series "Will the Real Jesus Please Stand Up." I was studying this topic and thinking and meditating a great deal about it and on February 16, 1996, I had a powerful visionary experience in my meditation. I saw Jesus coming towards me. I asked him this question, "Are you the way and the truth and the life?" The reply was, "I am. I am the way and I am the truth and I am the life because the way and the truth and the life is love. There is no other way and there is no other truth and there is no other life." Then spontaneously he went on to say, "…and the Buddha is the way and the truth and the life because there is no other way and there is no other truth and there is no other life except compassion."

115

What do we take this statement to mean, that Jesus is the way the truth and the life, particularly in light of the statement that comes immediately afterwards in the gospel of John in which he says, "Nobody comes to the Father except through me." I look at what we have done with that statement in the history of Christianity. I take this extraordinarily mystical statement of Jesus to mean that there is only one way to get to the Father and that is Christ consciousness or Buddha nature or love and compassion. That is the only way to get to the Father. There is no other way. We have turned this about into a belief system that if we are not baptized in the name of the Lord Jesus we are damned. The Catholic Church had its own phrase for it: "Outside of the Church there is no salvation." Anyone who attempted to marry someone who was not "in the Church" could not get married in the Church. They might be taken to the sacristy and married in the back room, but they could not be married at the altar in the church.

If a person was not a Christian, God forbid that he be allowed to be buried in a Christian graveyard. Is that what Jesus was about? It is not peculiar to Christianity. Every system has made this mistake. All the great mystical teachings of all the great spiritual leaders have been corrupted at some stage of the game into a literalistic mentality.

Judaism believed that it was the chosen people. What an extraordinary notion, that God would play favorites. Within Orthodox Judaism, if a person marries outside the faith, they sit Shiva for him or her, which is part of the funeral service, and they are considered dead to the community and dead to the understanding of God. Islam calls such people infidels, people without faith. Every system has attempted to take the mystical thinking of the great spiritual leaders and transform it into elitism where there is the "in" crowd and the "out" crowd. Is that what Jesus meant when he said, "I am the way and the truth and the life?" Now what did he mean? What do you think he meant?

My fourth point is this, when Jesus finally said, "I and the Father are one," what do you think he meant? He went on afterwards and said, "To see me is to see the Father. Have you been with me so long and you still do not understand? I am in the Father and the Father is in me." How can the Jesus who made these statements, if we take them literally, also make the statement, "The Father is greater then me?" Or how can he, in one of the other gospels, when he is asked "When will the end times be upon us?" make the statement, "Nobody knows. Not the angels in heaven nor the Son of Man but only the Father." How can we put these two sets of statements side by side? How can Jesus claim to be one with the father and then say, "The Father is greater than me?" As far as the end time is concerned, no one knows when the end time will come, not the angels of heaven and not the Son of Man but only the Father. How do you put these two sets of statements together?

I think the only way to put them together is to use a mystical understanding and it is the mysticism of the mystery between the immanence of God and the transcendence of God, between the God who lives within us in whose image we are born, and the God who is the creator of everything. God is the ground of our very being and the ladder on which our spiritual evolution is very firmly set. God is that ground. God is also the destination to which the ladder is leading us and God is the stuff of which the ladder is made. There is only God at every stage of it. So within Christian prayer, we talk about a Trinitarian formula where all prayer is the Spirit speaking to the Father through the Son. In other words, it is the experience of our groundedness or humanity addressing the experience of our transcendence through our very humanity. That is what it is about.

For me, these two sets of statements are not incompatible at all. Rather they are complementary. It is the dialogue that has to happen between the realization that we are built in the image and likeness of God but as fallible human beings. Since we are built in the image and likeness of God, each one of us can say "the Father and I are one," and "to see me is to see the Father." To really see another human being, is to see God in that sense of the word. You are a little articulation of God addressing the extraordinary magnanimity of the transcendent principle that causes all of creation. That is the dialogue that keeps us in the cosmic dance.

Life is like a jigsaw puzzle. You buy a jigsaw puzzle at a store and you open it up and you tumble all of the pieces out of the box. You first have to make an act of faith that everything that is necessary is present, and everything that is present is necessary. You are not going to have four pieces left over when you are finished. Nor are you going to lack three pieces when you are finished. Every single one of us has what it takes to realize our divinity. In constructing any jigsaw puzzle, there are a few clues that allow us to proceed on the journey. The first clue is to identify the straight

117

pieces that allow us to create the framework. Each one of us has to have some kind of framework, some kind of cosmology, some kind of belief system that allows us to situate our individual experiences and to contextualize them meaningfully for ourselves. That is the first clue we have.

The second clue that we have is the contours of the pieces. The third clue is the image we have of the finished puzzle on the cover of the box. How often have you been doing your jigsaw puzzle and after you labor for hours, you finally conclude that something is not right about it? You realize that you are going to have to undo your work because this one piece that seemed to fit is not creating the image on the box. You have to disassemble it and take this piece and put it up in the corner and that piece and put it down at the bottom. Then slowly when you have the courage to begin disassembling what is not working and reconfiguring the pieces, the image of God that is on the box begins to emerge. Every single one of us is God's masterpiece. Every single one of us is God's unique jigsaw puzzle. Everything you have is necessary and everything that is necessary you have.

16
SPIRIT

We didn't allow the girls to come with us. They pretended that they didn't care, but they were really jealous. Not that it mattered a whole lot to us, because we were just nine years old. What did we care about girls? But they weren't allowed to come with us because this was boy's stuff. I'm talking about going on hikes when we were small kids. It's always amazing to me that it took a lot of effort on our parent's part during the school year to wake us up at 7:30 in the morning. They'd have to call again and again and finally come up and shake us into wakefulness. But during the summer months when we could stay in bed all day if we chose to, we'd be out on the floor at 6:30 in the morning. There was important stuff to be done, we had to go play hurling, steal apples from somebody's back yard or hang out in the park.

Where I lived, there were 34 houses on three sides of a square and there was a big grassy field in the middle and all the kids would meet there early in the morning to decide the day's activity. Occasionally, if it was a really fine day, someone would say, "Let's go on a hike." We would say, "Yea, yea, let's go on a hike." So everyone would be deputized to bring some articles or other. We would need a big frying pan, a big hatchet to chop the wood, a box of matches, newspaper to start the fire, rashers, sausage, eggs, white pudding, black pudding, bread and butter, jam, and cookies. We'd also have to have hurlies in lieu of machetes to hack our way through the jungle. We'd need a whistle to get everyone going. We'd meet back in the park in a half-hour. That was the rule. Of course, there would always be some hold-ups, like Billy Flynn's mother deciding that we couldn't use her frying pan because we used it the last time and it never recovered. Or Michael Murphy would be discovered with a pound of sausage in his pocket and his mother would take the sausage back to the kitchen saying, "We need this for dinner." Stephen Flannery's mother would say, "Go in and dress your bed before you go!" He would have to go back three- or four-times to dress the bed to her satisfaction. There were always those kinds of hold-ups.

Eventually we'd get the show on the road and the girls would pretend to ignore us. We knew that they were absolutely mad with jealousy, but we didn't mind. The smaller kids would dance around us. They couldn't come because they were too small to walk the 150 odd miles for the day. It was a matter of honor that you couldn't walk on the roadways; you had to keep going cross-country. If you came across a paved road, by any chance, you'd have to go straight across it. It was a terrible indignity to walk on the road. We would always have to start off by going through Spillane's field. Spillane was a local farmer who had a big bull and about 25 cows. It was a point of honor for us to start the safari by going through this field. We weren't men; we weren't fit for the journey unless we could take on the bull and the 25 cows.

We'd climb up on the ditch. In Ireland, a ditch is not a hollow; a ditch is a big mound four- or five-feet high covered with brambles. We'd all get up on top of the ditch and we'd watch where the mad bull was. Bulls were always mad in Ireland. One by one we'd take off across the field hell for leather and clamber up on the ditch on the far side screaming at each other and alerting every cow in the countryside. When we got across we would compare notes on how the bull almost got us. That was the start of the safari.

Then we would go field by field and there would be one guy sent ahead to reconnoiter the terrain, because there could be pythons lurking anyplace or rabid jackals or man-eating tigers and we wanted to be sure that we were aware of them before we took them on. Finally, after we had traveled about 100 miles, we'd stop. Now if someone saw a road sign that said, "Cork four miles" we'd laugh at him, "Didn't he know that the natives in this part of the country would falsify figures to lure us into a false sense of security so that they could cannibalize us?"

We all knew that we were 100 miles from Cork; don't believe the signposts. Finally, we'd camp in a field and there had to be a river nearby. We'd collect a group of stones and we'd build a big fireplace. Then we'd put in the papers and some straw and for the next 45 minutes we would be blowing furiously to try to get it to start. Eventually the "God of Fire" would see that we weren't going to give up and finally it would start to light.

Then out would come the frying pan, a huge frying pan. Then we'd take about a half-pound of butter and throw it in on top until there was about an inch and a half of liquid butter in the frying pan. Then we'd throw in the spuds and the rashers and the sausage and the eggs and the white pudding and the black pudding and mix it up until the whole thing was a kind of liquid. Then we'd pour it into mugs and drink it mopping it up with a piece of bread. Then we would make tea, Barry's Tea, by putting a fist-full of tea leaves into a pot with a half pint of milk, three quarters of a pack of sugar, and stir it all together. We would pour it into the same mugs in which the other stuff had been and drink it down. I want to talk about that a little bit today.

I want to talk particularly about our frying pan, our liquid mess of sausage, rashers, eggs, white pudding and black pudding. I want to talk about that because that is what the Holy Spirit is not. Today is the feast of Pentecost. I want to make four main points. I want to talk first about a few definitions of spirit. What does spirit mean to us? Secondly, I want to talk about the spirit as a unifying force. Thirdly, I want to talk about the Spirit as renewal. Fourthly, I want to talk about the Spirit as the principle of love.

My first point is a few definitions. Let me set the historical background for this. Pentecost was a feast that long predated Christianity. Pentecost was a celebration of the fiftieth day after the Jews had escaped from Egypt in the year 1250 B.C. After having been in the desert for 50 days and having escaped their slavery, Moses goes to the top of Mount Sinai and is given the law, the Decalogue, a new covenant between God and the people of Israel. The Exodus on its own would not have resulted in the nation of Israel. It was the covenant on Sinai that welded a group of slaves into a nation for the first time. So in the Jewish cosmology and Jewish theology, Exodus and Sinai go together; they are inseparable. Passover and Pentecost are inseparable. . It was a celebration of the fact that 50 days after they had escaped they had an encounter with God who gave them a new constitution. That is what it represented. The Christians took over this feast

Can we define then what the spirit of that was? What do we mean when we talk about Spirit? Long before there was a nation of Israel and long before there was even a nation of Egypt, there was a primordial world view that has survived right down to the 1700's of our own era. This primordial view suggested that reality consisted of two orders. There was the invisible, sacred order and there was the visible, mundane or secular order. These two things interpenetrated. They interpenetrated in sacred places and in great historical events and in the lives of charismatic characters. My particular definition of

Spirit then is the divine intelligence that underlies the intersection of the invisible and the visible.

Spirit is the unifying force between these two that allows the intersection to happen. Great thinkers throughout history have given their own hits on Spirit, even if they did not call it Spirit. I think that when Plato was talking about the ideal realm from which all-physical reality finally manifests or from where all worlds emanate, in some sense he is talking about the same thing. There is an invisible order, the ideal realm; he calls it, from which all human phenomenology emanates. I think that is evidence of Spirit. Spirit is the divine intelligence behind that process.

Rupert Sheldrake, a modern day biologist, has taught about a phenomenon that he has entitled morpho-genetic fields. He believes that before any new life form comes into existence, nature creates some kind of a template and as the creative energy of nature flows through this template you get a new life form. I think that is Spirit. Spirit is the intelligence behind the template, Spirit is the intelligence behind the energy, and Spirit as the energy and Spirit as the template finally articulate as Spirit in physical matter. That would be a modern day hit on Spirit.

When Deepak Chopra talks about law, his definition of law is the best one I have ever come across. He says law is the process through which the unmanifest becomes manifest. Or, law is the process through which the invisible becomes visible. I would like to piggyback on that and say that my definition of Spirit is that Spirit is the information matrix, or that Spirit is the divine intelligence that sets up law in the first place and then uses law as a process through which all of the invisible sacred order can manifest on the visible, secular or mundane level. That is the first point, to make just a few random definitions of what Spirit may be.

Secondly, I want to look at the notion of Spirit as an underlying unifier. There is a great statement in the book of Wisdom, Chapter 1, which says to us, "The Spirit holds all things together." I want to look at that statement. I think there are two ways of looking at this. The first way is to take any physical thing and ask, "How does it hold itself together?" What creates the unifying principle of any physical, ontologically discrete object in the universe? I think it is Spirit. There is a Spirit inside every daffodil. There is a Spirit inside every earwig. There is a Spirit inside every moonrise. There is a Spirit inside every human being that somehow makes it a discrete, ontologically separate phenomenon. In that sense, the Spirit is holding that thing together in its unity. There is a second sense in which you could interpret that phrase. The Spirit holds all things together or binds all things together. I think the Spirit is the underlying unity that holds the entire cosmos with its billions of disparate elements together in some kind of universal unity. Everything is part of the fabric of a single painting or a single work of art. No matter how we separate things into their different, discrete little ontologically separate boxes, ultimately everything is one extraordinary canvas, one extraordinary masterpiece of God. Spirit for me holds the entire picture together, so in that sense, it is an underlying principle.

Then we can begin to understand what the story of Babel and the story of Pentecost are about, because one is the antithesis and one is the very essence of what this represents. Babel was the fragmentation of that unity consciousness. In the story in Genesis, Chapter 11, God became jealous because human beings were displaying so much chutzpah that they were actually attempting to build a tower that would reach the heavens. So God comes down, or more appropriately, the Gods come down, because there is a dialogue in Chapter 11 of Genesis suggesting that there is a group of Gods talking among themselves, and they say, "Let us go down and separate them lest they become Gods like us."

So they separate their tongues and for the first time ever there is this extraordinary diversity. In a way, Babel represents the disintegration of Spirit. In fact, Babel is the old Hebrew articulation of the second law of thermodynamics, entropy, which is that all things left to their own devices ultimately run down into chaos. Therefore, you could say that the second law of thermodynamics, the law of entropy, is the gradual withdrawal of Spirit from any article.

Pentecost is the very opposite of that process. Pentecost was the process by which all of the disparate parts without losing their ontological separateness somehow came back into some kind of cosmic unity. The interesting thing to me when I listen to the story of Pentecost in the Acts of the Apostle, Chapter 2, is not that Peter had mastered all the languages of his listeners. He did not. But rather that everyone heard them speak in his own language. It is not that God is trying to create this extraordinary mess in the frying pan of the world that as boys we created on our hikes. God is not into blenders. God is into smorgasbords and salad concoctions where you slice up all of the ingredients but you do not blend them. God never blends. Pentecost is not about blending. Pentecost is not about putting everyone into the same pot and messing around until you get a stew out of it.

There is a movie called "Bullworth." It is the story of an American senator who loses it and goes a little crazy, except his craziness makes a lot of sense. At one point, he is being interviewed on national television about how we can overcome the great intolerances of our world in our multicultural America. He had been taking pot before this particular program and he was really high and on a roll and he said on national television, "The way to end all of this is to let everyone make love to everyone until finally we all come out the same color. Then there will be an end to prejudice." That is not how the Spirit works. That is not what Pentecost is about. Pentecost is not about blending all colors, tongues and creeds together so you get this amorphous mass that all looks the same and tastes icky. That is not what it is about. It is about retaining our individuality in order to create the masterpiece of God's work of art. That is the second point I want to make.

I want to look then at the notion of Spirit as an underlying source of renewal. How does Spirit represent renewal? There is a great story from the Prophet Joel about 400 years before Jesus. Joel is prophesying the final times, the times of the messiah, and says, "In the days to come, I will pour out my Spirit upon all humankind. Your old men will dream dreams and your young men will see visions. Yea, even on your servants and on your handmaids in those days, I will pour out my Spirit." The first thing to realize is that in the Hebrew cosmology, dreams and visions are the very same thing.

When I was young, I pitied the old men who only had dreams. Visions somehow represented the future and dreams represented merely the past. Of course, that was not true at all. In the Hebrew cosmology, dreams and visions are synonyms. A dream is a vision you have when you are asleep and a vision is a dream you have when you are awake. God speaks equally powerfully through both. So Joel was not saying your old men have merely their past to remember where your young men have a future to envision. He is not saying that. He is saying in the final times that he will pour out his Spirit upon all human kind and all will be in communication with God through dreams and through visions, which are the very same things. He said he would pour out his Spirit on all humankind, young men, maidens, slaves and free. There would be no discrimination in this outpouring of Spirit. It would not be based on age. It would not be based on sex. It would not be based on race. It has nothing to do with class, color, creed or socioeconomic status. It is just about being a child of God.

Here is renewal in the Hebrew dispensation. Here is God renewing the face of the earth. But someone got there long before human beings. I believe that the most intelligent life forms on the planet are plants. Long before humans were born, plants learned to create energy for themselves through photosynthesis. After 1.5 million years, humans still have not figured out how to take energy directly from the sun as food. We cannot even do it at a second remove. Most of us have to do it at a third remove. So we have to eat the animals that eat the plants that convert sunlight into energy. We do it the third time. The plants do it directly – extraordinary intelligence. Plants have figured out a way of propagating themselves that is effortless and poetic. They do it through the wind. They make little helicopter seeds that spin down and move maybe 40 yards away from the parent tree. Or they create fluffy little dandelions that the wind takes hundreds of yards away. Or they create tumbleweeds that are driven before the wind in order to propagate. Or they use birds and bees to do their work for them, extraordinarily creative, extraordinarily intelligent and extraordinarily poetic. In fact, plants in my opinion, are the first missionaries of all. They were the first to bring the good news of life way beyond themselves. Therefore, it seems to me, this is one of the reasons why the wind is such a powerful image of Pentecost because Pentecost is about dispensing life to everyone. It is about bringing the message of good news and healing to the ends of the earth. That is why the Spirit came as this extraordinary wind on Pentecost. The Spirit wants us to be little helicopter pods who will take the word throughout the world. The Spirit wants us to be little dandelions that blow to the four corners of the globe. The Spirit wants us to be tumbleweeds bringing the message of love and healing to all parts. The Spirit wants us to be birds and bees, having the ability to cross-pollinate and give life to everything we touch.

The fourth point I want to make is about Spirit as an image of love which we read in the beautiful passage in Chapter 20 of the gospel of Saint John. In Jesus' first encounter with the disciples after they had betrayed him, denied him, ignored him, and run from him his message to them was, "Peace to you." He said to them three times in this passage, "Peace to you." He is not wagging fingers at them. He is not blaming them. He is not asking them why you did or why didn't you. He is saying, "Peace be with you." His first gift was peace.

His second gift was that he breathed on them. The third gift he gave them was the Holy Spirit. The fourth gift he gave them was the ability and the responsibility to forgive. He breathed upon them and he said, "Whose sins you shall forgive, they are forgiven. And whose sins you shall retain, they are retained." I want to say two things about this. It is a terrible pity that the church has constantly preached that the ability to forgive sins is the prerogative of a little oligarchy at the top of an institution that was meant to represent the community. Forgiveness of sins is not the prerogative of the institution. Forgiveness of sins is the responsibility of the community, every member of the community. That is why the sin against the Spirit is to refuse to forgive. There is no greater sin than the sin against the Spirit. The sin against the Spirit, in my opinion, is to refuse to exercise the gift of the Spirit that was the ability to and the responsibility to forgive sins. The interesting thing is that the statement is really true, "Whose sins you shall forgive, they are forgiven, and whose sins you shall retain, they are retained." Not that the institution has the power to bind or dispense, but that in human interaction psychologically and sociologically, when we refuse to forgive, we hold the entire system in thrall. We hold ourselves in bondage, we hold the object of our anger in bondage and we hold the whole human family in bondage. It is a very important responsibility if we are Christian to make forgiveness the touchstone of our discipline.

Therefore, my final definition of Spirit would be this. Spirit is the ultimate purpose through which God awakens the cosmic feeling of love, which is the origin of our life, which is the destination of our life, and which permeates and is the essence of our life.

17
Love

Yesterday morning I began a 21-mile race in preparation for a marathon that I will be running on June 17. I've been training with a team for the last four months and I've run several 12- 14- and 16-mile races. I enjoyed them all. I loved them all, until yesterday. The first 16 miles were great. I was enjoying it and feeling good, and then the last five miles I was hanging on by my fingernails. For the last few long races there has been someone whom I have befriended, part of the team, a young woman called Maria. Maria and I have done many of these races together because we are pretty much of the same pace. We take turns leading. I will lead for four or five miles and she will follow and then she will pick up and go ahead of me and I will follow for four or five miles. That way we keep each other going.

Yesterday, for the last five miles, I desperately needed her and she was there. Time and time again she would fall back and say, "How are you doing? Hang in there." I would say, "Maria, go ahead and finish the race at your own pace." She would say, "No we're going to finish this race together." She kept falling back to my pace and we finished the race together. As I saw what she was doing and as I was in pain and trying to hang in there to the end, I was reminded of a great Buddhist story about four people who are lost in the desert. As they crawl through the sand, sunburned and parched with thirst, they spot this huge wall. One of them climbs to the top and sees an extraordinary oasis with running water, food, palm trees, fruit, and shade. He yells, "Yippee," and dives over. The second guy climbs up to see what the excitement is and dives over in a flash. The third guy immediately follows. Then the fourth guy climbs up and he looks in and sees the pools, fruit trees and shade and he goes back down onto the other side of the wall and back into the desert to look for any other people who might be lost.

That reminded me of what Maria was doing with me for the last five miles. I want to talk about that. I want to talk about the notion of love. I want to make three main points. The first point I want to make is this; I want to talk about confusing law with love. Secondly, I want to ask myself the question, "Who is deserving of my love?" Then thirdly I want to ask a long question. "Does loving get easier or a whole lot harder?"

Let me talk firstly about the notion of confusing law with love. This morning in my meditation, I got this great insight that before there was law there was no sin. Now I realize, after I had this extraordinary insight, that Paul beat me to it by 2000 years in his letter to the Romans. But for me, it was a moment of insight, the realization that before there was law there was no such thing as sin. Are we capable, initially, of sinning or even telling lies? Children learn to tell lies when they are taught the rules. Only then do children begin to tell lies because lies go with the territory of being loved or not loved. So before children learn the rules, there is no need to tell lies. Unfortunately, when they tell lies, often love begins to be withdrawn. Since the thing that children crave most and since the thing that we all crave most is to be loved, we learn very quickly as children to manipulate people, situations, and truth in order to receive love and to prevent the withholding of love. Before there was law, there was no sin. Before there was law there were no lies. It was very easy to tell the truth until love became dependent upon doing what society or the individuals demanded.

We pick this up as adults as well. This is not true of children. It is interesting to me that the more laws we put on the statute books the greater the crime rate. There is a correlation between them. I think, in fact, it is not just a correlation; I think there is a causal connection between them. It is not the one you might first imagine. It is not that crime increases and therefore we need more laws to deal with the crimes. I have a thesis that as we put more laws on the statute books, we force more crime. It is the same extraordinary phenomenon that exists between population and food production. It is statistically well proven in developing societies that there are tremendous connections between population growth and food production. It is not the way you would think. It is not that as cultures produce more babies they need more food to feed the extra mouths. That is not how it happens. It is the opposite. As cultures learn to provide more food, the birthrate goes up. At some unconscious level it is like we need more mouths to eat the extra food. So the food comes first and then the population needs to grow to consume it.

I have a belief system that the same thing is true of law and crime. That the laws come first and the crime comes later. It is not that the crime increases and we need more laws to deal with the crime. It is that as we put more and more laws on the statute books, the crime rate is going to go up and up. This happens not just in the political arena; it happens in the religious arenas as well. Religions have tried this since the beginning of time: multiplying laws in the short-term works. In the long term, it really fails and eventually all you get is obedience, but you never get enlightenment, because if you think managed care is a disaster, you should try managed morality. It is a total disaster. We cannot manage morality. The only thing that really drives moral behavior is if it leads to love. Law has never managed to do it and law will never manage to do it. It is fascinating to me to watch. I presume that, in fact, there are more laws on the statute books of the United States of America than any other country in the world and we have the highest incarceration rate. Is there a connection between them? Is it because we have more criminals in this society that we need more laws? Or is it because we have more laws in this society that we have more criminals?

How might that work? For two reasons it seems to me. Firstly, when we multiply attorneys, jail systems, legislatures, laws and police then we multiply all the ways in which it is possible to break the laws. It is much easier to break laws as the laws increase. For that reason, it is much easier to be a criminal now than it used to be. There are lots more ways of doing it. You do not even have to be creative to do it any more. Secondly, and I do not mean this at all cynically, all of these people need jobs. Attorneys need jobs, legislators need jobs, jail staffs need jobs, police forces need jobs and if they succeed in their task, they will be out of a job. It is like the missionaries. We were told when we went to Africa that the job of the missionaries was to make ourselves redundant. We were going into a new area to preach the gospel and the idea was to create a local church that becomes self-sufficient. The idea was to work ourselves out of a job. Unfortunately, no one wants to be out of a job. Everyone wants to see that what he is offering to society is valuable and admired. So unconsciously, there is a need in all of us to make our job survive.

For these two reasons, it seems to me, that the more laws we make and the more police we have and the more legislators out there making the laws, the more criminals we are going to have in our society. We have not understood that you cannot legislate people into morality. It was a great philosopher who said, "To know the good is to do the good." As soon as you know what the good is and what the right is, then you will do it spontaneously, but it cannot be legislated. So often in the religious systems, political systems and social systems we have mistaken law for love. We cannot legislate people into moral behavior

My second point is this. I want to ask myself the question, "Who then should I love?" I want to do a very quick historical analysis of the evolution of this notion. It seems to me that we probably started out in some kind of hunter-gatherer society and very early on in that evolution the individual hunter, who was very accurate and could take down a gazelle, had a tremendous advantage. He got to eat for the day. Because food did not last in Africa, it got destroyed after 24 hours. There was no point in bringing down a gazelle because you could not eat all of it yourself in one day and you could not store it. Tomorrow some other guy might kill a gazelle and he got just one meal out of it and then it spoiled for him, too. So, pragmatically, it became important to cooperate in hunting and in sharing of food. We learned, very practically speaking, that it is much better to have a love relationship in a community than have individuals doing their own thing. We survived for thousands of years in that modality of cooperation of the hunt and the foodstuff.

About 10,000 B.C. there was a great horticultural revolution. And then around the year 3000 B.C. two extraordinary events happened that changed forever the techno-economic base of society and religion. One was the invention of the ox-drawn plow. For the first time, people could produce more food than they needed. And the second happened at the same time in China; they developed a kind of glazed pottery that allowed them to store food without water damage. Now this combination gave: the ability to produce much more food than we needed for today, and the ability to store that food so that it would not be destroyed. It totally changed the game. It proved to have extraordinary advantages and extraordinary disadvantages. The advantages were that there was plenty of food and we could hold the food for tomorrow and the day after. Another advantage was that we had much more free time to devote to more esoteric pursuits. This is when we invented mathematics, orthographies, and the ability to write. This is when we developed literatures and when we developed philosophy.

At the same time there were extraordinary disadvantages. Because we could store large quantities of food we could also destroy people's food source very easily. Because we could store food, people would learn to totally corner the resources. Because of this ability, for the first time in human history we were able to make war all year round. Up until then, we were so busy on a day-to-day basis trying to get food for ourselves, we could not engage in warfare for more that a few hours at a time. Now we could make war all day and all night all year round. Now for the first time an individual or small group could take control of all the resources. It affected family life. For the first time in history there is the possibility of polygamy, one man having several wives while many men did not get to have wives at all.

And then the worst cornering of resources of all was the cornering of information. When you corner information, you have extraordinary power. It happened again and again. It happened in religion. A whole priestly cast developed that cornered information and locked it into secret holes, esoteric unknown languages, Sanskrit for the Hindus. The ordinary people did not speak Sanskrit anymore. They spoke Pali. So the priesthood who cornered Sanskrit and the knowledge of Sanskrit had cornered the information about spirituality. The Hebrews did it in their language. The priesthood, who kept on to Hebrew after the great Babylonian exile in 587 B.C. when the ordinary people were speaking Aramaic, had cornered the spirituality. The Roman Church did it through Latin. When the ordinary people were now speaking a whole bunch of languages in Europe, the priesthood who had obtained the knowledge of Latin had cornered the information of spirituality and they kept apart.

The military did the same thing through propaganda. They have access to the kind of misinformation we need to hear in order to go along with the cause and kill people for whatever reason. The business community does it with the mass media. By cornering the mass media, they tell us what they think we need to buy and corner the business market. So the cornering of the resource information becomes one huge way in which we are manipulated into whom to love, and how to love and whom not to love and whom to kill. So today's reading is very important because it addresses this head on.

It is the story of Peter who for the first time is invited into a gentile household. For more than 600 years, one of the cornerstones on which Judaism had managed to survive many occupations of their country, including the most recent one by the Romans, was refusal to have table fellowship with anyone who was not Jewish. Here was Peter being invited into the house of a Gentile centurion, not just a gentile, but also a centurion, a soldier who represented the hated dominators. Peter is being invited to have food in this man's house. An extraordinary thing happens. As they are eating together and Peter is talking about Jesus, suddenly the Holy Spirit comes down on everyone present, including the gentiles, and they begin to speak in tongues of prophesy. Two huge myths got exploded in one mini-second, the myth of a chosen people and the myth of clerics. Now, in front of their eyes, they could see that God does not play favorites. Everyone is equally beloved of God. And the myth of clericalism; these people have not yet been baptized, how dare the Holy Spirit come down to and enter them before we the priests had poured water over their heads and said, "Okay now receive the Holy Spirit." For the first time in the Judeo-Christian scriptures you had the notion that God loves all of us equally and the Spirit cannot be parceled out by any human institution.

My third point is this. I ask myself the question, "Did loving just get easier or a whole lot harder?" So let us start off where allegedly God hands down 613 precepts to Moses in the Torah. Eventually, because it is too difficult for anyone to hold 613 precepts in his head, particularly in pre-mythic cultures, they got boiled down to ten. A lot easier, just use your fingers. Jesus at some stage in his life reduced the ten down to the two. He is asked at one stage, "Which is the most important law? Of all of the 613, which would you say was the most important?" He said, "Love God, and the second is, love your neighbor." So it went from 613 to 10 to 2. Now in today's gospel, on the day before he died he reduced the two to one. It has gone from 613 to 10 to 2 to 1. He says, "This is my commandment. Love each other." He did not even talk about the love of God at that stage, because he knew that if we really love each other, what allows us to love each other is the recognition of God's essence in each other. So when we love someone, it is because we recognize that he is God himself; therefore, I love God. So the two precepts collapse down to one. That was his final command to us, to love each other.

So, did loving get a lot easier, because we reduced it from 613 to 10 to 2 to 1, or did it in fact get harder? Christ went on to say, "This is the greatest of all, to lay down your life for your friends," which he was going to do in 24 hours. So what does it mean when Christ invites us to lay down our lives for our family? Maybe there are times in human history when you are really being asked to die in order to save someone's life. In war situations or maybe even in a drowning accident where you risk your own life or you give your own life to save someone, that is one possible meaning.

There is another meaning of it that is even more dangerous and more difficult. It is the Buddhist story of the bodhisattva. It is the notion of the human being that has become so enlightened as to merit getting off the wheel of karma, but chooses to take what is called a bodhisattva vow to keep reincarnating until every sentient being is saved. When we come to realize that true love does not have special relationships and that to love truly is to go "beyond" special relationships, i.e., personal individual relationships or community special relationships or ethnic special relationships or denominational special relationships. If we come to that realization then it must be that all living beings, since they are God stuff, deserve our love.   As long as there is one little wanderer pining in his desert someplace, if I were really a being of love, should I not need to come back for that?

I will tell you that in my paradigm, Jesus, the carpenter from Nazareth, did not visit this planet just once. Jesus, for me, is the bodhisattva of bodhisattvas. Jesus has been a human many times long before he became a carpenter in Galilee and long after he got crucified on Good Friday 2000 years ago.   Maybe he is a grandmother in Africa talking to a little grandchild. Or maybe he is a cab driver in New York City or maybe a fisherman off the west coast of Ireland. Who knows? Or who cares? As long as there are Christ figures in our midst that are weaving that kind of love into our environment, does it matter what color they are or what language they speak?

So the final question I ask myself and I ask you is, have you and I got the courage to climb back down on the wrong side of the wall and go back into the desert?   Are you willing to risk not winning the race in order to come back to help someone who is limping the last five miles?

18
Pentecost

I learned a new word this week, "meme" and I am going to talk about it today. Very simply, meme is a cluster of ideas that forms the blueprint for the evolution of culture. That is what it means. Meme is to culture what a gene is to an organism. Take DNA, for example. DNA becomes that cluster of information that forms the basis for the blueprint of the evolution of an entire organism. A meme does that for a culture. A meme is a cluster of ideas, a little like a paradigm, perhaps, that drives the evolution of a culture or the evolution of a society.

I am going to make four main points today. I'm going to talk about the meme generation. Then secondly, I'm going to talk about a brief history of Pentecost. Thirdly, I'm going to talk about Pentecost as a meme. Then fourthly, I'm going to ask the question, "Is Pentecost the final act in the drama?"

Let me start with my first point, the meme generation. If a meme is that extraordinary cluster of ideas or myths that becomes the blueprint for the evolution of an entire society or an entire culture, can I give you some examples? Yes I can. Nazism was a meme. It was a cluster of beliefs and ideas that drove an entire culture for a period of maybe 20 or 30 years. Like all memes, it had extraordinary power to unleash almost a nuclear-like reaction to take the energy of matter and transform it into an extraordinary explosion of possibilities. Like all memes it seems to have started off pretty well. It was an effort on behalf of an entire nation to drag itself up by its bootstraps from economic deprivation and the devastation of having lost the Great War. But very quickly it turned sour. It became the channel through which the lives of millions of people of this planet were devastated and in many cases annihilated. That would be a meme. That myth or that cluster of ideas drove an entire continent and, in fact, the entire world forward at a pace that devastated us, starting off with presumably good ideas.

Communism is a meme. Communism is that extraordinary cluster of ideas driving a belief system in the equality of all peoples, that everyone had a right to live, that people should be able to take from society what they needed, and give to society what they had. It was a great idea. Initially it was extraordinarily inspiring and then eventually it got corrupted and it became in fact the thing that oppressed the very people it was meant to serve. That would be an example of a meme.

Christianity would be an example of a meme. This extraordinary cluster of ideas beginning 2000 years ago radically transformed the course of human history bringing extraordinary compassion, love and justice and then getting corrupted and leading to inquisitions and crusades and outliving its usefulness as Nazism and Communism did. That would be a meme.

Science is a meme, an extraordinary systematic methodology that has evolved over the last 300 or 400 years that enables us to manipulate, control and predict our environment. But like all memes, there is a downside to it and like all memes it winds up doing damage. Like all memes it outlives its usefulness and needs to rethink itself.

Democracy would be an example of a meme, an extraordinary belief system in individual rights, not just the rights of groups, but the rights of individuals within the groups. It began here in the 1700's and drove forward a whole new experiment in human thinking. It conferred extraordinary benefits and made this an extraordinary country but it is devastating us at the moment, because it is leading so much to individualism that community is getting lost. We have two million of our citizens in prisons; we have an extraordinary crime rate, because in the meme of democracy, in the lauding and protecting of the individual rights, the community values tend to get lost. These would all be examples of memes.

I am going to say a heretical thing. A meme has built into itself the need to corrupt itself. Every one of these memes needed to fail precisely because it was a temporary solution phase of specific responses to extraordinary human crises. But like the trousers you wore when you were a little nine-year-old child, if you try to squeeze into them now they are not going to work for you. By wearing them, you destroy them until finally they become useless and then you have to buy new trousers.

Built into every meme and built into every great human idea are the seeds of its own corruption and the seeds of its own destruction. And that is not a bad thing. It is a very good thing because if it did not ultimately fail we would still be stuck in it and we would still be leading infantile kinds of existences. We would naively and innocently be trying to hold on to a life from which nature wants us to evolve and grow. We would be stuck in old ways of thinking. So inevitably all great human ideas, Christianity, Democracy, and science among them, need to fail because the very failures and the very crises precipitate the next great quantum leap in the human experiment. It is important that they fail. They will all fail every single one of them. We have to invent newer ways of thinking about science, newer ways of doing democracy, and newer ways of our Spiritual search; otherwise, we stagnate.

We are always going to need some kind of myth and we are always going to need some kind of meme. We cannot exist without some kind of meme and we cannot exist without a myth. What tends to happen when societies crumble, whether it is a regime like communism, a system like Christianity, or an experiment like democracy, is that confusion enters in and people get very upset and the danger is that we are rudderless and ruthless and one of two things will happen. Either there will be total fragmentation of the organism, or of the society, or else we regress to older recessive memes.

Whatever the old meme was that explained our prejudices and our intolerances; we try to go back very quickly to them in times of confusion. But there is no way back. There is no way of stopping the evolutionary thrust of the cosmos and there is no way of going back to old solutions. Old solutions are very temporary and they create more problems than they solve. But we constantly try it. We are looking for old political solutions. We are looking for old religious solutions. We are looking for old scientific solutions and they will not work for us any more. Only new creative thinking will work. As soon as we come up with some great idea that would bring the next quantum leap for the human community, built into it will be the seeds of its own destruction. And that is a good thing because it means that we never stop growing.

The worst thing of all is to be without a meme or a myth. Jesus had a very enigmatic story that addresses this issue. He said, "Think of this: there was a man who had an evil Spirit and he went to a healer and the healer exorcised him and left him clean. And this Spirit that had been cast out went about in the desert places and came back to the man's house and found it empty. Finding it empty, it took seven more Spirits even more evil than itself and they took up residence in his house." Nature hates a vacuum. You cannot be without a myth and you cannot be without a meme. The temptation

136

is to go back to the old myths and the old memes because they worked at some stage, but they will not work any more. The only way through is forward. The only way through is a creative response to the future and to life. That is my first point. That is what I mean by the meme generation.

I want to talk very briefly about Pentecost and then tie those two ideas together. When does Pentecost happen? There were many Pentecosts. The very first Pentecost, according to the Judeo/Christian scriptures, happened in the very first chapter and the very first page of the very first book of the bible, the Book of Genesis in Chapter 1. This is the first Pentecost. This is the first time when we read that the Spirit of God hovered over the chaos and from the chaos came order and organization. That is the essence of meme. Essence is the Spirit that converts the chaos and creates a new level of order – and that is Pentecost. The very first Pentecost did not happen when tongues of fire came down on the apostles. It happened thousands and thousands of years before that. It happened when the Spirit of God, that is mentioned in Acts, Chapter 2, converted the chaos of elemental cosmology and drew from it a blueprint and a meme for the total unfolding of God's plan for this universe. That was the very first meme.

The second one happened about 1250 years before Jesus after a group of serfs who had been slaves for 450 years escaped from the greatest empire of its day into the desert on the feast of Passover. Then exactly 50 days later, which is what Pentecost means, fifty days, God handed down a new constitution on Mount Sinai. Passover without Pentecost is useless. Passover means literally an escape from slavery; that is all it means. On its own, it would accomplish nothing without the Pentecost experience of having a new constitution, a new blueprint, a new meme to give meaning and possibility to further evolution and growth. That was the second Pentecost.

There was a third Pentecost and it is recorded in the Book of Ezekiel in the great vision that Ezekiel had when the last two tribes of Israel, now deported to the great empire of Babylon, were wasting away in exile. He had a vision where he saw an entire valley of dead, dried, bleached bones and God said to him, "Can these bones live?" Ezekiel said, "I don't know. You tell me." And as he watched, sinews and tendons began to join the bones together, and muscles began to form, and flesh began to grow on them, and skin began to

137

encapsulate the whole thing, and God asked him a second time, "Can these dead bodies live?" Ezekiel said, "I don't know. You tell me." Then God breathed on them and from this tangle of bones an entire nation is revived. That was the third Pentecost.

Then there is the Pentecost that we normally think of when we think of Pentecost – except that we have to figure which version we believe. If you read the gospel of Luke and Luke's Acts of the Apostles, Pentecost happened exactly 50 days after the resurrection of Jesus and if you read it very carefully, it happened at nine in the morning. If you read the gospel of John, Chapter 20, Pentecost happened exactly the same day that Jesus was resurrected. It happened at six in the evening. So there was 49 days and 12 hours difference between them.

So what is Pentecost about? What was that extraordinary wind that gripped the house and shook it? It was not a monsoon. It was not a hurricane. It was not a typhoon of any kind. It was the brainstorming noise of ten billion neurons in each of 120 heads firing together. We have approximately ten billion neurons in the brain. There were approximately 120 people gathered together according to the Acts of the Apostles. There were the brothers and sisters of Jesus, the apostles and the disciples, and Mary the mother of Jesus all gathered together after Jesus had ascended, brainstorming. The sound of Pentecost was the sound of 1.2 trillion neurons firing simultaneously creating a whole new myth, a whole new meme, dreaming a whole new constitution, dreaming up a whole new notion of nation and dreaming up a whole new notion of neighbor. That is what it was about. So let me tie these things together.

My third point is this. I want to talk about Pentecost as a meme, as this myth, an extraordinary social experiment during which we got catapulted from one phase of thinking as a society into a totally different phase of thinking as a society. The original Pentecost story, according to Moses, started with the Passover. Passover was an escape from slavery but Pentecost was the beginning of freedom because escaping from slavery is not the same thing as finding your freedom. The Jewish nation for the first 50 days was merely escaped slaves. They were not free people. They had no unity. They had no blueprint. They had no myth. They had no constitution. They had no sense of identity. They were just a bunch of escaped slaves. Pentecost gave completion to Passover.

Passover originally was a planting festival; a time for setting seeds. Pentecost was originally a harvest festival, a time for gathering in what had been sowed. You cannot have one without the other. The extraordinary thing is, however, the cycle. It is not that one is the beginning and the other the end, because what you harvest this year provides the seed for next year's planting. That is how it works. Most of the seeds you harvest this year go into food and nourishment, but a quantity will be set aside for providing the planting for next year's crop. That is the cycle. There is no first Passover and there is no last Pentecost. That is the final point I want to make.

I want to ask the question, "Is Pentecost the final act in the drama?" We have the birth of Jesus. We have the private life of Jesus as a man. We have the public ministry of Jesus. We have the death of Jesus. We have the resurrection of Jesus. We have the ascension of Jesus and then we have Pentecost. Is that the end of the story? Is Pentecost the end of the story? Not by a long shot. There is no last Pentecost any more than there is a final revelation or ultimate scripture. There is no ultimate scripture and there is no final revelation because there is no last prophet. Mohammed, in spite of what Islam believes, in my opinion, is not the seal of the prophets. He is not God's final oracle. Jesus, the carpenter from Nazareth, was not God's final oracle. Christ consciousness, in my opinion, has come on to our planet again and again and again since the carpenter of Nazareth and continues to come.

The Spirit of God coming among us did not have its final articulation in the carpenter of Nazareth nor in a desert Bedouin in Arabia. There is no final Pentecost. There is no final prophet. There is no final revelation. Every generation wants to believe that it is the apex. It wants to believe that it is the ultimate expression of the evolutionary thrust whether it is a political system or medical model, or scientific model, or a Spiritual or religious model. Is this is as good as it gets? Has God finally spoken and this is the end? I do not believe it for a moment.

The evolution proceeds and Christ consciousness continues to pervade our universe and to give us prophets not just in religion but in medicine and education, agriculture, politics, and mass media. Everywhere the human experiment exists, the Spirit of God continues apace. Or rather, let me put it another way. Every place the Spirit of God breathes, human discipline and human activity takes off and improves exponentially.

The final injunction of Jesus, according to this gospel, happened in five phases. They are: the human dilemma, the divine response, the human reaction, the breathing of God and then finally the understanding of mission. So we start the story with people gathered in fear of the authorities. Their leader has been killed and crucified. They had experience of him and then he went, and now they are totally on their own. They had never been more alone in their lives. That is how the story starts, in fear in a locked room because of the authorities. The response of God is, "Peace be with you." After God grants them peace, God commissions them and sends them forth. In order to empower them for this commissioning, we are told God breathed on them. God gave each one of them the Spirit of God. The final injunction was, "Whose sins you shall forgive, they are forgiven. Whose sins you shall retain, they are retained." I have constantly disagreed with the Catholic Church's teaching of this issue.

This was not Jesus commissioning the Roman Catholic Church to have the power to dispense from sin, to forgive sin or even to retain sins. It has nothing to do with that. It is simply the divine teaching and the human realization that when we truly forgive, forgiveness permeates our world and when we retain and hold back that our world gets stuck. It is about liberation and the power to liberate. It is not about some dude sitting in the confessional with a stole around his neck saying, "In the name of the church I forgive." It has nothing to do with that. It has to do with each human being having the Spirit of God within and the ability to allow this process to move forward; for the evolution to continue so that we all experience liberation, not for any one of us to dig in and to hold the process back.

My prayer for us this morning is this: that each one of us, having within us the peace of God, might be a little "mini Pentecost" in every community of which we are a part.

140

19
Getting Walloped When You're Not Ready

Did you ever crack a rib? It's a very sore thing. You're afraid to cough. You're afraid to sneeze. You're afraid to laugh. You can't lie down and it's very difficult to sleep. Cracking a rib is the pits! The last time I cracked a rib was September 1990. I remember the occasion very well. I was home in Ireland on vacation with my little brother, Páraic, who was then in his 40s, but he's still my little brother. We were watching the All Ireland Hurling final. For you philistines who don't know what hurling is, hurling is an ancient game that goes back at least 2500 years and it's played with a stick that looks a bit like a hockey stick. It's a cross between American football and ice hockey without any of the padding. It's a very tough game, a really tough game.

My team, Cork, where I come from, was in the final game against Galway. The score was all tied up and there was just one minute left to play when Cork got a goal. Páraic and I jumped up and we hugged each other with such energy that he cracked my rib. I paid dearly for Cork's 1990 success. No one limped off the field sorer than I did at the end of the hour. I couldn't laugh, sneeze or cough for about three weeks.

That is what happened to Jesus in Mark's gospel, 5:21-43. That is what I want to talk about. I want to talk about getting walloped when you are not expecting it. I want to make three main points.

The first point I am going to call, "Embarrassment or empowerment." Secondly, I want to talk about the fertility life cycle. Then thirdly, I want to talk about re-framing death.

I'll begin my first point with the story of Jesus walking through a crowd minding his own business, his mind several miles away. He has been invited to go to the home of a little girl who is dying and he is thinking about what lies ahead of him. Suddenly this woman who has been hemorrhaging for 12 years sneaks up behind him and surreptitiously touches the hem of his cloak. He swung around in the crowd and said, "Who did it? Who touched me? Power has gone out of me."

There are different kinds of healing. Healing, in my opinion, is meant to be the mediation and the channeling of the power of

God. As long as we are healers, as long as we realize that we are not the source of healing for others, that we are merely the conduits, channels and the media for healing for others, then when we mediate and channel healing to others not only do we not get depleted, we get empowered in the process. But if in healing we think we are the source, if we are reaching out and touching someone else to bring healing to them then we get zapped, we get depleted in the process. Healing involves extraordinary, mindful intentionality. When energy goes out of you in any guise when you are not expecting it, it hurts the entire system.

I want to talk about the extraordinary story of this poor woman who had been hemorrhaging for 12 years. She had gone to many doctors and spent all of her savings and she was still no better. She thought that if somehow she could touch the hem of this healer's garments, she would be fine. She snuck up behind him and there was a large crowd pressing in on him and she touched the hem of his garment and she was healed immediately. Jesus knew that something had happened. Why did Jesus do what he did? Why didn't he just let her go off silently and enjoy her healing? He didn't because he had something much more important in store for her. According to the gospel, "He looked around and said, 'Who touched me?'" Peter said, "Give us a break already, there's 500 people jostling and you want to know who touched you." Jesus said, "No, someone touched me. Someone touched me intentionally and I want to know who it was because I have a message for him or her." Fearfully the woman went down on her knees in front of him and confessed because she had realized what had happened.

Two things had happened. The first thing is that she realized she was healed. The second thing, and a much more embarrassing thing, she realized she had defiled Jesus. According to the patriarchal Judaic system at the time, any woman within her menstrual cycle or any flow of blood was unclean. Everything she touched or everyone she came in contact with was made unclean. So this woman had a double realization. She realized that after 12 years of suffering she is healed and she also realized that she had defiled this man in the process. This is the reason Jesus brought her forward. Jesus had two things to teach her. Jesus was going to teach her firstly, that being a woman was not a defilement, and secondly, her healing came from herself. Jesus said to her, "My daughter, I want to say something to you. I want you to know this; it is your faith that has healed you."

For years and years, every time I read this phrase, I presumed what Jesus meant was, "My daughter it was your faith in me, Jesus, that healed you." Then I got it several years ago that he was not saying that at all. He was saying to her, daughter, I want you to realize that it is your faith that healed you. I did not heal you; your faith healed you. You are as much a child of God as I am a child of God. If you understand this, you do not need me or you do not need anyone because you too are built in the image and likeness of God. So when I think of this story, I think about Jesus not embarrassing this woman but empowering this woman. He could have let her go off with her healing. But only her body would have been healed. Jesus intended to heal her psyche and he intended to heal the society. He had a much bigger plan in mind than just merely a physical healing of one human being.

I love to put this story side by side with a story in the gospel of John, Chapter 8, where another unfortunate woman who had been caught in the act of adultery is dragged before Jesus and Jesus is asked to pass judgment on her. There is a group of men standing around condemning her. Forget the fact that it takes two to commit adultery and that the guy was off someplace else, but the woman was caught and she is in the middle. The patriarchal system is going to pass judgment on her; she deserves to die, according to the Mosaic Law.

You know the story of how Jesus handled that situation. The two of them, in my opinion, are very similar. In both cases, Jesus protected the woman. In both cases, Jesus healed the woman. In both cases, Jesus empowered the woman and in both cases, Jesus threw down an extraordinary challenge to a system that would demonize women and demonize fertility and demonize the ability of women to conceive, carry and birth life. That is what the story is really about. This was Jesus empowering this woman, not just healing her. This was Jesus empowering a whole class of people, not just healing them. This was Jesus laying down an extraordinary challenge to the thinking of the time that would demonize any child of God or any human attribute.

The second point I want to make is this. I want to talk about the fertility life cycle. I do not think it is accidental that both of these women had the issues they had and that the number 12 comes to both of them. The little girl who died was 12 years old. Why does Mark tell us that? In my opinion, this was a little child on the verge of puberty coming perhaps into her first menses. This woman who was bleeding continuously very possibly was approaching menopause. The entire fertility life cycle is held between the two of them.   I think there is an extraordinarily beautiful message here about femininity and about fertility and about the ability to conceive, to carry and to birth life.   It is no accident that it is a blood-related issue for the woman, that there are 12 years of suffering and that this little girl was 12 years old. She died just as she was about to become a fully-fledged woman capable of conceiving, carrying and birthing life.

I want to talk about that for a little bit because this represents, in some sense, the extraordinary feminine ability of creativity. The co-creativity of the feminine to take, nurture, birth and nourish human life and the physiology that prepares a woman for this mental and Spiritual exercise is an extraordinary ability. It is an extraordinary physiology that allows a woman to menstruate every month so that, to use computer technology, she refreshes her screen on a regular basis. She is literally insuring that when the time comes to conceive life she has a brand new environment in which to do it. It is an extraordinary physiological ability. Much more important than that, it is also a metaphor for all of us that that is what the human soul and that is what the human heart are about. The human heart is meant to be the womb in which we conceive, carry and birth the word of God. Like the womb of a woman, it is meant to be refreshed on a regular basis. We are meant to have the courage to constantly examine our thinking, our paradigms, our worldview and our prejudices so that we can constantly create a fresh environment in which the word of God can take seed.

It is no accident then that 700 years ago a very famous Christian mystic called Meister Eckhart said; "Of what value to me is it that my savior was born of a woman 1300 years ago if he is not born again in my time and in my heart. Every single one of us is meant to be the mother of God." That to me is the importance of this little girl and this woman in this story. They are beautiful metaphors not just about the physiology that prepares womanhood for creativity, but about the fertility in the human soul and in the human heart that allows us to conceive, carry, birth and to nourish the word of God.

The third point is this. I call it, re-framing death. This little girl had died. Possibly this is the first case in literature of a childhood near-death-experience. For those of you who are aware of the literature since the 1970's, there have been over eight million Americans pronounced clinically dead and because of modern technology have been resuscitated. There is an extraordinary literature growing out of that phenomenon.

Very possibly, this story, in the gospel of Mark, Chapter 5, is the first recorded case of a near-death-experience in a child. This child came back from death. What happened to her in the interim? Very briefly, what near-death-experience research suggests is that at the moment of death there is a journey through a tunnel, there is a light at the end of the tunnel, an extraordinary beam of light that encompasses one in absolute love. There is some kind of life review, which is instantaneous and chronological, and it is detailed perfectly, except it has one extraordinary extra dimension. Not only does it seem to present every detail, thought, word and every action of their lives, but it simultaneously allows them to experience the effects of their acts, thoughts and their belief systems on everyone else involved. You get the extraordinary ability to be able to empathize with everyone who has been touched by every detail, thought and word of your life.

When these people come back, they come back totally changed. Their cosmologies are different. Their response to the planet is different and much more importantly, their attitude toward death is totally different. So I want to try to reframe our thinking about death precipitated by the death and resurrection of this little girl.

In the first reading, which was a reading from the Book of Wisdom, we are told, "God did not create death. God created us to be imperishable. God created us in his own image." At the end, there is this statement, "Through the envy of the devil, death entered into the world." What does that phrase mean? Obviously, it is couched in the cosmology of 2200 years ago where there is this evil disincarnate entity called the devil or Satan who introduces all the bad stuff in the world. In my opinion, this is merely the classical personification of the illusion under which we labor. There are two great illusions that are pertinent. There is the illusion about life and there is the illusion about death. Our illusion about life is that life is composed of material objects that are separate from each other and our illusion about death is that death is the end. The truth is, if we open our eyes even to evolutionary biology we begin to realize that from raw matter at some stage in the 4.5 billion years of this planet, life evolved. And somehow at a later time some of this life managed to manifest consciousness or mind. From this conscious mind, much later, some great avatars came among us like the Buddha and Jesus who developed soul and from this soul has evolved Spirit. So from raw matter comes life, from life comes mind, from mind comes soul and from soul comes Spirit. The reason it emerges in this fashion is that it has always existed there. The devolution has been from Spirit to soul to mind to life and to matter.

So the truth is, we are living in an illusion. In the West, particularly, for the last 300 years, our scientism and our materialism is living in the illusion that the only thing that is real is matter and we are separate little identities. Then the second great illusion is the illusion that death destroys all. My belief system is that there is only one life and there is no such thing as death. There are merely different articulations of the same life. In my cosmology, I believe that we come back many times. Since I believe very strongly in reincarnation, I am convinced that in this eternal continuum of life we articulate differently by sometimes incarnating and taking on spacesuits. Eventually we let go of the spacesuits when our mission is complete and we go back to living in a disincarnate form until our next mission is prepared for us. So there is only one life.

Even if you come onto this planet ten thousand times and die ten thousand times there is no death because there is only one life. It gets even more complicated. There is only one life because the apparent discrete ontological separateness of us is also an illusion. There is only one life. There is only Spirit manifesting as daffodils, dinosaurs, butterflies, and human beings and as Tim, Pat, Mary and Seán, there is only the one Spirit.

There is only the one life breathing through all of that and this to me is the great message of Jesus as he reaches out healing hands. Jesus wants to heal, not just our physical illnesses, he wants to heal our Spirits, he wants to heal our psyches and more than anything else he wants to heal our cosmologies. So my prayer for myself and for all those of us who are ill in some way or other is that all of us really begin to get it that there is only one life. There is the life of God within us and every single one of us is evidence of the

146

extraordinary creativity and the manifestation of this Spirit and physical form

20
Eucharist

I have been saying mass now for over 28 years. I believe that I have said mass more than 9000 times since I was ordained a priest in 1972. On every occasion, for me personally, it is an extraordinarily transforming experience no matter where it happens. I have said mass in the weirdest places for the most unusual of congregations in a host of different languages. My very first mass after I was ordained was in my mother tongue, Gaelic. Afterwards, I began saying mass in England in English. Then I went to Kenya and said mass in Swahili, Kipsigis, Nandi, Tugen and occasionally I say mass in Latin. So I have been in the most diverse congregations in the most diverse places for over 28 years. I can honestly say that the most upsetting mass I ever celebrated was in Palo Alto, California, six or seven years ago. At that time, I was associated with the Catholic Diocese of San Jose. We ministered to five churches and I was moving from church to church being assigned to a different church each Sunday. I was also assigned on a semi-regular basis to say the Latin mass for the community at Saint Anne's Church. I love the Latin, and the Gregorian chant brings back lots of happy memories.

On this particular Sunday, I was assigned to say the Latin Mass at Saint Anne's. There was a small congregation and we had begun the mass. I came down to give the homily as I usually do standing by the second or third pew. As I was speaking, I saw out of the corner of my eye someone in the very first pew reading a newspaper. It was not that this guy was bored with what I had to say. It was obvious that he was making some kind of protest. He was not just reading the newspaper; he had the newspaper held aloft and was turning the pages noisily.

I continued with my homily and when finished I went back up to the altar. For this "Gregorian group," the liturgy was arranged so that the sign of peace comes right before the offertory. While the preparations were being made for the offertory, I went down to the congregation to give the sign of peace. I went to the front pew where the guy sat with his wife and four very frightened Dad-dominated little kids. I greeted the first child while he held himself very stiffly and the same with the second, third and fourth child. The wife was obviously wondering if she should or if she shouldn't exchange the peace sign with me. When I came to the guy, I went to hug him and he crossed his hands over his chest. I put out my hand to greet him and he said, "No." I was absolutely shocked. I said to him, "Can you tell me why you were reading the newspaper during the homily?" He said, "I totally disagree with what you were saying." I said, "Okay, are you going to give me the sign of peace?" "No," he said, "I refuse to give you the sign of peace." Everyone is watching this performance as everyone had watched the newspaper. I went back up to the altar and I said, "I've been a priest for 22 years. I have never in my life had anyone in the congregation refuse to give me the sign of peace. I don't know what to do."

I remember the teaching of Jesus when he told us, "If you go to offer your gift at the altar and you remember that you have something against your brother or your brother has something against you, leave your gift at the altar and go back and be reconciled with your brother first and then you can come and offer your gift." So I said, "You have all seen what happened, I can't continue with mass, I'm going to do one of two things. I'm going to go back down to my brother in the first pew, and I'm going to offer him the sign of peace again and if he gives it to me, fine, we'll continue. If he refuses to give me the sign of peace, I'll take off my vestments, go into the sacristy and go home." And I would have. I went down to him and put out my hand and he put out his hand and he said, "I'm only doing this because you forced me to." We continued with the mass.

I have said mass for the Kipsigis, the Nandi, and the Maasai and that had never happened to me. In fact, among the Maasai if there is a dispute in the village and the priest goes in to say mass, mass cannot start until the elders resolve the dispute, because the Maasai understand what the Eucharist is about. But obviously that particular man did not understand what the Eucharist is about. Most of you have celebrated Eucharist maybe more than 9000 times in your lives. Often it is celebrated mindlessly by people who do not know what they are doing. They do not think about what they are doing. I thought today, given the reading, obviously a preface for the Eucharist, that I would talk a little bit about Eucharist and what it means to me and maybe share some ideas and let you take from it what is of importance to you.

149

Very briefly I want to make four main points. Firstly, I want to talk about what I call a trinity of parts. I'm going to divide the mass into three parts. Secondly, I'm going to ask myself the question, "In whose name are we celebrating this Eucharist?" Thirdly, I want to look particularly at the notion of forgiveness because this comes at the very first part of the mass. Then fourthly, I am going to ask myself the question, "Why do we do what we do?" I am going to try to address those four areas.

I am going to divide the Eucharist into three parts. For today's homily, I will concentrate on the first part and address the other parts on subsequent Sundays. I will call the first part the preparatory or introductory phase, which is from the time we enter the church until we begin the readings.

The second phase of the Eucharist is called the Liturgy of the Word and consists of a reading from the Hebrew Scriptures (Old Testament), then typically a psalm from the Hebrew Scriptures followed by an epistle from one of Paul's writings or from some other New Testament writings. The last reading is a gospel reading. After the gospel reading, we have the homily by the priest or someone else from the congregation and we finish the Liturgy of the Word with the prayers of the faithful where we offer our prayers and our petitions to God. That ends the second part of the mass.

The third part of the mass we call the Liturgy of the Act and that consists of an offertory procession where we bring the gifts forward (an offering of the bread and wine), a preface, the Eucharistic Prayer, the Our Father, the distribution of communion, and then finally, what is called the Dismissal, where we are told to go forth and spread the good news.

Secondly, I want to ask myself; "In whose name are we celebrating this Eucharist?" As Catholics, we begin almost every kind of spiritual function or every meal by making the sign of the cross, "In the name of the Father, and the Son and the Holy Spirit, Amen." If you're a real Catholic, when you go to a movie and you want to find out which actor is really a Catholic, you know that the guy who very mindfully makes the sign, "In the name of the Father, Son and Holy Spirit, Amen," is not a Catholic; you know that immediately. The guy who does it too quickly and very sloppily is a Catholic. So the first thing I want to emphasize is that very often the action we begin with should be calling us to mindfulness. So when we say, "In the name of the Father, and of the Son and of the

150

Holy Spirit, Amen" at the beginning of the Eucharist, what exactly are we doing? In whose name are we now entering into this liturgical celebration? We are going straight into one of the most extraordinary mysteries in any religious system.

We are calling upon a notion of a Trinitarian God, yet we cannot, obviously, know who God is. God is the ineffable Ground of our Being. Any category we attribute to God, even the category of being or non-being is meaningless. But we have to do it because we have an intellect and we have words and it is the only way we know how to communicate. We try to understand God by creating some kind of model of how God may be experienced. The way many systems do it is to create some kind of Trinitarian formula. In the Christian religion, we talk about God the Father, God the Son and God the Holy Spirit. What does that mean?

It is not that God has gender, that there is an old guy with a long gray beard, and there is another guy with holes in his hands and feet, and that there is another that looks like a pigeon. Obviously, we do not believe that. This is a metaphorical expression of the fact that the Father somehow represents "is-ness" or "being," that Jesus represents God's total self-knowledge and that the Spirit represents the love that God has for whom she knows herself to be. So there is being, self-knowledge and self-love.

The Hindus have exactly the same notion; Sat, Chit, Ananda, (being, full consciousness, and total bliss). When we begin our celebration, it is a realization that all of us are God stuff, that nothing exists apart from God, and that fact is represented by fatherhood or generativity in some fashion. However, things exist without knowing they exist. Presumably, daffodils exist without knowing that they are daffodils. Presumably, but maybe they do. Certainly when we get to the human species you have a self-reflective group. As far as we know, the universe became self aware with the evolution of the human species. Personally, I don't believe it. I am totally convinced that there are other life forms much more advanced than we in other places. But as far as we know in our little anthropocentric model, we believe that the entire universe came into self- knowledge with the evolution of the human species.

Let us at least honor that insight by the realization that we are only profoundly human to the extent that we are mindful of our existence and of our actions. To the extent that we act mindlessly, we are not being fully human. So the notion of Jesus as the second person of the trinity is the constant call to mindfulness, to the realization that existing without knowing that we exist, is almost meaningless. Once we know who we are, the only response that makes any sense is to totally accept and to love who we find ourselves to be. In fact, the Trinitarian model in Christianity is not a weird flaky, esoteric theological thing; it is a practical manual for psychological self-development. We all exist. Most of us do not know who the hell we are and those of us who spend any time finding out who we are do not particularly like what we find and we are stuck.

The model of trinity suggests to us that we are, that we have a duty to be mindfully aware of who we are, and we have a responsibility to love what we find. That is the model of trinity. The Hindu model does exactly the same thing. There is a Hindu trinity called Trimurti, (Brahma, Vishnu, and Shiva.) Brahma represents again the creativity or the creative aspect of God, the evolutionary blueprint. Vishnu represents the sustaining quality of God, the God who protects, sustains, nourishes and keeps us alive. Shiva represents the destructive force of God but not destructive in the sense of someone willfully laying waste but, rather, someone who constantly reconfigures new possibilities out of the void, breaking down old configurations in order that even more exciting possibilities might emerge. This is the notion of Shiva in the trinity of the Hindu system.

We find the same three great laws in the physical universe. For me, the three great laws of physics are firstly the law of evolution, a blueprint that is driving inexorably this movement from matter to life to mind to soul to spirit. There is a second principle that we call the law of homeostasis that is desperately trying to hold on to the status quo. Every system, when it is perturbed, tries terribly to hold itself in the position that it found itself in originally. You cut a body and it starts to bleed. The body is constituted in such a way that the blood coagulates in order to stop the bleeding. You get too cold; your body will make you shiver to generate heat. You get too warm; your body will sweat in order to cool it down. The second great law then is the law of homeostasis. This is Vishnu. This is Jesus.

The third great law of the universe is the law of entropy, except that as entropy is expressed in the law of thermodynamics, I have never believed it. I do not believe for a moment that the

152

universe is running itself down into chaos. I believe, rather, that the evolutionary spirit itself is taking apart old configurations in order to create even more exciting new ones. And that is Shiva in the system.

So when we begin the Eucharist, "In the name of the Father, Son and Holy Spirit" and we do it so mindlessly, what are the possibilities we are missing? We are missing the entire evolutionary thrust. We are missing the possibility of participating mindfully in an extraordinarily sacred action. We are missing the possibility of creation. We are missing the possibility of homeostasis and we are missing the possibility of reconfiguring our world, our paradigm and our belief systems. So the very simple act of beginning Eucharist is lost too often upon most of us. That is the first thing I want to say about it.

In whose name then are we offering Eucharist? We are doing it in the name of Brahma. We are doing it in the name of Vishnu. We are doing it in the name of Shiva. We are doing it in the name of evolution. We are doing it in the name of homeostasis. We are doing it in the name of entropy. We are doing it in the name of the Father. We are doing it in the name of the Son. We are doing it in the name of the Spirit. That is how we begin our Eucharist.

My third point is forgiveness. There is this extraordinary prayer which we begin by saying, "I confess to almighty God and to you my brothers and sisters that I have sinned..." It sounds like a real downer. I kind of "beat my breast" saying, "I'm a schmuck, I'm a schmuck, I'm a schmuck." It has nothing to do with that. What we are doing at this stage, in my opinion, is to consciously create sacred space. It is the equivalent of taking off your sandals. It is Moses meeting the burning bush and being told by the power of God take off your shoes because the ground on which you stand is holy ground. We have a special word in Gaelic, "Caol Áit" which means, "a thin place." It means a place where the veil between the sacred and the secular is temporarily diaphanous: where the veil between the unmanifest and the manifest is temporarily diaphanous, where the veil between the seen and the unseen is temporarily diaphanous. We all know of such places.

In some systems, we take off our shoes when we encounter such a place. In other places, we wash ourselves when we encounter such a place. Within Hinduism, that is the system, daily bathing. If you are lucky to live near the sacred river, the Ganges, the daily bathing is recognition of the fact that you are on sacred ground. If you are a Muslim, it is prostration five times a day with your forehead to the ground so that for once your head is lower than your heart. That is the recognition of a sacred space.

This prayer is about the recognition that we are now consciously creating sacred space. Therefore when we say, "I confess to almighty God and to you my brothers and sisters," the realization is that I live so much of my life in misalignment. It is not that I believe that I am unworthy of God's presence; it is that I am unmindful of God's presence. This prayer for me is not self-abnegation; it is not obeisance in front of some kind of distant demanding deity who is wagging fingers from the sky. It has nothing to do with that. It is a recognition of the fact that I live so much of my life, not unworthily, but unmindfully and I recognize that I do this vis-à-vis the transcendent aspect of God and that I do this vis-à-vis the horizontal or immanent aspect of God. In my opinion, the cross represents this. The vertical arm of the cross represents my relationship to the transcendent aspect of God. The horizontal arm of the cross represents my relationship with the immanent aspect of God, my bothers and sisters and all living things, not just the human species, but also all living things. The intersection of the two represents my relationship to myself because I can only be meaningfully in relationship to myself to the extent that I am in relationship to the transcendent ground of my being and at the same time in a relationship to all sentient life forms. That is what I am representing and therefore, when I become aware that I am creating sacred space, I am immediately reminded of the fact that, unfortunately, I live most of my life out of harmony and in misalignment with this vertical dimension and this horizontal dimension.

If there is only my relationship to the transcendent aspect of God in my life, I am a mere esoteric flake. If there is only the relationship with the immanent aspect of God, my brothers and sisters, if this in my life, I am merely a secular humanist. But when I bring the two of them together, I am a totally rounded human son or daughter of God. That is what the prayer represents for me. It is recognition of the fact that I live so much of my life in mindlessness or in misalignment, not that I am unworthy, but merely that I have been unmindful. I realize that I do this in four ways. So I say to you, "I confess that I have sinned in my thoughts, in my words, in what I have done and in what I have failed to do."

Sin for me is choosing to do the selfish thing. It is not about transgressing commandments. It is not about breaking any laws. It is about being out of alignment with God, self and others. I recognize that I do that in four ways: I do it in how I think, I do it through what I say, I do it through my deeds and I do it through my inaction. So I need to bring myself back into realignment in all these four ways. The great laws of Karma in the Hindu and Buddhist traditions say exactly the same thing. There is this great adage that says, "Sow a thought and reap an act. Sow an act and reap a habit. Sow a habit and reap a character. Sow a character and reap a destiny." Every single one of us is the net result of everything we have thought and said and done and failed to do.

But it is a little bit more complex than that because I believe that we inherit a world which is the result of the thoughts, words, actions and the inaction of billions of people throughout all of human history. We inherit a milieu and an environment that has been created by the conscious and the unconscious actions, thoughts, words and deeds of everyone who preceded us and everyone who co-exists with us. This for me is the meaning of original sin. In some sense, Augustine was right and in many senses he was wrong. I do not believe original sin is stamped on a baby's soul at the moment of conception because of the way that we conceive babies, this horrible thing we call sex. I do not believe that for a moment. But I do believe that Augustine was on to some kind of truth that every baby born into the world is not coming in as tabula rasa and is certainly not inheriting a world that is tabula rasa. Every baby coming into this world is inheriting a world that is already the production of all that people have ever thought, said, done or failed to do. This is what we acknowledge when we say, "I confess to my brothers and sisters that I have sinned in my thoughts, my words, in what I have done and in what I have failed to do."

I do not believe in the future. I do not believe there is such a thing as the future. If by future you mean, the fated, inevitable outcome, I do not believe such a thing exists. I believe, rather, that there are millions of possible outcomes and that the outcome is like the wave equation in physics. We collapse it to the particular by the specific choices we make. As a community, as an entire human community, as smaller communities within that big body and as individuals, the way we think, how we speak, how we choose to act and how we choose to refrain from action is creating our future as

155

individuals, as societies, and as an entire human culture. We acknowledge that from this great prayer.

What do we do about it? "And therefore I ask you Blessed Mary, ever virgin, and you my brothers and sisters and all the angels and saints, to pray to the Lord our God for me." Is this a kind of pious poppycock that we are going to call on some kind of heavenly denizens to come down here and rescue us? It is not that at all. It is the recognition of the fact that we are part of a seamless garment. That everyone who has ever existed and that all life forms from the lowly snail to the archangel that sits before God's throne, if such a configuration exists, that every possible manifestation of the creativity of God is a single thing. It is a single masterpiece, every part interacting with every other part. And the realization of that is the breaking of the greatest illusion under which we labor as a human species, the illusion of separateness.

To me, the first sin in the Garden of Eden by our fore-parents, Adam and Eve, was not a sin of disobedience, it was that for the first time ever they bought into the illusion of separation and so they were separated. They were kicked out of the garden. Not that God evicted them but that the illusion created the distance between the transcendent aspect of God and their own experience of their own humanity.

That was the beginning of the separation. Subsequently, there was a separation between the male version of that creativity and the female version of it. Afterwards, there was the separation between language groups, ethnicity, race, socioeconomic status, and between religious affiliations. This separation continues to bifurcate again and again. This prayer is about the shattering of the illusion. It is about the invitation back into the fabric of the seamless masterpiece. That is why we call upon the "Blessed Mary ever virgin, all the angels and the saints and you my brothers and sisters..." It is the realization that there is only one-ness. There is just God stuff creating and experiencing what it creates.

So when we finally ask God to "forgive us our sins," in some sense, it is a meaningless thing. If we think there is some kind of transcendent being in the sky who is basically a Certified Public Accountant, some kind of dude who adds up figures, we have it all wrong. God is the only one in the universe who cannot forgive, for the simple reason that in order to forgive, you first have to hold a grudge and then let go of it. Since God is love, there is no grudge

156

possible for God. Therefore, when we ask God to forgive us our sins, we are calling upon the God within all of us. We are calling upon the God within our brothers and sisters to forgive us our misalignment and our buying into the illusion of our separateness. That is what we are asking ourselves to do.

Finally, in the last part of this first section of the mass, we break into this glorious hymn, "Glory to God in the highest and on earth peace to people of good will." Here is the realization now that the illusion of separateness was a fallacy. Here is the ecstatic utterance of the realization that we are one family. Not as separate individuals but as only one being. If you are a hunter in the forest and your left hand gets snared, there is no point in your right hand making fun of your left hand and saying, "See I'm free." If the left hand is snared, the entire body is snared and the right hand is snared with it. The best thing the right hand can do is to free the left hand because in freeing the left hand, it is freeing itself. This is the great tragedy of cancer. Physically, cancer is a system whereby a group of cells replicate again and again greedily not realizing that their success is their downfall because in killing their host, they kill themselves. Much more importantly is the cancer of the illusion of separation because to the extent that we become more and more efficient at being separate from each other we inevitably kill the host that sustains all of us. This prayer is the realization that all of that needs to change.

Therefore, I ask you, my brothers and my sisters, I ask you Mary, I ask you saints and angels, I ask all aspects of this extraordinary canvas of God's work of art to be one again.

My fourth point is this. I want to ask myself the questions; "Why then do we do what we do? Why do we come here on Sundays to celebrate this Eucharist?" Obviously, we are not here to fulfill a Sunday obligation. If all you want is to fulfill your Sunday obligation, you are in the wrong place for the wrong amount of time. It is not about that. Nor is it that we are here in little hermetically sealed containers, i.e., "Don't ask me my name and don't touch me and don't offer me the sign of peace. I'm here because this is between God and me." That is not what Eucharist is about. Neither is Eucharist about something I do on Sunday that is divorced from the rest of my life. If my Eucharist is not spilling into my ethical behavior throughout the week, I do not understand Eucharist. If my Eucharist, my community celebration, is not spilling over into individual theophanies whereby I experience God directly through my meditation, through nature, or through watching the eyes of a baby or however else you choose to do it, then I have not understood Eucharist.

So what is Eucharist about? Eucharist is about three different things. It is firstly an opportunity to learn and to educate myself through the readings I hear and perhaps through reflections I hear from people in the congregation on the readings or the homily. Secondly, it is about the building of community. I do not mean the community as a group. I mean that too, but I mean the individual friendships that arise out of community and the way in which people meet each other and the way in which people become resources and outlets for their needs and for their talents within community. I mean that too. Thirdly and most especially, Eucharist is about the group articulation of, the honoring of, the celebrating of, and the facilitation of the individual experiences of the numinous. That is the most important aspect of all. That Eucharist should help us create the kind of environment and the kind of symbology that allows us individually, as well as a community, to touch God directly without the need for concepts and without the need for words.

I'll finish with a little incident from one of my favorite movies, "The City of Angels." For those who have not seen it, it is about an angel who wants to become a human being in order to experience what being human is like. It is a very difficult process. It is a very complicated movie in that sense. There is this one beautiful scene where Nicolas Cage, all dressed in black, as any self-respecting angel should be, is trying to understand what it is like to be a human. Meg Ryan, with whom he has fallen in love and who has fallen in love with him, does not realize he is an angel and he does not want to communicate that to her just yet because he still hasn't made the transition. He is watching her eat a pear. As an angel, he has never had a sensual experience in his life including eating food. He says to her, "What does a pear taste like?" She says, "You don't know what a pear tastes like?" He tries to cover his tracks very quickly and he says, "Well, I don't know what a pear tastes like to you."

That is what Eucharist is about. If you do not know what God tastes like to yourself, then you have not understood Eucharist.

21
Baptism

Image One: He flies a journey of 12, 000 miles averaging 200 miles a day. He will spend two months getting there and two months living there and then make the return journey, another two months, another 12,000 miles. He spends one-third of the year actually in flight not to mention daily fishing expeditions. He is called the Arctic Tern. He has an extraordinary homing instinct and will return to the exact same spot in the Arctic and the Antarctic every year.

Image Two: She lives in a huge cave in Spain with two million others crowded on top of each other and if you enter this cavernous vault, there is non-stop, earsplitting cacophony. Every night she goes forth to seek food for her young. Her food is blood. She is called the vampire bat. While she is out, the big sisters of the babies watch over millions and millions of little creatures screaming their heads off. When the mother comes back into this cavern she finds with unerring precision her own baby in the midst of this absolute pandemonium. How in God's name does she do it? She has an extraordinary homing instinct.

Image Three: The Buddha and the bagel. The Buddha did not use the word bagel. The bagel had not been invented as far as I know, but I am going to use the word bagel. Statistics had not been invented and probability theory had not been invented. The Buddha who lived 2500 years ago said, "The probability of incarnating as a human is the following: Imagine that there is only one turtle in all of the oceans of the world. This one turtle swims in the ocean and is totally blind. It surfaces only once every 1000 years. Floating somewhere in the ocean there is a small bagel with a hole in the middle. What are the chances that when this turtle surfaces his head will come up through the hole in the bagel?" The Buddha said, "That is the probability of incarnating as a human being." What an extraordinary homing instinct and what an extraordinary achievement – and every single one of you has managed it! What brought you here?

Image Four: Quantum electro-dynamics that tells us that there are ten to the power of 27 brand new universes called into being every second per cubic centimeter of 11 dimensional primordial space. That is a lot of universes. How in God's name did you

159

find this one? When you found it, you came into a universe that had one hundred billion galaxies. How in God's name did you find the Milky Way? When you found the Milky Way, you found 100 billion star systems. How in God's name did you find this little one? Of the nine planets rotating around this little star of ours, how did you find planet Earth? What an extraordinary homing instinct! I want to talk about that. I want to talk about baptism as a symbol of this extraordinary homing instinct of ours. I will make five main points.

My first point I will call RSVP. The second I will call the contract. Thirdly, I will say what I think baptism is not. Fourthly, I will say what I think baptism is. And fifthly, I will talk about six water symbols.

The first point then, RSVP. In a few moments we are going to baptize a little baby by the name of Ronan Patrick Burns. Ronan Patrick Burns was exactly three months old yesterday. He was born on the eighth of June in 2001. He was exactly three months old yesterday on the very day that his grandparents celebrated their 50th wedding anniversary. But Ronan Patrick Burns sent out an invitation to every single one of us to attend his baptism today in Palo Alto many, many years before Bob and Mary Burns even had faces.

Is that just a cute little statement? Or could it be true? In my cosmology, it is very true. I believe that every soul is as ancient as every other soul. There are some souls that are much more advanced than others, but every one of us is as ancient as everyone else. These souls, in my cosmology, move in cohort groups and we make what I call preconception contracts with each other to be part of each other's lives and drama as parents or grandparents or siblings or friends. We move through our lifetimes in these cohort groups. Long before we take on these spacesuits that we call our bodies, we make contracts with each other to appear in the same place at the same time for significant episodes in our life. I am serious when I say that many, many years before Bob and Mary Burns had faces, their grandson, Ronan Patrick Burns issued an invitation to us to attend his baptism today in this church – and you came. That is my first point.

Secondly, the contract: What is this preconception contract that we make together? This baby, this extraordinary organizing genius has brought Jews, Christians, Hindus and Buddhists into this church this morning. As I look around, and I know all of you, I see that this little child has brought people from three different

160

continents into this church this morning. There are people from North and South America, the European continent and there are people from Asia. I know there are people who have come here for this baptism from Ireland, Scotland, Spain, Austria, Peru, Ecuador and Colombia. This is an extraordinary achievement by a three-month-old baby. What was he doing? What was the contract and what is the job? The contract and the job are this, in my opinion. It is the realization that it is not okay to let peers and mass media raise our kids. It is the realization that we need intentional communities of like-minded people who model the kind of spiritual values in which we believe. That is the contract. We contract to bring together a group to nurture us and to help us to evolve and develop.

There is an extraordinary tribe of people in West Africa. When a woman of this tribe is about seven months pregnant the elders of the tribe take her into a special hut, sequester her, and induce in her an altered state of consciousness. They put her into a trance. Then they speak not to the woman but to the baby in utero. They want to know two things. They want to know what the baby's name is supposed to be so they can properly identify it. And they want to know the baby's mission. That is what baptism is about. Baptism is an inquiry on behalf of this intentional community, this cohort group, to find out the name of this baby, not so it can just hang an identity tag on it, but to discover this baby's mission and what our mission is vis-à-vis this child. I am totally convinced that this extraordinary arrangement of parents and children is an elegant design. Children are God's way of reminding adults that we are basically spirits in space suits. Parents are God's compassionate way of helping the children who come in to learn how to use their space suits. Children tell us we are <u>spirits</u> in spacesuits and parents tell us we are spirits in <u>spacesuits</u>. That is the arrangement, which is an extraordinary design. It is almost as though periodically God sends prophets into our midst to try to unstick the clogged wheels of human evolution. We call these prophets babies. It is as if we are in a Super Bowl and in the last minutes God sends in three or four substitutes to try to raise the flagging spirits of the losing team. That is what the contract is about.

My third point is to establish what baptism is not. Baptism is not about saving a baby from limbo or from hell. That teaching is an extraordinary corruption of the teaching of the compassionate carpenter from Galilee. In the 16th century, a Catholic theologian at the University of Paris claimed that if a Christian woman died pregnant she could not be buried in a Christian graveyard since she carried a pagan within her. She would literally have to be eviscerated and the little pagan dumped someplace else so that her undefiled body could then be buried in a Christian graveyard. Baptism is not about that. Nor do I believe that baptism is about saving a baby from original sin as if this little creature had come into this world stained and sullied. It is definitely not about that. Baptism, in my opinion, is not just about a cutesy naming ceremony where we dress the little baby in white and we sing songs and we party and that is the end of our commitment. Baptism is not about that. Nor is baptism about the induction of a baby into some kind of club, some kind of international religious organization that we might call the Roman Catholic Church or whatever. It is not about inducting a baby into a bureaucracy; it is not about that.

Fourthly, what then is baptism? If baptism is not about saving a baby from hell, what is it about? It is about saving us, in my opinion, from the apathy and the lethargy that happens to the best of us. It is about waking us up to who we really are so we can create the kind of world in which the child can blossom. It is about sin, but it is about the sin of apathy and intolerance and prejudice. If baptism is not about original sin on the part of the baby, what is it about? It certainly is about sin. We have inherited a world and this baby is inheriting a world that is almost five billion years old and has had billions of human beings making violent, prejudicial and selfish choices and thus creating an ethos in which the child will encounter sin, prejudice, violence and selfishness. If there is original sin in the world it is about us recognizing it and trying to clean that before this child has to contend with it. If baptism is not just a cutesy naming ceremony, what is it about? It is, in my opinion, really naming the mission. It is about identifying the purpose for being in spacesuits on planet Earth and waking up to that realization. If baptism is not about inducting a baby into a religious bureaucracy, what is it about? It is about us waking up to the recognition of this symbolism that invites us to excellence in the course of our own spiritual evolution.

Fifthly, I want to talk about six water symbols. As we go through the baptism there is one prayer where I am going to take this bowl of water and bless it and I am going to talk about six different symbols from the Judeo/Christian scriptures. You have heard this many times and as I read through them you probably will not hear them so I will tell you what they are. The symbols are: one, water as creation from the first Chapter in the Book of Genesis; two, the symbol of the flood, (Book of Genesis); three, the Israelites crossing the Red Sea as they escaped from Egypt; four, the Israelites crossing the Jordan as they go into the Promised Land; five, Jesus having water flow from his side on the cross; and finally; six, the symbol of baptism itself. What is that about?

This is what I think baptism is about. I think it is a beautiful evolutionary model of how the human spirit has developed. The very first symbol in Genesis is water as creation. It is true. The very first animal life forms on planet Earth, 700 million years ago, happened in water. The very first creatures were sea creatures. About 400 million years ago they first ventured onto dry land. But there was a big problem. How does a creature that has been born and bred for millions of generations in water live on desiccated terrain? There were two extraordinary solutions to it. One entire group of reptiles went back into the water every time they wanted to conceive and birth their young. They are still among us, frogs and salamanders still do it. Mammals had an even more extraordinary hit on it; mammals carry the sea with them. In every mammal, human beings included, the saline content of human blood is precisely that of seawater. We have taken the ocean with us. The female mammals carried a veritable ocean within them called the amniotic fluid of the womb. They conceive and nurture their babies in the ocean within. When we talk about creation coming out of water, it is still happening. It did not just happen years and years ago, it happens every day.

The second symbol is the symbol of the flood, the great flood where God allegedly wiped out everything saving only Noah and his wife and their three sons and their three wives, eight people. Is that what it is really about? In my opinion, it is a symbol of the fact that even after creation we were still drowned in the unconscious, unawareness of our destiny and our being. We were just drowned out. We did not understand what it meant to be children of God. We drowned in our own ignorance.

The third symbol comes in the Book of Exodus in the Hebrew Scriptures. It is the notion of an enslaved people who for 450 years had been exiled in Egypt, breaking away from the greatest empire of the day and escaping into the desert and symbolically crossing the Red Sea. What does that symbolically represent? It was

163

the first awakening of the human spirit to the realization of its right to be free and its duty to be awake. It was the first dawning of that recognition, but it was only the beginning. These groups of escaped slaves did not really believe it themselves. When they reached the Promised Land within six weeks, they were afraid to go in because their spies told them that the people in that country were giants and would eat them up. So they turned back into the desert and wandered for 40 years and only then did they cross the second river, the Jordan.

Symbol number four is the crossing of the Jordan River. What does that represent? The human species for the first time came into full realization of its patrimony; the full realization that we are, indeed, children of God. That was the first deep understanding of that patrimony. They were still a long, long way from the end of the process.

Fast forward 1250 years and you have an extraordinary Jewish Rabbi dying on a cross, crucified by Roman soldiers, and to make sure he is dead, one of them jabs a spear into his side and the body that has been bleeding continually for three hours now produces only water. Traditionally, theologians have seen the water and blood symbolically, as the mixture of divinity and humanity.

Symbol number five is the realization of an extraordinary avatar, not the first to realize it and not the last to realize it; an avatar who realized that at the core of his being, that he, indeed, is the Son of God. An extraordinary realization!

The sixth symbol is that most of us Christians are prepared to leave it at that and say, "Jesus was God's son. Wow, what a man!" Baptism is not about that. Baptism is the final stage in the process because baptism is the invitation to every single one of us to wake up to the very same realization. The avatars are merely the advance guard of the movement of human evolution that invites all of us to the realization, "That thou art." When we baptize this baby today we are asking ourselves, "Can we, too, go that extra step?" Can we really believe that at the core of our being, not by our name, nor by our spacesuit, but by the core of our being we are God stuff? Can we believe that we are spirits in spacesuits? If we can realize that, and I do not mean just to cognitively appreciate it, I mean to make it real in our lives, then we will see the same God in others and the world will be very different. The world that Ronan Patrick Burns will inherit will be a very different world.

Many, many years ago I got an invitation from Ronan Patrick Burns to attend his baptism on the ninth of September in the year of our Lord, 2001 in Palo Alto and I said yes and I showed up. The question is, do I have the courage and the commitment to make the kind of changes in my life that will create for Ronan Patrick the realization of his divinity?

Many years ago every single one of you got an invitation from Ronan Patrick Burns to attend his baptism and you said yes and you showed up. The question is, do you have the courage and the commitment to try to make the kind of changes in your life that will allow you to create the kind of world in which Ronan Patrick Burns can realize that he, too, is really another Son of God?

22
The Evolution from the 911 Tragedy

It was an extraordinarily elegant exercise and it involved groups of four people at a time. It happened every July in Kenya. A family of four people would go out. The first person would dig a little hole in the ground every six inches with a stick. The second person would put two seeds into every hole. If one seed failed, the other would certainly take. If the family was rich and could afford it, the third person would have a bag of artificial fertilizer and would put a spoonful of fertilizer into each hole and then the fourth person would cover up the hole with his foot.

After three weeks, when the young maize sprouted, they would go back and weed. After about six weeks, when the young corn was higher, they would weed it for a second time. At the end of two months they would harvest the maize.

These were people who had been nomadic all of their lives and had no tradition of agriculture. I was a city boy from Ireland and I didn't either. Together we were trying to figure out how to make it work. I held seminars for the farmers. I was their teacher in agriculture. After three years of doing agriculture I asked the farmers, "If you had a choice and you had to choose between fertilizing the seed and weeding, and you could only do one, which would you choose as the more important, the fertilizing or the weeding?" After three years doing it, no one had the slightest doubt. Weeding is much more important than fertilizing. Fertilizer is blind; it gives growth to everything it touches. The weeds and grass just grow and the corn gets smothered and you are very lucky if you get a few ears from a few different stocks. If you weed it very carefully, even without fertilizer, you get a very good crop. If you can combine them, you obviously get the very best crop of all. I would say to the people that that is what Jesus meant by the teaching, "Love your enemies." Jesus understood that this was not just being a patsy by lying down to be walked over. He was perhaps the greatest psychologist planet Earth has ever seen. Jesus knew as a great psychologist and Jesus knew as an enlightened human being that there are two things that make us grow fertilizer and weeding.

The fertilizer corresponds to the love that we receive from those who support us and unconditional love from our family or

166

friends. It is vital for our growth. We cannot develop healthy egos or healthy self-images as individuals, as communities or as nations without that kind of support. However, if that is the only kind of support we get, then our ego grows apace. Jesus also knew there needed to be times of weeding in our lives. This happens in our interpersonal, inter-communal, international and global relationships. There are times in our lives when we need to weed. I want to talk about that today because of the tragedy visited upon all humanity this week.

I want to make six points. My first point I will call: He taught it, he lived it and he died for it. Secondly: They died for it; can we live for it? My third point is this: Act first and think later. My fourth point is the evolution of the human family. The fifth one is the evolution of the notion of priesthood. Sixth will be the way forward from here.

He taught it, he lived it, and he died for it. This is possibly one of the most extraordinary spiritual teachings of all time. If there is one theme that comes through in the teaching of Jesus again and again it is the extraordinary notion of forgiveness. It is one of the most important spiritual teachings of any tradition of any kind and it is not just meant to make patsies or doormats of us. It is to offer a blueprint for our evolution.

We have heard this text many times in this country. We have realized its potential and we have asked the people in Northern Ireland; "Could you please pay attention, you Christians who are killing each other in Northern Ireland, please listen to this text and let it into your hearts." We have taken this text and we have said to the people of Eastern Europe, Serb and Croat, "Christians, could you take this text and could you really make it your own and act upon it?" We have taken this text and we have said to the warring parties in the Middle East, Israelis and Palestinians; "Could you take this notion and could you begin to incorporate it into your relationships with each other?" When we did that we did it with conviction, hearts filled with the realization that Jesus was a way or even the way.

Last Tuesday we got the opportunity of taking this text and wondering could we, too, take it seriously. Either Jesus was all wrong or this is the most important single blueprint for the evolution of the human species ever to come through in any spiritual tradition. It is either one or the other. It cannot be just one way

167

when it is happening in Northern Ireland, Croatia, and the Middle East. It cannot be just that then and something else now. Either Jesus knew what he was talking about and he was an extraordinary human being, or we have been extraordinary hypocrites, all of us Christians throughout the world, by pretending that this is a valid text except when it happens in our back yard. I am convinced that if you searched all the scriptural traditions you will not find a single chapter of any scripture that so eloquently and so totally addresses where the human species is being invited to move more than this text. He taught it, moreover, he lived it. I do not believe that Jesus came onto planet Earth to die for our sins. I do not believe that for a moment. The blood of Jesus is no different from your blood or my blood. Jesus came to live and to teach his truth. His death came because the leadership of the time and the prevailing paradigm of the time could only respond to him in fear and anger. He died unnecessarily but when it came to dying, he died as he lived with love and forgiveness in his heart. He was not lying down and becoming a doormat or a patsy. He lived and he walked his talk right up to the very end. He acted upon it.

I do not believe that though Jesus died because of the fear of others that that justified in any way what they did. I do not believe that this extraordinary loving life and loving death of Jesus justified Peter's denial of him. I do not believe that this extraordinary life and death of Jesus justified the apostles' cowardice in running away and abandoning him. I do not believe that this extraordinary life and death of Jesus mitigated Judas' greed in selling him. I do not believe for one moment of my life that this extraordinary sacrifice of his life and of his death in any way justifies Roman brutality in crucifying him. Nor do I believe for one moment that this extraordinary life and death of Jesus in any way justifies whatever complicity there may have been among Jewish religious leadership in his death. Throughout Christian history when we have remembered his love, we have been great. When we have dwelt upon the fear and dwelt upon the anger, we have had institutionalized religiously sponsored terrorism in the Crusades, the Inquisitions and in the Conquistadors. That has been our history. We have been great when we remembered Jesus' love and forgiveness. We have been terrorists when all we remember is our fear and our anger.

They died for it, could we live for it? Let me run something by you. You know the notion of cohort groups and preconception

168

contracts. In the core of my being it is my belief system that we come onto this planet many times. Every soul on this planet is as ancient as every other soul on this planet. There is no soul on this planet that is younger than the soul of Jesus. There is no soul on this planet that is older than the soul of the newborn infant. We are all as ancient as God because we are God stuff. I believe that groups of these souls that I call cohort groups travel from lifetime to lifetime with each other to present a human drama that allows us countless different opportunities to respond to life with love. What if, before these people who died on last Tuesday were ever conceived, they made an agreement to live their lives and their deaths as an extraordinary sacrifice to try to wake up the human race from its "business and violence as usual."

Once we come onto the planet, amnesia is created for all of us. What synchronicity happened that these chosen ones were in the same place at the same time in order to offer that sacrifice? As I said, with the death of Jesus, this in no way justifies the terrorism involved in it. This in no way says that it was okay for anyone to take innocent lives, more than Peter abandoning Jesus, or Judas betraying him, or the Romans crucifying him. This extraordinary sacrifice of this band of souls in no way justifies the agenda, the tactics or the mindset of those very sick people who killed them. If they died for the fear and the anger of the terrorists, and even if they died in fear and anger in their human spacesuits, we are totally undoing their sacrifice if we believe it was _for_ fear and _for_ anger. They may have died _by_ fear and anger; they may even have died _in_ fear and anger; but they most certainly did not die _for_ fear and anger. If their only legacy to planet Earth is more fear and anger, then this extraordinary sacrifice, this extraordinary preconception contract has been washed down the tubes. We have totally missed the boat.

My third point is, "Act first and think later." In 1981, I personally came close to dying. I was living in a remote mission in Kenya and I had contracted typhoid. I thought it was malaria and was treating myself for malaria and after 14 days and about 40 pounds lighter I suddenly realized what was happening. I remember one day while lying on my bed shaking and full of fear, a voice deep inside me said, "You are not your body. Your body is doing what bodies are built to do. It is trying to shake itself into recovery. It is saying no to the disease. It is trying to heal itself. That is what bodies do. But you are not your body. You are not your heart or

169

your emotions. Your heart and your emotions are doing what hearts and emotions do. They experience anger, fear and sadness, but you are not your emotions. You are a spirit being as ancient as the universe itself." From that moment to this day I have never had the slightest fear of dying under any circumstances. I have no doubt whatever that I am not my body, though I have a body. I am not my emotions, though I have emotions. I am not an intellect though I have an intellect. I am not even a personality, though I have a personality. I am a spirit being on safari on planet Earth.

This entire nation has a body. This entire nation has emotions. At this time, after this extraordinary tragedy, the body of America is doing what bodies do, even great bodies like America. It is shaking and trying to heal itself. We have to listen to it, but that is not who we are as Americans. We have to listen to the fear and the anger generated nationally in the psyche of America, but that is not America. There is a soul to America. If we listen only to the body of America and only to the emotions of America and do not listen to the soul of America, we will miss an opportunity to be part of the wave that takes the human species to the next stage of our evolution.

My fourth point is this. I want to talk about the evolution of the human species. I have been personally convinced for over 25 years that the entire human species is on the brink of some great evolutionary breakthrough. It will be a leap in human consciousness so that we will really get it, not just mentally and not just in the heart, but at a soul level. Ethnicity does not define us. Denominational affiliation does not define us. Class does not define us. Nationhood does not define us. We are defined by the fact that every single one of us is God incarnate. My knowledge of human history and my knowledge of evolutionary biology tells me that never in the course of evolution is there a significant quantum leap in functioning that is not precipitated by some kind of extraordinary crisis. People do not change dramatically unless there is some kind of an extraordinary trigger to act as a catalyst. As a psychologist I see this with individuals in therapy. I see it with couples in therapy, and I see it with families in therapy. As a person who reads history and studies evolutionary biology, I see the same thing happening again and again. Three years into my priesthood, at a meeting of the elders, I was stopped in my tracks by an old man who said to me, "Why is it that for you Europeans your only response to a problem is to want to solve it?" It sounded to me like a Zen koan. What the

170

hell else would you do with a problem except solve it? He said to me, "No, a problem is an invitation to self-transcendence. When you get that, the problem will clear itself up. If you do not get it and you merely solve the problem, then life and evolution will just give you another bigger problem to try to wake you up."

This is an extraordinary opportunity for planet Earth to do life on this planet as a human family such as we have never done it before in one million years of our history as a human species. For the last 5000 years we have tried violence. Since the beginning of the agricultural revolution, the development of the mechanized ox-drawn plow in the year 3000 B.C. we have had the leisure time and the ability to hoard food and for the first time ever to develop philosophy, mathematics, orthographies, literatures and classical warfare. We have tried for 5000 years to beat people into submission. It will be more of the same if that is our only response to it. I have to believe from my studies of these systems that part of our invitation through this extraordinary crisis is to begin to dismantle our mythologies because our founding myths are part of the problem. There is not a single country on planet Earth that has not violently carved its national identity on the backs of aboriginal people.

I watched in horror and fascination several years ago during the Los Angeles riots, when the first wave of looters went in and ransacked the shops and took what they could take and ran home with it. Then the second wave of looters came in and they realized at this stage that the police were not going to be able to intervene so they went into the stores and they took things out and stockpiled them on the pavement and went back in for more. The third wave of looters came and because there was nothing left in the shops they started stealing things from the sidewalks and the second wave and the third wave got into it with each other. "How dare you steal my stuff!" There is not a country on planet Earth that is not involved in that conflict. There is not one of us that is not involved in a second wave versus third wave confrontation as to who owns what kind of stuff. It is about time we woke up and realized it is all our stuff. The mythologies of every country are mythologies of violence. Every single nation's founding myth is about the bloody revolution that brought freedom, got rid of colonialism or captured the Promised Land for us. There is not a single major religion on planet Earth whose founding myth is not a bloody myth. Unfortunately, even the

171

Christian foundation myth is a man dying in agony on a cross. That is the Christian myth. How would the history of Christianity have been different if our founding myth was a mother nursing her infant at her breast? How different might it have been?

We need to take this opportunity to create new myths, a myth for the planet, not a myth for individual religions, not a myth for individual nations, but a myth that brings all of us together. We need a new flag. Not a flag that tells me I am Iranian, or Pakistani but a flag that tells me I am a child of God on safari on planet Earth. When I heard reports this week of a sub-group of Palestinians jumping for joy and handing out candy and singing, "Allah be praised," and I heard reports of Americans waving flags and singing "God Bless America," my response was, this only works if God suffers from multiple personality disorder. We have called God to witness all sides of all conflicts throughout human history. Enough already! God must be called upon as the Father and Mother of all of us with a founding myth and a founding flag that makes us brothers and sisters throughout the planet, not one that fragments and differentiates between us.

I am totally convinced that as far as humanity is concerned there have been prototypes sent among us in order to tell us where the future of humanity is headed. The question is to guess who the prototypes are. Some of us are convinced that the prototypes heralding where the human race is headed are Hitler and Genghis Khan and Stalin and Osama bin Laden. Some of us are convinced that they are the prototypes where we are headed and some of us are prepared to follow them into terror and counter terror and violence and counter violence. There are some of us who recognize that the great prototypes who have been sent among us for the last 5000 years are people like Jesus, Gautama Siddhartha, Mother Teresa and Mahatma Gandhi. The question is where are you going to cast your vote? Will it be for the likes of Genghis Khan and Osama bin Laden or will it be for those like Buddha and Jesus? Will you cast a vote or will you just cast a stone? That will determine who you are and it will determine where the world is headed.

My fifth point is the evolution of priesthood. The priest is not just the man who is dressed like a woman saying mass. That is not a priest. A priest is any leader whom we follow whether it is a military leader, political leader, industrial leader or someone who tells us that he knows where he is going. That is the priest. There are

172

many kinds of leadership on a spectrum of leadership. I see five different points. There is the leader who is elected and uses his office for personal self-aggrandizement. They are the worst of all. There are the leaders who are elected and use their office merely to repay their backers who got them into power. They are the second worst of all. There are the leaders who are elected and they spend their time answering only the needs of those particular people who elected them but not the rest of their constituency and they are the third worst kind of leaders. There is a fourth kind of leader who is elected and tries to represent the needs of the entire electorate. But none of those four are great leaders. A truly great leader is the leader who thinks of planet Earth long-term. He thinks about the effects of the decisions made and the influence for the seventh generation yet to be born. They are the leaders. They are the priests.

I have come to the conclusion that the notion of priesthood will undergo four evolutionary shifts. The first stage of priesthood would be the mother priest. At some early stage in the evolution of human consciousness we did not understand the connection between coition and conception. Suddenly, every so often a woman of the tribe would bring new life into the group. It was a very important miracle. The first priests were the mothers who brought new life to the tribe.

As the human race expanded and we began to argue with each other for resources, a second order of priesthood evolved. I call it the warrior priesthood, the man who is prepared either to take the life of the enemy or to give his own. It was a very appropriate response. It was an extraordinary response, but, unfortunately, it is a very old and outdated response. Priesthood as mother, in my opinion, is now passé. If priesthood is only about bringing new children into the world, I have bad news for us; we are over breeding. If priesthood is just about bringing new souls unthinkingly on to planet Earth, then the priesthood has run its course. If priesthood is only the priesthood of the warrior, it has run its course. Given its head for another 10 or 15 years, the warrior priesthood will bring us to ecological and nuclear disaster. It is passé. The good news is, in my opinion, that there are two other kinds of priesthood waiting in the wings. There is the healer priest whose function is to soothe and calm wounded humanity. We need to evolve immediately into stage three, priesthood, and we need to aim at stage four priesthood.

Stage four, priesthood is the prophet priest. Not the one who brings new life into the group and not the one who takes life on behalf of the group or even gives his life. Not even the person who can cure the life of the tribe, but the person who can call the entire human family into a totally different understanding of life. The priesthood we need to be aiming for is a priesthood that can tell us what life is really about and will invite us and seduce us into making that a reality.

It is very important for us as a human family and particularly as an American family to feel our sadness but not to define ourselves by our sadness. It is important to feel our fear but not to define ourselves by our fear. It is important to feel our anger but not to define ourselves by our anger. The greatest tragedy of the year 2001 will not be remembered as Tuesday the eleventh of September. It will be remembered as October if our only response is fear. It will be remembered as November if our only response is anger. It will be remembered as December if our only plan is war.

If my words have any power to move you today and to shift your fear into faith, that is very good, but it is not good enough. If my words have any power to move you from despair into hope, that is very good, but it is not good enough. If my words have any power to move you from your anger into love that is very good, but it is not good enough. If my words have the ability to somehow encourage you or even inspire you, that is good, but it is not good enough. If my words have the ability to allow you to be thinking a wider, deeper, more profound cosmology that can contain all of the events of this last week that is very good, but it is not good enough. If every one of us does not become a leader of the evolution, then my words are wasted and the people that died have died in vain.

In 75 minutes, a group of dedicated fanatics fueled by a fundamentalist fervor changed the course of world history. They were not the first to do it. The question is will they be the last to do it? Long before these 19 fanatics changed the course of human history it had been done before. The Buddha did it 2500 years ago single-handedly. Jesus did it 2000 years ago single-handedly. This was not the first time it happened. The question is, will it be the last? The question for you and for me is this. Are you prepared to make it happen again? Are you and I prepared to join the evolution of the human species so that human beings modeled by Jesus and the Buddha become a reality in our lifetime?

23
The Evolution of Religion and the Nation as a Holon

Because I am a male member of the species my preferred mode of entertainment is not a good movie, not even good food. If I really want to get turned on, I watch heavy equipment dig holes in the dirt. Last Tuesday morning I sat in the forest for five hours watching a guy on a backhoe dig a septic system. I was in ecstasy. As I watched him, I began to think about the evolution of dirt and dust and humans and technology. I remembered that according to the best modern estimate, we inhabit a universe that is 13 billion years old. Planet Earth spewed into existence 4.5 billion years ago. Planet Earth was in existence for a long time before the first land animals came into being. They only came into being 400 million years ago. It took the land animals a long time to evolve. It took homosapiens 400 thousand years to invent horticulture, a digging stick. It took us another 10 thousand years before we had the great avatars, the great wise ones who came among us, Socrates, the Buddha, Jesus and Mahavira. In just the last 250 years, we invented industry and very lately we invented information technology.

I want to continue to address what has been happening in our world beginning on September 11 and what the invitation to us might be. I'll make four main points. I'll talk about holons and epigenesis in those terms. Secondly, I'll talk about the nation as a holon. Thirdly, I'll talk about religion as a holon. Fourthly, I'll talk about commerce as a holon.

Firstly then, holons and epigenesis. The term holon was coined by Arthur Koestler to refer to an entity that is itself a whole and simultaneously a part of some greater whole. There is nothing in the universe that is not composed of sub-pieces and which itself, is also not part of a greater whole. The universe does not consist of atoms. It does not consist of sub-atomic particles. It does not consist of quarks or leptons or any of these things. The universe consists of holons. Everything in the universe is composed of sub-parts and is part of a greater whole. Every cell is composed of molecules and every cell belongs to some kind of an organism. Every family is composed of individual people and each family is part of a larger community. There is nothing in the universe except holons.

175

Holons evolve in an extraordinary fashion. One thing about the evolution of holons is that holons evolve epigenetically. That means that every subsequent stage includes but transcends all of the previous stages. In the process of evolution, nothing ever gets left behind. Evolution, properly speaking, goes beyond, but incorporates what it has come from. Like a tree reaching toward the clouds or toward the sun, it never loses contact with its roots. If it loses contact with its roots, evolution stops. If the branches do not continue to reach toward the sun, evolution also stops. If there is no transcendence, it is the end of evolution. If there is not contact with the roots, it is the end of evolution as well. Evolution always proceeds in the fashion of epigenesis. Every next stage includes but transcends all of the previous stages.

Problems begin to happen when this breaks down. In this process of transcending and including, there are three stages. The first stage is symbiosis, which is the inability to distinguish self from other. It is stage specific and it is correct in its time.

Stage two is differentiation. This is the ability to recognize self and to recognize that self as an individual among the group.

Stage three is integration where the individuals, recognizing their autonomy, come together in a greater collective. That is how the process proceeds. However, there can be difficulties at every one of these three stages. If we get stuck in symbiosis, then what appears to be oceanic bliss just becomes a stagnant morass; there is no way forward. If we get stuck at the differentiation stage, what looks like liberation just becomes total anarchy. If we get stuck at the integration stage, then we simply form bigger groups to make war on other bigger groups.

How is the process meant to evolve? What are some examples of holons and their epigenetic evolution? Every single one of us started out as a zygote, a single cell where one sperm met one egg. That is symbiosis. At some stage, in order for evolution to continue, this cell has to split in two, then in four, then in eight, and then in sixteen. That is the differentiation process. If differentiation continues on its own, all you have is just splitting and more splitting, confusion and anarchy. At some stage, groups of cells come together and form organs and ultimately organisms. That is the reintegration stage. That is an example from biology.

I'll give you an example from sociology. Every baby born into the world is born into a symbiotic relationship with its

176

environment. It is totally at one with its mother. It cannot distinguish between mother and self. That is the stage of the first year of our life, a total symbiotic relationship with the mother. Later we begin to differentiate out. We recognize our own name. We begin standing up, walking and saying, "NO," which is the first most important differentiation. We become teenagers and the only word we know is "NO," that is differentiation. At some stage we become adults and we have an adult relationship with our parents and our family. There is the integration, sociologically.

If you take a jigsaw puzzle and you tumble the pieces out on to the table, you have symbiosis; just a total mess of pieces all lumped together. At some stage you have to start the differentiation process. You take out the corner pieces, you take out the straight-edged pieces, and you take out the colors that look the same; you are differentiating. The integration is when you take all of these pieces and you fit them together to match the picture on the box cover. That is how the process is meant to go. We are always striving for greater complexity, but always honoring our roots and that from which we have come.

In the context then of what has been happening in our world the last three weeks, I want to propose that the way forward is not to impair the process at any level. It is to totally embrace the greatest possible holon for planet Earth. It is to radically bring together great thinkers. If I had any kind of position of authority where I could make this happen, I would bring together the greatest thinkers on planet Earth. I would gather economists, ecologists, politicians, educators, media people, and spiritual people, and I would put all of these great minds together and ask them to please start thinking globally.

What have we been doing wrong in religion? What have we been doing wrong in politics? What have we been doing wrong in economics? What have we been doing wrong in the mass media? Can we do these things better? Can we create a holon which incorporates and transcends all of the stages that have gone before us? Can we differentiate out the pieces at this stage from the morass of symbiosis, and can we start reintegrating at a higher level?

Specifically, for the next three points, I want to take smaller areas and begin to treat those as holons in their own right. Let me talk about the nation as a holon. When you look at the evolution of human life on this planet for the first 400 thousand years, we were

177

almost individuals, everyone looking out for himself. At some stage in the process, we got the notion that in order to optimize our existence and our survival, it was important to operate as family systems. The males began to take responsibility for child raising practices and for child protection practices. This was an extraordinary leap in human consciousness. For the first time we transcended mere individual pursuits of security and food sources and banded together into little families.

At some stage, we began to realize that even that grouping had its drawbacks and we began to group together as clans. After a while, the clans became tribes, and as this happened, you could see a movement in the techno-economic base of it. From a sociological basis, we went from individual considerations to family concerns, to clan interests, to tribal agendas and finally, we got to the notion of a state and then to a nation. My question is, who claims that nation is the ultimate divinely revealed unit of holon evolution? Why would we think that all of this evolution that has brought us to this point would stop here? Why would we think, in our right minds, that God meant for the whole epigenesis and the entire evolution of human community to stop at national boundaries? It is crazy; it doesn't make any sense. It is not going to happen. Evolution will not allow it to happen. We can be dragged kicking and screaming beyond our national boundaries or we can embrace the possibility of looking at how we do life as an entire species on this planet.

When you have unenlightened male energy there is always the trend to embrace the more complex holon and to sacrifice the less complex holon. Unenlightened male energy will embrace the tribe and sacrifice the family for the sake of the tribe. Unenlightened female energy will embrace the less complex holon and sacrifice the more complex holon. Unenlightened female energy wants to protect the family at all costs and let the tribe look out for itself. What we need in our times is the union of enlightened male and female energy. We need the enlightened energy that allows us to totally honor, nurture, and celebrate the less complex holons of our sociological evolution. For instance, we need to honor and celebrate our families, extended families and clans, incorporate, honor and celebrate the previous stages, but aim to create even more complex models to go beyond and transcend. If we do not accomplish that, evolution will proceed without the human species.

My third point is religion as a holon. When you look at the extraordinary evolution of religion on this planet, our ideas of God have come a long way from Gods who are distant, unpredictable, demanding deities, zapping us left, right and center. We have come from Gods who are regional deities totally partial to particular ethnic groups. We have come from Gods who are particularly addicted to specific portfolios; a God of war, God of fertility or a God of the arts. We have come finally to a God who is monotheistic; but one believer's monotheistic version is very different from another believer's monotheistic version. We have landed on a place of denominational religion as if that were the final stage of the evolution of religion on our planet. If it is, we are lost.

There is a place way beyond that which we are now discovering for the first time. The great avatars that came among us many years ago have been constantly pointing out the way forward for religion. It is spirituality. It is the mystical core that transcends mere dogma or denominational affiliation. That is not to say that this is not important because we are talking holons and epigenesis. We are talking "transcend and include." We are not talking "transcend and abandon." We are certainly not talking "stay stuck and forget transcendence." If religion does not evolve into real spirituality, we are going to kill ourselves. Since September 11, it has been extraordinary how many people have gone back to religion, which is very good. If we go back only to religion we will die very slowly, but die we will. If we do not go forward to spirituality, we will never continue to thrive as human beings. The way forward is spirituality. It is a path that has already been mapped out; it is not totally uncharted territory. Great people like Mahavira, the Buddha, Jesus and Socrates who came among us have mapped it out for us. It is the deep mystical core leading us to a non-dualistic understanding of God where there is only God. It is not we worshiping God; we are all God stuff. It is the Namasté of Hinduism, the God in me recognizing and honoring the God in you. The way forward must mean the embrace of that. Spirituality, in my opinion, is the individual encounter with the numinous ground of our being. All that means is this; that every single one of us has the right, in fact, the duty and the responsibility to encounter God. Religion, when it is good, honors, celebrates and facilitates that process for us. Religion, when it is bad, substitutes dogma and creed imposed by hierarchies on the masses instead. That is not the way

179

forward. That is a huge part of the problem we have created on planet Earth.

My fourth point then is this; I want to talk about commerce as a holon. It would appear that the way world trade is moving is very much a holon. Isn't it a bigger and bigger embracing of more and more complex wholes? Not true! In my opinion, much of world economic expansion is merely a wolf in sheep's clothing. It is the wolf of economic greed masquerading in the sheep's clothing of world free trade. "World free trade" is one of these euphemisms like "collateral damage" that hides the truth. Collateral damage really means innocent people being killed. There is no such thing as world free trade. There is a cost to everything we produce. There is a cost to everything we deliver. There is a cost to everything we consume. I am not saying that is bad or good; I am saying that that is a fact. There is a cost to the ecological systems on which we depend for our life. There is a cost to families and family relationships when we produce, deliver, or consume, and there is a cost to international relationships as well. Every time we produce and every time we deliver and every time we consume there is a price being paid, and you cannot put a dollar amount on it. You have to look at what the results are for small communities in India that are reduced to total poverty. You have to look at what the price is for the planet that is paying the ultimate price for it. You have to look at what it does to international relationships when we use commodities like oil as international bargaining tools. There is no such thing as free trade, it is a euphemism, and we have been led blindly by the nose into accepting that it is a good thing.

When I look at organizations such as the World Trade Organization, on the surface it appears to be this holon embracing more and more of us in the ability to trade more and more freely. For two reasons I would claim that organizations like that are not holons. They are not holons because the essence of holon is that it transcends and includes. The essence of the current alleged World Trade Organization, "Free Trade," is transcending very definitely, but it does not want to include, in fact, it is taking steps to totally annihilate everything that has gone before. There are conglomerates operating on our planet at the moment that have made it illegal for Indian farmers to save their own grain from their own harvest and plant it the following year. It is illegal; your farm can be confiscated for attempting to do it. You have to buy new seeds, hybrids, every year from some large monolith. For that reason, such economic trade is not free trade and it is not a holon. Moreover, they have succeeded in legalizing their game and making it the only game in town. It has become illegal to practice agriculture as formerly understood. Is that free trade or is that holon? That is a total aberration of the evolutionary process. It is as if all of the long distance runners were to get together and pressure the Olympic Committee saying, "You know, the Olympics started off as a marathon race of 26.2 miles, therefore, we insist that in the future all Olympics consist of only marathon events." But you try as a swimmer, gymnast or a weight lifter to run 26.2 miles if it is not your skill, and you will never succeed. Only the long distance runners will ever appear on the stand and get a medal. In this alleged free trade model in which everyone is free to participate, why is it happening that fewer and fewer people are receiving the medals? Why is it happening that fewer and fewer people are standing on the podium getting gold or silver or bronze? Everyone is free to join the race, but we do not have the skill to do it and the models constructed in a pyramidical fashion make it impossible for everyone to be at the top at the same time. We need to radically reassess our economic models.

I have heard the word, "bio-terrorism," being bandied about for the last few weeks. I have news for you, bio-terrorism is devastating, but we have been living with bio-terrorism for the last 40 years. We simply have not recognized it. We have used euphemisms to protect ourselves from it. We have destroyed more than 30 percent of the waterways of the United States of America such that 30 percent of our rivers, lakes and ocean fronts are unsuitable for fishing or swimming; that is bio-terrorism. We have done it to ourselves. We have destroyed the quality of the air we breathe and the water we drink and the food we eat; that is bio-terrorism. As someone said once, "We have found the enemy and it is "us," we have found the bio-terrorists and they are "us." It is untrammeled capitalism going for bigger and bigger profits at higher and higher costs to our own children because they are paying the price of it.

We have a glorious opportunity on this day the 30th of September in the year of our Lord, 2001. It is not the awesome possibility of nuclear devastation; nor yet the possibility of an outbreak of anthrax; it is the possibility of breaking, not the sound

181

barrier this time, but the light barrier. We have been noisemakers for a long time, let's become light breakers and light makers instead. Are you ready today to join the charge of the light brigade?

24
How Human Beings Manage God and Grow God

If you were to look at the past, the present and the projected future and you were to bet as to what would be the greatest non-event in the history of planet Earth, what would you say it was? I'll tell you where my money would go. As the greatest non-event in the history of planet Earth, it would be the last judgment. There are going to be a lot of very disappointed people. A lot of people are hoping for this grandstanding, cosmically televised event in which one by one we shamefully confess our sins and God will say, "Out louder," and we are given a microphone to confess our sins, while over in the corner, a group of smug, religious bureaucrats who knew what the truth was all the time were just waiting for God to create an appropriate event to tell everybody else who was right and who was wrong. There are going to be a lot of very disappointed people.

The thing about the last judgment is, it's a "DIY," a "do it yourself." There is going to be no grandstanding, no grand inquisitor, no grand inquisition, and no shame-faced people being paraded in public in front of the scoffing multitudes. There is only going to be this personal understanding for the first time perhaps in our lives of the fact that we are all just one and that to sin against anyone is to sin against myself. It will be the ability simultaneously to feel the effects of all my thoughts, all my words, all my actions and all my omissions on every living thing that we have shared this planet with. It will be very much a private affair and it will be very much a soul-searching understanding of what it means to be a child of God.

There won't be any group left at the end of it who will say, "See we told you all along. It is us. We are the chosen ones." There won't be anyone embarrassed except for the embarrassment that comes from the understanding of how misaligned we have been from what God was offering to us. I want to talk about that. I'm going to just make two main points.

The first point is this. I'm going to call it a brief history of the management of God. And secondly, I'm going to call it growing up, growing wild and growing God. It will be obvious what I mean as I go through it. Firstly, let me give you a very quick, brief synopsis of the history of the management of God. I'm going to do it chronologically.

In the first story today, from the Book of Numbers, 11:25-29, we have this great event in the lifetime of Moses when Moses is God's anointed prophet. But suddenly, Moses is feeling very democratic and very egalitarian and he decides to register, that is the word that is used, to register 72 more elders who will also have permission to speak on behalf of God, or to sing ecstatically in prophetic utterance. There will be 72 more who have this kind of permission. Except on the day as will typically happen with human situations, two of the guys were late so when it came to the grand gala and God was going to pour herself out in this spirit on these other extra 72, two of them were missing. They forgot to make it. But God visits them anyway and they began to break into ecstatic utterances. Someone who heard them was absolutely shocked. It was upsetting enough that Moses, who was God's anointed, had decided to share the goodies with 72 more, that was hard enough to take for people who had this tradition engrained in them that there was only one voice of God in the planet. Bad enough that that had happened, but now that these two guys who didn't have their watches and their alarm clocks set on time, they too were having the chutzpah to begin to speak in ecstatic utterances. That was too much and so they complained.

Joshua, who was Moses' aide de camp, rushed out to where Moses was and he said, "We got problems, major problems. These two guys, Eldad and Medad, you know they were registered but they didn't make it, they're back in the camp and they're uttering prophesies like everyone else. My Lord, Moses, you've got to put a stop to it immediately." It was interesting that Moses' response was this. He said, "I wish to God that God would pour out his spirit on all human beings all over the world." What an extraordinary statement! So Moses, nearing the end of his life, is finally getting it. God cannot be confined, cannot be managed in any way and God, perhaps is not even just for the Jewish nation.

What is interesting is that this was not Moses' own insight. Moses' wife, a lady called Zipporah, was the daughter of a Midianite priest, sometimes called Jethro and sometimes called Reuel. It was this Midianite priest, Moses' father-in-law, who had seen Moses go overboard trying to manage this huge group of people who said to him, "Why don't you put people in charge of the hundreds and

184

thousands and back off a bit and let God do his stuff." So this great insight was not even from Moses himself; it was not even from the culture or from the religion of the Hebrews; it came from a priest totally outside of the system, a priest of Midian. But at least, Moses had the ability to recognize and to break into maybe the most prophetic and the most extraordinary statement of his entire career, "I wish to God that God would pour out his spirit upon all human beings."

For the first time in his life perhaps, and maybe for the last time in his life, Moses got it in some kind of prophetic utterance that God is not bound by ethnicity or gender or age or even by registration. God can think outside of the box. It is not even those who just register who can have the power of God work through them. That was Moses' great hit on it. Afterwards, this prophecy was taken to a whole new level by a prophet called Joel. Joel, calling on God or allegedly speaking on God's behalf said, "In the days to come, I will pour out my spirit on all human kind. Your young men shall see visions and your old men shall dream dreams." In case you think that all that the old men have are memories of the past while the young men have visions of the future, that is not the meaning of the Hebrew. In Hebrew, a vision and a dream are the same thing. A vision is a prophecy or a theophany you have when you are awake and a dream is a theophany you have when you are asleep. They are exactly the same. So Joel is saying, "I will pour out my spirit on all humankind and there will be no age barriers. Young or old, it won't matter a damn to me." He goes on to say, "Yea, I will pour out my spirit even on your handmaids and servants and slaves." So there is going to be no gender divide nor is there going to be any socioeconomic status divide between the landed gentry and the slave class.

Jesus came 400 years after Joel. What did Jesus have to say about it? Jesus told us that our whole thinking needed to be turned upside down. If we think we have understood God, and if we think we can manage God and tell God to whom she may speak, under what kind of circumstances, and in what language, we have it all wrong. Through Jesus, God says, "The first shall be last and last shall be first. Everything you thought was true is false and everything you thought was false is true." In other words, your thinking needs to be totally upscuttled if you think you can micromanage God in any fashion. Jesus will go on and say in one of

185

his strongest statements of all, "Woe to you religious leaders because you have locked the storeroom where the treasure of God's gift is held. You have not gone in yourself and you will not allow anyone else to go in." Is that not true so often of all religious organizations including our own at our own time? Some people, "allegedly in charge of the word of God, God's conduit for planet Earth," have closed this off and not gone in and not been immersed in the mystery of the ineffability of the ultimate ground of our being, and won't allow anyone else in there either. That is what Jesus had to say about it.

Obviously, Jesus is not in favor of the status quo mentality that thinks God always writes between the lines. Sometime after Jesus, James made an extraordinary statement where he talks about the rich and the poor and social justice. He talks about people going to bed at night after they have defrauded laborers of their wages. He talks about saving up treasures until the end of the world. I think this is very true in our socioeconomic model and our political systems, but today, I want to give it a totally different interpretation.

I want to suggest that this is equally true and perhaps even more importantly true of our spiritual treasures. It is bad enough to hoard the physical and the financial resources of the world and let people go hungry. But it is far worse to attempt or to purport to have the power to hoard the spiritual resources of the world and to tell who may and who may not have access to them. To think that any organization can claim that they can hold these treasures inviolable, keep them to themselves and dispense them according to some kind of human rules, is ludicrous. It is absolute futility and absolute arrogant stupidity for any group to think that God is bound to honor any kind of human laws of the tiny, hard-hearted, small-minded minutia of human regulations that have been so much a part of religious systems throughout history. To associate God's word with that nonsense is the ultimate hypocrisy.

Peter talks about the very same notion. Peter, who was not much of a speaker at the best of times, goes forth in this ecstatic homily on the day of Pentecost quoting Joel and saying, "You heard what the prophet Joel said, 'In the days to come I will pour out my spirit upon all human kind. Your young men will see visions and your old men will dream dreams, yea, even on your handmaids and your slaves, on those days I will pour out my spirit.'" And Peter said, "It is happening even as you listen." It took extraordinary redaction and rewriting of history to presume that Peter was talking about only 12 men.

There were 120 people gathered in the upper room waiting in fear and expectation after the time that Jesus died until the time of Pentecost. Probably most of them were women. To think that the spirit came down and said, "Oh, oh, you know this is a woman, can't speak to her." To think that the spirit parceled out its power depending on gender or depending upon being an apostle is absolutely ludicrous. The spirit visited everyone who was waiting. Indeed, the prophecy of Joel was really happening in Pentecost and Peter recognized it. Unfortunately, we shut down the door very quickly.

The history of religion on this planet, all religions, unfortunately, has been pretty much the same. I'm going to take three of them very quickly, the three monotheistic religions. You have Judaism starting off with the belief system that they are a chosen people, that the chosen language is Hebrew, and there is only one revelation of God and it is the Torah. Christians, coming some hundreds of years later, said Judaism got it totally wrong. They blew it! God has rejected you. Now we are the new chosen people and there is a new sacred language. There is a new chosen revelation for all times and it is the New Testament.

Islam came around 600 years later and said, Judaism and Christianity blew it! The reason they blew it was that God did not speak directly to them. He inspired them but he did not actually tell them exactly what to write. But now through the prophet Mohammed and the angel Gabriel, we have the heavenly book. God literally dictated it line by line, sentence by sentence, comma by comma and period by period. So we have the truth. The Muslims are the new chosen people. There is a new sacred language, it is Arabic and there is a new final revelation of God and it is the Koran. We have done this again and again and again. I think God varies between laughing uproariously at the temerity of this and scratching her head in wonderment as to when we are ever going to get it. And we do it in our own times.

Cardinal Joseph Ratzinger delivered two salvos in the month that I was on vacation. His timing was great. The first one was against our sister churches. He informed us that we cannot use the word sister churches anymore because there is only one church and it is the mother church. All of these allegedly "sister churches," like the protestant denominations are not really churches. They are not in communion with Rome because they don't accept the primacy of the Pope. So we are not allowed to call them sister churches anymore because there is only one mother church. Then as if alienating a half-billion people was not enough, he decided to alienate another four billion people by saying that the non-Christian religions were even worse. He claimed that our separated brethren who used to think that we were sister churches at least knew about Jesus, but these other schmucks, God love 'em, don't even know Jesus.

What is it going to be like on the last day when these guys arrive at the gate of heaven expecting to get in? I call this the accordion effect. There is an in and out movement throughout our history where we have these extraordinary prophetic utterances that we are all equally beloved of God and that God is not interested in gender, ethnicity, race, creed, or socioeconomic status. We get that and the accordion is pulled to its fullest extent. But it is quickly squeezed back in again and we get this narrow fundamentalist thinking that "we are the only chosen people and we will tell God what language to use, what to say, when to say it, and who will say it."

My second point is this. I want to talk about what I call growing up, growing wild and growing God. I am convinced in my own study of this phenomenon that it goes through ten quick stages.

The first stage is a mystical experience of God.

The second stage is that in order to retain some kind of memory of the mystical experience we invent symbols that signify the experience we have had.

Stage three is that in order to be able to talk to each other or to think through what the symbols might mean we invent concepts.

Stage four is that we invent theologies and philosophies in order to create a dialogue with each other.

Stage five is that a community comes into being as a result of these experiences and these theologies.

Stage six is that an institution forms on top of community.

Stage seven is that on top of the institution a little oligarchy forms that grabs all power.

Stage eight is always that intolerance develops within the system and outside the system.

Stage nine is that if the institution has the power to do it, it will excommunicate people from within, and persecute people from without, sometimes even physically persecute them if they have the power to do it.

Stage ten goes right back to the beginning. Someone within the system will have a new extraordinary, mystical experience of God and the whole cycle will start again.

That is how it is done. In order to be really open to the spirit of God, we have to think beyond the box. We have to think beyond religious institutions. We have to think beyond all the old patterns. I believe that in order to be truly spiritually evolved people we need to become serial murderers. We need to commit four murders in order to be truly aligned to "Is-ness."

The first murder is I have to murder my father. I have to have the courage to step outside all the traditions I got from my family of origin and think for myself. That is very hard for us to do.

The second murder that has to happen is I have to murder my ego, i.e. the little fearful part of me that feels that I am distinct, ontologically separate from all of the other tiny skin-encapsulated egos on the planet.

The third murder is I have to murder my guru. No matter how good my teacher is, my teacher is only a temporary guide on an eternal journey. There is no teacher and there is no guru who does not need to be surpassed in my own personal journey. We need teachers and gurus, but they are no substitute for the ultimate experience of God.

The final and the most difficult murder of all is that I have to murder God, because any notion I have of God is totally idolatrous. No matter how esoteric it may appear, no matter how much it has been honored in history, it is always idolatry and all the great thinkers and all the great mystics understood that.

Buddhism has a saying, "If you meet the Buddha on the road, kill him." In other words, if you think you have understood God, ultimately, you are hopelessly lost. Meister Eckhart, the Christian mystic of the 14th century said, "I pray daily to God to rid me of God because there is no notion of God and there is no theology of God which is not made up." There is no substitute for the individual, mystical experience of God. God does not give us teachings, God does not give us theologies, and God does not give us institutions or rules. All these may evolve and they may be useful

to some extent, but there is no substitute for the individual soul
having the courage to step outside the box, registered or unregistered
and have a direct experience of the ultimate ground of our being.

25
A Time of Transition (Death)

My uncle, Michael O'Leary, is probably the most colorful character in four generations of the O'Leary clan. All his life he had been "very fond of the craytur," that is an Irish euphemism for a predilection for alcoholic beverages. Most of his life he lived in Birmingham, England. He was a great driver. He drove everything from cranes to buses to articulated lorries. There are definitely more stories about Michael O'Leary in our family than about any member of the group for the last four generations.

At one stage, he was the driver of a double-decker bus in Birmingham. These old double-decker buses had a driver's section that was cordoned off and there was a little panel you could slide back and stick your head through. One day, as he was wending his way through the streets of Birmingham, a cousin of his, Paddy O'Leary, got on the bus full of passengers, walked up to the front, slid back the panel, stuck his head in and said, "Mike, there's a party." Mike said, "Where?" And Paddy said, "Keep going, I'll show you." So he left his route completely, went up several side streets, parked his bus where the party was and said to the passengers, "I'll be right back." He went in to the party and came back four hours later and was really upset to find his bus was gone. Some irate passenger had phoned the depot and they had sent out the inspector and the inspector took the bus back. Michael got fired. He couldn't understand why.

My favorite story about him was when he was a long-distance truck driver. He was working for a meat company based in Birmingham. He was given five days every week to make a trip from Birmingham up to the north of Scotland and back. He would have an empty lorry on the way back. Michael thought that this was a terrible waste of gas, time and space to be driving all the way back from northern Scotland with an empty truck. So Michael started doing what we call in Ireland "foxers," little jobs you do on the side when you are supposed to be working for somebody else.

So Michael would carry stuff from northern Scotland to anyplace in England for anyone who would pay him. He was a very good driver and he could make his trip very easily in three days instead of five. He would pick up an order of pipes or bags of cement and he would bring them to Wales or anyplace. On one of these trips, he was in western Wales about 300 miles off his mandated route when he looked out of his window and there was one of the company cars with the company logo passing him. He recognized his boss. He didn't bat an eyelid. He drove into the next town, looked at the signs for hospital, drove up to the hospital, parked his truck, went into the emergency room and told them he didn't know who he was, where he was or who the Queen of England was.

He was brought in immediately and was kept inside for ten days. When the hospital attendants saw his truck, they contacted his company, and his wife. When she came up to the hospital, Michael had no idea who she was. They had to be introduced to each other all over again. So Michael got three weeks leave with full pay. Michael O'Leary died on Wednesday of this week in Birmingham and is going back to Ireland to be buried.

Yesterday I had a meeting with one of the most extraordinary women I have met in my life. She wanted to know if we could think of some way of honoring a very dramatic event that happened in her life exactly this time last year. Her brother and the brother's girlfriend, the girlfriend's parents and a housemate, this woman's sister and her husband and this woman's mother were all killed this time last year in the Egypt Air plane crash; eight members of her family and friends gone at one time. She wanted to know if there was some way that we could honor them in some kind of ceremony.

This morning, at 6:15, I got a phone call from South Carolina from a friend of mine who is an eighty-year-old woman I have known for many years and who is in ICU dying. She has been trying to contact her son who lives in Los Altos and he was not answering the phone and she wanted to know if I could contact him. I rang his home. I could not get her son so I drove across to Los Altos and threw stones at his windows and woke him up and got him to contact his mother. He spoke to her and he is on his way to see her. I said to her, "Loraine, you have to wait until Patrick arrives," and she agreed. That is my prayer that she will wait until Patrick arrives.

This all happened in one week. So today I want to talk about our time of transition. I am going to make four main points. I'm going to talk about death and ask myself the question, "Is death a radical uprooting or is it a gentle evolution?" Secondly, I want to look at the notion of models of body, how they parallel models of the afterlife. Thirdly, I want to look at the notion of moral development, stages of moral development and how they parallel our belief systems in the stages of the afterlife. As my fourth point, I want to talk about stages of human evolution and how they are paralleled in our notion of stages of heaven and hell.

Let me begin with the question, "Death, is it a radical uprooting where everything changes in the blink of an eye, or is it some kind of gradual evolution?" I have to tell you that, personally, I do not believe for a minute that at the moment of death everything changes radically and unalterably, and suddenly we are in one state of being, and then afterwards we are in a totally different reality with totally different parameters. That has not been my experience around death or in my meditation or in my work with people who are dying.

It seems to me that we create the stages of our further evolution by the way in which we live and by the way in which we die. We ease into the next stage of our evolution as spirit beings in spacesuits according to the way we live our lives and according to the way in which we die our deaths. It is not this radical uprooting where everything is different and suddenly in the twinkling of an eye everything is changed. I do not believe that is true. I believe that the way we are, the way we think, how we believe, how we act, and how we exit this life are pretty much how we enter the next phase of our being.

So the ways we prepare for our dying and the ways we do our living are very important indicators of what the next stage of our life is going to be. I have seen many people die. I have had the privilege of being with many people as they made the transition. People make the transition in very different ways. I remember one parishioner in this parish, and I was with her when she died. Five of us were with her; her husband, her son, her daughter, the doctor and I were there. She could not speak at the very end but she was conscious. Her last living act was to turn to each one of us, and just mouth the words, "I…love…you…" to each one of us, her husband, her son, her daughter, her doctor and me. That is how she transitioned.

I have no doubt whatsoever that that woman transitioned and what was waiting for her was where she left off, an understanding that life was about love, death is about love, and the afterlife is about love. That was the beginning of the next phase of her life.

I also know a friend of mine whose wife died a year ago. They had been separated for over a year. It had been a very acrimonious separation. This woman, God love her and I mean that, God love her, spent the last six months of her life trying with a whole bevy of lawyers to entangle their resources and their finances so that her husband would never have access to them after her death. A year after her death and a team of lawyers since, he still has no access to funds that he needs because he, too, is terminally ill and cannot get at them. What a way to transition! What a next stage of an afterlife to create for herself! With her dying breath and her last six months on this planet she was so caught up in revenge and anger that she spent all of her last days trying to tie up an inheritance to keep him from having access to it. What a terrible way to enter the next stage of her existence.

I began to reflect on how do we stay connected to people who are disincarnated and who are continuing with their existence on "the other side." What are the things that hold them to us and hold us to them? I believe that there are many ways and many reasons why people stay connected to us after they disincarnate.

For some people it is fear. Some people are so discombobulated and confused by the experience of their transition that they do not know what is happening and they cling tenaciously to what they know. They cling to people or they cling to places. You may call them ghosts or apparitions. That is one of the reasons why people come back to us. Another reason that people cannot transition adequately is because of addictions. People who have died with unresolved addictions need a physical body in order to experience the addictions and so they try to come back and hang around places that are associated with their addictions. That is another reason why people stay attached.

A third reason, in my opinion, is that people stay attached because of their concern for the ones who are left behind. They come back sometimes to console us and to tell us it is okay and to help us be brave. This happens many, many times. There is a great story about Jesus when he met Mary Magdalene after his resurrection. Mary flings herself at Jesus and clings to him and Jesus says a very strange thing to her. He says, "Do not cling to me Mary because I still have not ascended to my Father." So the temptation even for Jesus is to want to hang around to console his beloved people and it seems from scriptures that he did that for about 40 days. Forty is a symbolic number in Hebrew cosmology and in Christian cosmology. But the belief system was that Jesus, too, hung around because he was concerned for us.

The fourth reason why people might hang around is because of our need for them, our attachment to them. Sometimes it is very difficult for us to let them go to continue with their journey back to God. These are some of the reasons why we keep disincarnate human beings around us, some very good reasons and some reasons that are not so good. But for me, death is not this radical uprooting. Death is gradual phasing in to the next stage of our journey.

I am just going to take a few different models from our human experience and see how these might have impacted the models we have created of the afterlife. The first model is the model of body. How does our thinking about the physicality or our body impact our belief systems about what happens to us after death? Obviously, if you live in an atheistic western culture that believes that this is it, there is only this body, there is nothing else, then there is no problem. It is a very simple model. There is nothing afterwards. This body dies. It gets recycled back into the eco-system and that is it. So if our model of body is so poor that we think body literally means the physicality of us, then obviously our model of the afterlife is a very simple one. It is zero.

However, many different people in many different cultures and many different theologies have had much more sophisticated and much more esoteric models of the human body. For instance, in many literatures, they talk about different stages of heaven. I want to look at the Hindu model of body which for me, is probably the most sophisticated model of body that human beings have ever come up with. I want to suggest that the seven stages of the Hindu body parallel what we sometimes call in many esoteric mystical systems the seven stages of heaven, and the different levels of heaven.

In the Hindu model of body, there are seven levels, each of which is vibrating at a different frequency. The lowest frequency is vibrating in the range of 400- to 700-nanometers, in other words, between the infrared and the ultra-violet levels. It can be seen very easily. Hindus call this the gross body. This corresponds to the western model of what total body is. That is pretty much it. If you believe in this model of body as just one stage you get a totally different understanding of the afterlife. In the afterlife, people who are stuck in this phase of body, stuck in the physicality of it, of course, would be discombobulated afterwards.

There is a second stage of body in Hinduism called the ethereal body or the subtle body and it is composed of pure energy. Some people are able to see this body. We call it the aura; most of us cannot see it. It is vibrating at a higher frequency than 700 nanometers so most of us cannot see it. Some people can; they call it the aura. The belief system is that when the physical body dies and is recycled molecularly, this subtle body gets redistributed back into the universe as pure energy. If I am stuck in this level of body, then there is a corresponding level of heaven. That is a level of heaven where it is not the physicality of me that matters, it is the energy of me that matters and I am stuck at the energy level.

There is a third level in the Hindu model and that is called the astral body. The astral body is the level of emotions, sometimes called the emotional body. It is also the dream body in Hinduism. It is the body we inhabit when we are dreaming. In this model, we have a different kind of body when we dream. When you find yourself in the middle of Africa in your dream, it is not that you are just imagining it; you are there in a different level of your body, in your astral body, in your dream body. If this is how far my thinking goes, then the corresponding stage of an afterlife would be a place where there are emotional attachments. This would be a phase of my growth. It is the phase of heaven, according to my thinking, where we encounter our beloved ones. We want to know that when we die father, mother, grandmother, or Uncle Michael is going to be there to welcome us. It is the emotional attachment to family and associations that is another level of heaven. It is a phase, but if I get stuck in it, then I am stuck in it for a period of time. That is my model of heaven.

There is a fourth level of body in the Hindu model that is called the mental body. It is the place of ratiocination, the place of cognition, the place of thinking thoughts. This is the level of body where we create the perceptional world or our reality. If I get stuck at this level of my evolution in the afterlife, this is the place I am going to encounter either monsters or angels. If I choose to get stuck in that place for a period of time that would be my experience of heaven or hell, the monsters or the angels which are my mental perceptions and cognition of what reality is.

There is a fifth level of body for the Hindus called the causal body. It is the first truly transpersonal dimension of the human being. This is the place in which psychic abilities reside, precognition, psychokinesis, mental telepathy, clairvoyance, and all those kinds of things. If I am stuck at that level of body then the afterlife would be a place of magic for me. It would be a place of extraordinary gifts and there is nothing wrong with any of these levels except that none of them is complete. These are all transitional phases. Sometimes we get stuck at that level and that is what heaven means to us. It means a place where miracles happen every day and psychic abilities are the norm.

There is a sixth level of body in the Hindu system called the Atman or individual soul. It is much higher, obviously, than the other five. If we create heavens in which Atman would be the end, then we have the Christian model of heaven. The Christian model is that we are all discrete, ontologically separate entities sitting in concentric circles with harps or flutes or clarinets around a divinity in the middle that we are adoring. That is as high as it gets and that is a beautiful model. But it is not the final story in my opinion.

There is a seventh level of body in Hinduism called Brahma, cosmic consciousness or universal soul. There are many names for it. This is the realization that ultimately, everything else is a dream. It is simply God dreaming her dream. It is God creatively making this extraordinary dream and casting it with these extraordinary individuals who interact in these extraordinary dramas until finally the players in the drama get it that the illusion is that they are real or separate and that ultimately there is only God loving God. When we create that model of heaven, then ultimately there is only God, however we define God. That was my second point.

Thirdly, if I were to take a model of human development based on our moral evolution, here is what heaven and hell might begin to look like or the afterlife might begin to look like. According to Lawrence Kohlberg the famous psychologist at Harvard University, there are six stages of moral evolution. They are broken into three basic categories. The first category has to do with egocentric thinking. When a child keeps the rules either because he is afraid of being punished or he wants to get rewarded, I call that egocentric moral thinking. It is moral thinking based on the notion of reward and punishment for me, myself. When we are at that stage of moral evolution as a group of people or as individuals that is the kind of heaven and hell that we create, in my opinion. That has been the model of heaven and hell that we have created very often in the Christian religion; the idea that salvation is an individual matter and that the afterlife is a place where individuals are either rewarded with heaven or punished with hell.

Part of the reward of heaven, according to the medieval Christian church in its disgusting corruption of the teaching of Jesus, was that the beauty of heaven was that we got to have ringside seats to look down to see the suffering of the damned in hell. I cannot think of anything more disgusting, anything more at variance with the teaching of Jesus, but this was the teaching of medieval Christianity. This is a model of heaven based totally on Stage One and Stage Two model of moral evolution, i.e., the idea of individual reward or individual punishment.

When we move on in our moral evolution we enter the second great category that you could call ethno-centric moral thinking. I am thinking not just of myself as an individual. I am behaving because I do not want my group to be punished or I want my group to be rewarded, the idea of "my country right or wrong" or "my religion right or wrong." When we are stuck at that stage or that phase of moral evolution, we create corresponding heavens and hells. The heavens in that model look like places in which there are chosen groups. We are Jews and therefore are especially beloved of God and as a group God loves us and does not give a damn about anyone else. Or Christianity has pushed Judaism out and we are the new chosen people of God and in order to get to heaven you have to belong to the Christian family. That is moral thinking and that is theological thinking based on that stage of moral evolution. Any group that thinks it is special in God's eyes and thinks that membership in this group qualifies anyone for some kind of reward in the afterlife is stuck in the second great phase of moral evolution.

The third great stage of moral evolution is what might be called eco-centric moral thinking. It is thinking of the entire system, all sentient life forms; every butterfly that has ever lived, every dinosaur that has ever died, that all of these participate and that no one can be saved until everyone is saved. In that model of heaven or hell, there is no possibility of ultimate merging with God until all of my brothers and sisters have come to the realization that only love is real. This is the level at which some people will take a bodhisattva vow to keep coming back again and again until every living being has tasted the essence of God. This is the model of heaven that comes from such a style of our moral evolution.

The final point I want to make is this. I want to take a model of the evolution of the whole species, again borrowing from Hinduism, and see how heaven or hell might parallel that thinking. I want to make this statement first. Purgatory, in the Christian thinking, is an extraordinarily beautiful teaching. It is the realization of the fact that our on-going evolution continues long after we are incarnate beings. We step through various levels of understanding of ultimate reality dispensing one at a time with all of the illusions of our physicality, emotionality, intellectuality, personality, Atman or whatever. Purgatory represents, in some sense, that entire process. Whether it happens through reincarnation onto this planet or happens in a disincarnate form is not that important. It has to do with having the courage to face the illusions and going beyond them. The illusions are myriad in our world and they are getting to be more and more seductive.

I came to an extraordinary conclusion as I was thinking about this. I realized this morning that there are more people who have never died in the 20th century than there are people who have died in the 20th century. Therefore, you can be forgiven for thinking that this generation is never going to die. There are more people on planet Earth in the year 2000 who have never died than there are people who have died in the previous 100 years. The population of planet Earth in the year 1900 was one and a half billion people. The population of planet Earth in the year 1960 was double that. It was three billion people. The population of the planet Earth in the year 2000 is six billion people. So if the life span is roughly 75 years for human beings living now, then statistically speaking, it is a fact that there are many more people who have never died than there are people who have died in the 20th century. That allows us the illusion of thinking we are the lucky ones. We are the ones who are never going to die. It is as if death was a bad thing, or birth was a bad thing, or somehow our existence in the womb is the ultimate paradise. As if the womb of planet Earth and the physicality of us are the ultimate destinies, and that there was not some place beyond in our evolution, so we can be forgiven for buying into the illusion that this is the lucky generation that will never see death. This would be a very unlucky generation if that were true because the result would be that you would never really see life. We would be stuck and fixated at a very primary level of our ongoing evolution back to God. So what does that model look like if you accept that?

Hinduism teaches that in our continued evolution as a species and as individuals within the species we step through four wants. The first one is sensuality. The second is power. The third one is service. The fourth one is what we call Sat, Chit, Ananda or Moksha, ultimate liberation. Sensuality is the belief system that the ultimate reward or the ultimate sense of well being has to do with gratifying all our sensual needs whether it is food, wine or sexuality. Hinduism says all of those are beautiful, every one of them is beautiful. It even teaches you a way to appreciate good wine or many ways of making love that are even more exotic than anything you have ever dreamed of, but the point is that ultimately the realization comes through that it is not finally satisfying. If all you believe in is Stage One, what kind of heaven and hell will you create? We see in the Koran that the notion of heaven is this earthly paradise where there is lavish food, great girls, lovely palm trees, and a shaded oasis. If that is our expectation, that sensuality is as good as it gets, then heaven is a place of sensuality and that is as good as it gets.

Stage two however, in the Hindu model, is power and privilege. Once you have realized that ultimately sensual pleasure does not really cut it for all time, you need something more and that is the sense of privilege or power or prestige. Hinduism says there is nothing wrong with that. If you can exercise power, privilege and prestige in a moral way, there is absolutely nothing wrong with it. But ultimately you will realize that that too palls. What happens if you are stuck at that level? You create a John and James model of heaven. Here are John and James coming to Jesus (they are his cousins), and they say to him, "We want you to grant whatever we ask of you." Jesus says, "What do you want." They say, "We want that when you come into your kingdom, one of us will sit on your right and the other on your left." Their model of heaven is a place of power, privilege and prestige. That is as far as they go. Jesus very quickly debunks that for them.

The third stage in our continuing evolution as a species is the place of service. In Hinduism, it says that once you realize that

200

sensuality does not do it for you and even power and prestige do not ultimately do it for you, then you come into a place of service. You begin to realize that you need to be of service to all your brothers and sisters. This may look like the end of the process. It is not. What does heaven look like in that model? It is a place where we are all looking out for each other. It seems to be Jesus' teaching. He says, "The one who wants to be the first among you must become the servant of all." That looks like the ultimate teaching of Jesus. It is not. It is only stage three of the model.

The final part of the teaching of Hinduism is the Sat, Chit, Ananda which has to do with total being, supreme consciousness and moksha which is ultimate liberation. That is the final stage. What does heaven look like in that model? It is another teaching of Jesus at the end of his life when Jesus had fully evolved. It was the Jesus who was able to say, "I and the Father are one." There is no need for a physical body and sensuality. There is no need for mental or emotional body and power and prestige. There is not even a need for Atman in individual service to anybody else. There is ultimately only God loving God. Then, with Jesus, every single one of us can say without any hubris whatsoever; the Father and I are one.

26
Role and Identity

Most of you probably lived here at the time, maybe even one or more of you were students and well aware of the experiment or maybe even took part in it. Certainly all of you who live in Palo Alto have probably heard of it. I'm talking about a very famous or a very infamous, depending on how you choose to look at it, experiment that was conducted by a social psychologist at Stanford University, Philip Zimbardo.

In the summer of 1971, Zimbardo set up this extraordinary experiment. He took over one of the basement floors in the Psychology Department of Stanford University and converted it into cells for prisoners, rooms for guards and a place for solitary confinement called, "the hole." He advertised in two local newspapers for people to volunteer. They would be paid 15 dollars a day for taking part in this experiment that was supposed to run for two weeks.

There were many interested applicants and he screened them very carefully. He ran the applicants through a battery of physiological and psychological tests to make sure they met his qualifications. He chose 21 men for his experiment. He randomly divided them into two groups. Ten of them would be the prisoners and eleven would be guards. The ten prisoners had to live in the cells for 24 hours a day for two weeks. They were given just a smock and rubber sandals to wear and their ankles were chained.. They were allowed no freedom whatsoever. They had an exercise yard where they exercised once a day. They had no right to leave the place. They could receive visitors twice a week. They were given a toothbrush, tooth paste, towels, and bed linens. They had no right whatsoever to any kind of privacy.

The 11 guards were given uniforms, night sticks, a whistle and dark reflective sun glasses so that the prisoners could not see their eyes. The rules were that the guards could visit their will upon the prisoners. The guards worked eight hours a day and then they were free to go home. The rules were that the prisoners had to know how to behave themselves. They would be rewarded or punished according to their behavior.

Within three days, five of the prisoners told Zimbardo that they could not take it any more and dropped out. The other five stayed. At the end of six days, Zimbardo dropped the experiment because of what he witnessed. Both the prisoners and the guards got so totally into their roles that the five remaining prisoners evidenced all the signs of chronic depression and the guards evidenced all the signs of being out and out sadists.

He advertised very widely what had happened and he got lambasted by the press and by the other psychologists for the experiment. Most people claimed that he did not screen the participants very well, which was not true. The single biggest finding, according to Zimbardo, was that people very quickly identify with roles. If you create a system of roles and rules and people buy into that system, most people very quickly become the role they are given.

That is what I want to talk about today. I want to make three main points. I want to talk about the difference between role and identity and the confusion between role and identity. Secondly, I want to talk about what I am going to call a partial God and then thirdly, I want to ask myself the question: Incarnation, why? So I will start with my first point.

I want to talk about the difference and the confusion between role and identity. Most of us, throughout our lives buy into roles. It seems to be part of our culture and our socialization process. As I watch a child unfold developmentally, it is interesting to see that when the ego begins to constellate somewhere between 12- and 18-months the first notion of identity that the child acquires is the idea of a personal name. Children identify with their names and it is very important to them. It is very upsetting to them if you cannot remember their name. And it seems like a game to an adult, but it is really serious to a child.

A child has struggled for a year and a half to try to find a sense of self. It takes 12- to 18-months of psychic evolution for a child to create the idea of identity. It centers around the notion of a personal name. That is the first test of identity that we have. Subsequently, we begin to identify with relationships. "Who are you?" "I'm Patrick ÓLaoire's son, or I'm Séamus ÓLaoire's brother." So we begin to identify ourselves according to our relationships. At a subsequent stage of our evolution, we begin to identify with our vocations. "Who are you?" "I'm a policeman."

"Who are you?" "I'm the school janitor." As if that explains the essence of who we are, particularly the relationships and jobs we do. These are both roles. And it becomes so easy for us to identify with roles and that creates problems.

I think perhaps the most important question Jesus ever asked in his entire life is recorded in the three synoptic gospels. It is a story of Jesus on the road to Caesarea Philippi. He is walking a few paces ahead of his disciples. He is obviously deep in thought, and he turns around suddenly and he lets them catch up with him and he says, "Who do people say that I am?" And they said, "Some people say that you are John the Baptist come back from the dead. Some people say that you are Elijah. Some people say you are one of the old Hebrew prophets come back from the dead." And Jesus said, "Okay, that's what the people who don't know me say. You've been with me for three years; who do you say that I am?" Then Peter gave an answer. But there is a third question that is not addressed in the gospel and which I believe Christ was working on during the lead up to those two first questions and it was a question Christ was asking of himself. "Who do I believe myself to be?" And it is the single most important question I will ever ask of myself. "Who do I believe myself to be?" Because if I keep coming up with the wrong answer for that, if I keep coming up just with a name, or I just keep coming up with relationships or I just keep coming up with jobs I do, I will never really make progress.

There is a great teaching in Hinduism; it is called Sat, Chit, Ananda. It is the equivalent of the Christian trinity. It is the notion of being, knowing and bliss in Hinduism. Or it is the notion Father, Son and Spirit in the Christian dispensation. It is the notion that every one of us has existence. We are. Most of us have no clue who we are. And those of us who go to the trouble to find out who we are don't particularly like what we find. The model of trinity is not just an esoteric theological concept. It is an extraordinary pragmatic blueprint for psychological evolution. You are. You have no choice over it. Do you know who you are? And when you find out who you are, can you love who you find yourself to be? Because it is only by loving who I am that I can become that of which I am capable. The trinity or Sat, Chit, Ananda, is about asking myself the questions, "Who am I really?" and, "Can I love myself and grow from where I am?"

The problem is we are constantly seduced into believing we are our different roles. Roles are very important. It is very important when you go into a shop that you know how the green grocer is going to behave. It is very important when you go into a hospital that you know how the doctor is going to behave. It is very important when you climb into a bus that you know how the driver is going to behave. I am not saying that roles are not important, they are very important. But when we identify essence with roles we get into trouble. This is the whole point, it seems to me, of the extraordinary parable in which Jesus tells about the Pharisee and the Publican. He talked about humility and he said, "Those who exalt themselves will be humbled and those who humble themselves will be exalted." What is humility about? Humility is not some kind of self-deprecating attitude towards life. Humility is about ego management and role recognition. Humility is about truth. Therefore, when Jesus talked about prayer he said, "Real prayer is what aligns me with essence rather then confuses me with roles." That is the whole point, it seems to me, of this story. Prayer and humility are about aligning myself with essence rather than confusing myself with any roles that I might play.

My second point is about a partial God. Do you believe in a partial God? By partial, I mean a God who is not really God or by partial I mean a God who favors one group over the other. Obviously, God, the ineffable ground of our being, cannot possibly be partial in any sense of the word. That kind of God cannot be a small entity or a part entity and neither can that kind of God favor one group over another. This God, in my opinion, neither defers to nor despises the rich, neither favors nor rejects the poor. In fact, I would say, if there is one kind of attribute of God, anthropomorphically speaking, that I might attribute to the ultimate ground of our being, I would say it is role-less-ness, that God is ultimate role-less-ness.

There is a fabulous story in the Hebrew Scriptures from Chapter Three of the Book of Exodus, where Moses has a theophany of God and the burning bush. God wants to send him back to Egypt to liberate the children of Israel and Moses wants to know who it is that is sending him. And Moses says to God; "Can you identify yourself, so that when I go back and I tell the people of Israel that God has sent me and they ask me which God am I talking about, how am I to identify you?" God answered in Hebrew which is mistranslated into English as, "I am who I am," or "I am that I am." There is no present tense of the verb "to be" in Hebrew. We get around it by the technique called predication without a verb, but strictly speaking, there is no present tense of the verb "to be" in Hebrew. What God actually said was, "I will be who I will be." In other words, he is telling Moses I am role-less; I am not confined to any particular modality. I will be whatever the situation demands of me. And so, for me, God is ultimate role-less-ness. In other words, God can choose to operate in any modality in which he sees fit.

My third point is this: What is the purpose of incarnation? Incarnation, why? Why, in God's name, would any spirit being in its right mind want to come onto planet Earth? The answer, I believe, is for the same reason that anyone would want to go backpacking. Why would anyone in his right mind want to leave hot and cold running water, color TV, water bed, microwave oven, and walk into the boonies, sleep on the ground, get bitten by mosquitoes, have to cook outside, and freeze to death? Why would you do it? Because in doing so you develop a kind of resiliency and kind of ability to harmonize with nature that you didn't even suspect you had until you began this experiment.

That is why, in my belief system, we incarnate. As spirit beings without incarnation we have none of the limitations we experience on planet Earth. Therefore, we cannot break through any prejudices because the prejudices have not arisen. As soon as I decide to become a human being, I have to make choices; am I going to be born male or female, am I going to be born into a rich or poor family, have an IQ of 180 or 85? Am I going to be born Catholic or Protestant; yellow, black, brown or red? I have to take on all of these self-limiting choices. Why would I do it? Because it is only by self-limiting that I can discover prejudices and it is only by discovering prejudices that I can go beyond prejudice. People who have not met prejudice are people who have not broken through prejudice. The trouble is that when we meet prejudices we often get stuck there. There is a difference between someone who has not yet met a prejudice and someone who is stuck in the prejudice and someone who has gone beyond prejudice. Incarnation is the invitation to go beyond prejudices. That is the whole point of our being on this planet, in my opinion.

We are here because each one of us is on a mission, a unique God-given mission. There are extraordinary paradoxes in this mission; it seems to me, because, in some sense, the artifacts of my birth, ethnicity, gender, socioeconomic status or my denominational affiliation, are total accidents. I could just as easily have been born this time female and black and Muslim as I was born male and Irish and Catholic. Just as easily, so in some sense, they are total accidents. So why should I get stuck in the prejudices of being male and Irish and Catholic?

On the other hand, it is not merely accidental that I chose these because they best suited the mission I was setting myself. Here is the paradox; that birth circumstances are totally accidental, it could have been any one constellation or any other configuration, but, on the other hand, these were tailor-made and I chose these for myself because I had a particular mission to perform. It goes hand and hand, I believe, with the paradox of karma. Karma at one hand is extraordinarily impersonal; it is merely the law of cause and effect. It operates also in the physical domain. Every cause leads to an effect and for every effect there is a prior cause. So in some sense this is a totally impersonal law of the universe. On the other hand, it is a tailor-made program suiting who God is inviting me to become this time around. Now if you believe this in a reincarnational sense or you believe it merely as subsequent stages of the same lifetime, it certainly is operative.

I want to finish with a kind of vision experience I had. I had this image of myself waiting with some kind of a heavenly teacher who was preparing me for my next incarnation. I recognized this teacher. He was someone who debriefed me many years ago after my last Earth incarnation and tried to bring me beyond the self-recrimination of the mistakes I had made and my egocentric striving for holiness, because even the striving for holiness sometimes can be egocentrically driven. He was taking me beyond those and was preparing me for my new entry. We were reviewing what the possibilities might be and one of the things he told me was, "You will be part of four different communities."

"The first community you will be part of is the community of the self." This sounded like a conundrum until he explained it. "The community of the self is the coming together of all of the people you have been in previous incarnations, sometimes male, female, Jewish, Christian, Muslim, black, white, rich and poor." All of those individuals I had been are going to be my base community.

First I have to learn to live with that accumulation of wisdom through all of those personifications.

My second community would be what I call in my language, "Anam Chara." The English equivalent is soul mate. Soul mate in my language is not necessarily a lover, or somebody of the opposite sex that I am attracted to physically or romantically. In my language, "Anam Chara" can be a mentor or a parent or a best friend, someone who is destined to walk in a very special way with you on this earth safari. So it is more accurately translated as "soul friend."

The third community was the cohort group. All of those other beings who at this very same moment are sitting at the feet of other heavenly teachers being prepared for their next incarnation because we are going to be coming onto this planet within a few Earth-years of each other. All of these will be significant people in my life. Some of them will be friends, some of them will be family and some of them will be enemies, significant enemies.

And the fourth group, he said, is the group of all sentient beings you will find on the planet when you arrive. There would be everything from butterflies to buffaloes from earwigs to elephants and from serpents to songbirds. The last thing he said was this, "I will create amnesia in you for all these things. You will forget your mission. You will not recognize the face of your beloved. You will not know who your cohort group is and what they mean to you and you will forget your kinship with all living things because ultimately the whole point of the mission is to discover it and become it." As I hurtled through space looking for the next womb to occupy for the next incarnation I had the words ringing in my ears, "I will be who I will be."

27
The Essence of a Person

The first time I met Sally Struthers was in the summer of 1981 in Kenya. At that time Sally Struthers was the national chairperson for the Christian Children's Fund. She came to Kenya to make a promotional movie. The Christian Children's Fund is an organization whereby individual people sponsor a child somewhere in the third world. Because I was involved with physically disabled children who lived on our compound I got drafted into being a part of the promotional movie. Sally and I became good friends.

Three years later she was making another promotional movie for the CCF in Atlanta, Georgia. She invited me to take part in the movie with her. When we finished the movie Sally invited me to go to California with her. When we got to Hollywood she asked me what I would like to see and I said, "I would love to go to Disney Land and I would love to see Mickey Mouse." The next day we went down to Disney Land and I caught sight of Mickey Mouse and I followed him around for hours. I was totally fascinated with him. What I really wanted to see was who stepped out of the Mickey Mouse costume at the end of the day when he went back to his dressing room.

As you know, all of these characters are not allowed to speak. They can greet you, shake hands, smile and wave but they cannot speak to you. Unfortunately I was not allowed to go into the dressing room so I have no idea who it was in the Mickey Mouse costume. That is what I want to talk about today

I want to make five main points. I want to talk about what I call "Operation Planet Earth."   Then I will about "cross-dressing."   Then I want to talk about something I call, "I'm not prejudiced, I'm principled."   Then I'll talk about; "I really want to sleep with you." Finally, I'll talk about "Jesus the transpersonal psychologist."

For my first point, in my personal cosmology, we are here because this entire group, our entire cohort group agreed long before we took incarnation to play a significant role in each others' lives. We agreed to specific roles and we agreed to the rough outline of a plot except that none of us was given a script. We were sent down onto this little green/blue jewel of a planet and we took up our roles and we got into the assigned plot, but since we did not have a script we had to wing it. Unfortunately, when you do not have a script, very quickly you get caught into a socially induced hypnotic trance called persona.

In the Greek Theater, the actor had a group of masks that he could wear. When coming on stage he chose a particular mask to clue the audience as to what kind of show it might expect. If he came in with a smiling mask, it would be a comedy. If he came in with a frowning mask, it was going to be a tragedy.

In Latin this mask is called "persona." Persona literally means that through which you speak, "per" meaning through and "sona" meaning like sonic, sound. The masks had holes so that the actor could sound through them. That is where we get the words person and personality in English. The problem begins when you start identifying with the mask. We think that a person's personality is the essence of who he is. Not realizing that even personality is simply the mask through which we make our sound. My own definition is that personality is merely the interface of essence with the environment. It is the mask that connects the essence with the environment. We are constantly mistaking the person or the personality for the actor inside. We are constantly thinking that the costume of Mickey Mouse is going to open up and little Mickey Mouse is going to hop out from inside. Of course, it is going to be just a human person. We are constantly mixing up the mask and the costume for who is inside.

One of the most dramatic representations of this happened in the year 1971 with the famous psychology study by Philip Zimbardo. He assigned a group of students to be policemen and some to be prisoners for a period of two weeks. They had to abandon the study after less than a week because the students so identified with their roles that the ones who were prisoners became craven, cowardly and got depressed. While those assigned the role of policemen became so brutal and so offensive that the experiment turned into bedlam and was abandoned. It is so easy for us to identify with the masks and the costumes we wear.

Operation Planet Earth was the invitation to take part in an extraordinary drama that would allow the essence of each one of us to develop love, compassion, integrity and courage. Instead of that, we have gotten identified so often with the masks and costumes we wear.

My second point is this. I am totally convinced that the cross upon which Jesus died was not just a symbol of torture and death. It was a symbol of relationship. The vertical arm of the cross stands for our relationship to the transcendent, our relationship to God. The horizontal arm of the cross stands for our relationship with all living beings, i.e., all of the human beings and every other species with whom we share this planet. When you bring these two pieces together the intersection where they meet represents my relationship with myself. I believe that I cannot be in a meaningful relationship with myself unless I am in a relationship with God and in a relationship with others. If all I have is a relationship with God, I am merely an esoteric flake. If all I have is a relationship with others, I am a merely a secular humanist. It is when I bring the two together that I truly can be in relationship with myself. All love is "cross talk." So when I talk about cross-dressing I mean dressing in order to know what the cross is. Cross-dressing means being equipped to face life and to face love, the vicissitudes, difficulties, problems and successes. Cross-dressing is equipping myself for the journey to the cross, the journey of relationship to God, the journey of relationship to others and the journey of relationship to myself.

And now for my third point; as a mathematician, I always try to operationally define the terms I am using. The difference between love and compassion is the same difference between mathematics and engineering. Compassion is to love what engineering is to mathematics. Mathematics is the pure underlying language of all science. Whatever science you are doing, mathematics is the underlying language of it. However, in order to translate pure mathematics into practical science, you need some kind of an engineering modality. That is what compassion is.

Love, in some sense, is a very subtle attitude. In order to know whether or not I am walking my talk and really loving, I have to translate it into action. Love in action is compassion. There is no faith without good works. Faith on its own is absolutely useless. No matter how much belief I have in God, if it does not translate into walking my talk, if it does not translate into compassion for all of God's little ones, it is worse than useless. It is self-delusion. One of the greatest forms of self-delusion is prejudice.

Prejudice is mixing up the costume and the mask someone is wearing for the actor inside. Prejudice is thinking that there is a little Mickey Mouse inside the costume of Mickey Mouse.

In the movie, "The Silence of the Lambs," Anthony Hopkins plays a psychopathic killer, Hannibal Lector, an absolutely vicious character. I know people who see Anthony Hopkins in other movies, even movies in which he represents extraordinarily sensitive characters, and they cannot get beyond the fact that they saw him once as Hannibal Lector. They say to me, "I can't get it out of my system, whenever I see Anthony Hopkins I think Hannibal Lector, so I can't go to any movies in which he appears. All I can think is Hannibal Lector." That is prejudice. That is looking at someone and seeing that he is black or female or male, or looking at someone and knowing that he is gay or straight and beginning to identify the particular costume he is in with that someone who is inside; mixing up the masks with the essence. That is what prejudice is about. So often people who think they are acting in a principled fashion are acting instead in an extraordinarily prejudicial fashion. We are constantly allowing the illusion that the mask and the costume are the essence.

The truth is that everything about the costume is accidental. The color of it, the creed of it, the religious affiliation of it, the social status of it, the ethnicity of it, all of these are artifacts of the costume and none of it has anything to do with the person inside. Prejudice is thinking that the costume is the person.

My fourth point is this: "I really want to sleep with you." It is probably the most misunderstood statement in all of romantic literature. If I say to you, "I really want to sleep with you," the last thing I want to do is sleep with you. I may want to sleep afterwards with you, but when I say I really want to sleep with you, that is not what I mean. When I say it spiritually, that is not what I mean either, because you cannot love when you are asleep. You can only love when you wake up. As a spirit being, if you are asleep, ipso facto, you cannot love. Only someone who is awake is capable of loving. This is the whole schtick of the Buddha. The Buddha called himself the Buddha; which means the one who is awake. It was precisely because he was awake that he was able to have compassion for all living beings.

Jesus said again and again, "Blessed is that householder whom the master finds awake when he returns. He will set him over all of his property." Jesus hammers out this fact that in order to love you have to be awake. If I think I am loving when I am not awake, it is merely mawkish sentimentality or self-serving egocentric aggrandizement. That is all it is. It is masquerading as love but it has nothing to do with love.

Moses lived about 1250 years before Jesus and he lived at a time when Judaism and most of the world religions did not believe in life after death. This life was it. What you see is what you get. Moses said, "The essence of the law is to love the Lord your God with your whole heart and your whole soul and with your whole mind and with your whole self." The reward is here. Moses is stuck not in a love model; Moses is stuck in the reward model because Moses has no better place to go, there being as yet no notion of an afterlife. What did Moses promise? He said, "If you love the Lord your God with your whole heart and whole soul, this is what this God will do for you. He will bring you to a land flowing with milk and honey. He will increase your numbers. Your own personal family will get bigger and bigger. You will have 17 children where you used to have only 11. The nation will improve and increase and it will prosper." It is a model of love based very simplistically on physical delights and the delights of family.

Hinduism took it much further. Hinduism claimed that there are four great things that human beings want. In subsequent incarnations when we have lived through the earlier needs and realized that they do not ultimately satisfy us, we go for greater and greater needs. The first need in the Hindu model is for sensual delights and there is nothing wrong with that, except that ultimately it does not fully satisfy. Love of self is what this is about. The second stage of Hinduism is about prestige, power and privilege. We want to be in powerful positions and we want to have money so we can win elections or influence people. Hinduism says that there is nothing wrong with that if power is exercised in an ethical fashion but ultimately it does not satisfy either.

These first two have to do with love of self. Hinduism says that the third stage is that every one of us finally gets to realize that it is much more important than sensual delight and more important than power, privilege and prestige to be of service to others. Now we are talking about love of others. Not just love of self, but love of others. But that is not as good as it gets in Hinduism. Hinduism says that there is a fourth level that human beings move towards when they are fully enlightened. They call it moksha, liberation. Even service is not important anymore, because service is predicated on a model of separation. It is predicated on a model that you are

213

different from and separate from me. Liberation is the realization that this is an illusion and that there is only God loving God. Now we have love of God. The first two stages were only self-loving. The third one was love of others and the fourth one is love of God, real love of God. So to really sleep with someone is meaningless. It is to wake up for someone that is important.

For my final point I want to speak about Jesus as a transpersonal psychologist. Transpersonal psychology, when I was learning it, taught that the human being consists of five parts. They have since extended it to six. A human being has a body. A human being has a heart, i.e., emotions. The human being has an intellect, mind. The human being has a soul or spirit. A human being is an entity in relationship to others. That is exactly what Jesus was saying when he was asked, "What is the most important law of all?" There were 613 laws within the Torah and he is being asked which is the most important. He gives the two most important. He said the first one is this, "Love the Lord your God with your whole strength, with your whole heart, with your whole mind, and with your whole being. And the second one is this, to love your neighbor as yourself." In other words, love God with your whole body, your whole emotions, your whole intellect, and with your whole soul and to be in loving relationships with others. He very adroitly outlined what transpersonal psychology is going to take 2000 more years to figure out, that being truly human is to be fully alive consistently honoring my body, emotions, intellect, soul and relationships.

The final thing Jesus will say about love is this. There is no greater love than to lay down your life for your friend. You could think that this is Jesus saying, "I am prepared to go to the cross and die for you," but there are two other different meanings. For Jesus to go up on the cross did not mean just laying down his physical life, it meant being actually living and hanging on the focal point between a relationship with God and a relationship with others and a relationship with himself. Jesus, in some sense, was a personification of and the incarnation of the intersection of our relationship to God and our relationship to each other. That is maybe one of the things that Jesus had in mind when he talked about laying down his life for his friends. But there is another meaning, and, in my opinion, an even more important meaning. It is not that Jesus was willing to give up physical life on planet Earth because he had so much love, it was a much bigger sacrifice. Jesus was prepared to give up his divinity and to isolate himself in a little spacesuit and come onto this planet. That is the real death. The real death is not leaving here and going back. The real death is leaving there and coming here. The extraordinary thing is that every single one of you and I have also done it.

Paul in his letter to the Philippians in the famous Chapter 2, 6-11, says, "Have that same mindset in you that was also in Jesus. Although he was God, he did not cling to his divinity with God but he took on a spacesuit and came down to planet Earth." Have that same mindset in you. There is not a single one of us who has not done what Jesus has done. There is not a single one of us who did not come from God as Jesus came from God. There is not a single one of us who did not abandon our divinity and take on physicality and humanity out of love. Now can we return? Can we go back in the journey? Or are we going to get caught in the illusions of being here? To the extent that we are caught here, we are here for one of three reasons, in my opinion.

We are here because we are attached to ego and we are afraid to let go of it. Or we are here because we are attached to something on this planet, relationships, or food, or sex, or drugs, or power, or prestige or whatever it is. Or we are here because we are taking the bodhisattva vow that Jesus took. We are here because we have so much love in us that it is inconceivable that we go back and merge with God while there is a single sentient being living under the illusion of separation from God. How different would it be if you were to believe that you are sitting here today not because you are afraid to go back and not because you are attached to anything in this life, but because you signed up to come back here out of love? How would your life change if you really believed that you are here today in this spacesuit not out of fear and not out of attachment but out of an extraordinary love that you have for this planet? What if instead of saying to this planet, "I would love to sleep with you," you say, "I would really love to wake up for you."

28
Death and Resurrection

I don't remember it but I'm told that I was born in the afternoon of October the eight, 1946. I weighed in at nine pounds, some few ounces. The first person to greet me was my great-grandmother, whom I called Muddy when I learned to speak because I couldn't pronounce her name. I was her first great-grandchild, and she and I were very close. I was almost ten years old when she died on June 7, 1956. I was living then about three miles away from where she lived which was quite near the school I attended. And so occasionally after school I'd run up to her house. She lived with her own daughter, my grandmother. I remember about two or three weeks after she died, deciding to go visit grandmother, and running up from the school and coming to the front door and trying to get in but the door was locked, which was very unusual. No one locked his doors in Ireland. I ran around the side of the house to try to get in the back door. The back door was locked. I pounded on the door quite loudly and no one came. I figured that perhaps my grandmother had gone shopping and would be back in a few minutes. I sat in the backyard with my head against the window, leaning on the windowsill. It was a beautiful, sunny afternoon, as I sat waiting for my grandmother to come home. After a few minutes, something happened that made the hair on the back of my neck stand up. Someone was inside less than a foot away from me, inside the back window, wiping cutlery into a drawer, which is exactly what my great-grandmother would do. There was a little pantry and she would take a fistful of cutlery and come back in with a cloth and wipe them and drop them into the drawer as she wiped them. Someone was doing that by the window. I froze and I freaked, and when the energy came back into my knees, I got up and bolted around the side of the house out into the front and waited. And in about fifteen minutes my grandmother came back. She opened the door and let me in. There was no one else in the house!

Thirty-seven years passed and I had a second visit from my great-grandmother. It was October 25, 1993, and I had a very powerful dream. It was a very short dream, but it was so powerful that when I woke up what she said to me in the dream was burned into my consciousness. She said a very strange phrase that took me a week to figure out. In the dream, she said to me, "To me, I am. To me, I am." I had no idea what it meant. I work a lot with my dreams. I spent a week trying to figure out what it meant. Then I had another dream and I finally got it. My great-grandmother was telling me after 37 years, "I am not a figment of your imagination. I'm not just a memory from your past. I'm not just a dream element. I have an existence all in my own right. 'To me, I am.'"

I want to talk about that this morning. The first reading and the third reading this morning talk about death and resurrection. I want to make four main points. First, I want to give the context to this story about the Maccabees. Then I want to give context to the gospel reading about the debate between Jesus and the Sadducees. Next I want to talk about theories of the afterlife. And finally, I want to talk about theories of the self.

So let me begin with the context of the first reading. This is really a horrific story. This excerpt from the second book of Maccabees, Chapter 7 is an absolutely vicious account of a murderous torture of a mother and her seven sons who refused to convert to a particular religion. Alexander the Great, possibly one of the greatest military geniuses in the history of the world, conquered the entire known world between 333 B.C. and 323 B.C. Beginning in Greece he swept right across the Middle East and to the gates of India conquering everything before him in a ten-year campaign. Possibly, he might have gone right across even to China except that his soldiers revolted. After ten years on the campaign, they figured enough already. And so, at the gates of India on the eve of a great battle, they decided they had had enough and he had to begin his journey back to Greece. He died en route. Since he was childless, his mighty kingdom was divided into three segments. One of his generals got Greece and the hinterland. Another general, called Ptolemy, took over Egypt and that region, and a third general, called Seleucus, took over Syria and east of Syria.

The story today is about the eastern part of the Greek kingdom. About 150 years after the death of Alexander, the king at the time was Antiochus Epiphanes, an extraordinarily cruel person. He intended to visit Greek culture on his entire kingdom, and to do this he wanted to whip people into shape. One of the troublesome spots, as usual for him, was the little land of Israel; so, he set about trying to force these people to the worship of his own Gods. This gospel story is about trying to get a family of Jews to eat pork as a symbol of the fact that they were rejecting their Judaism. One by one, all seven children and the mother are finally persecuted and executed. The extraordinary thing is, as the children are being executed, each one proclaimed a belief in the afterlife and a belief in resurrection, except it is the resurrection only of the just. As the fourth son was about to die he said, "I believe I will rise from the dead, but for you, the persecutor, there is no resurrection from the dead." Now the extraordinary thing is, this oppression and torture, in some sense, is indirectly the work of Alexander the Great. But the paradox is that indirectly the belief of the Maccabees in life after death and in resurrection is also indirectly the work of Alexander the Great.

Judaism did not believe in life after death until about the time of Alexander. Because he had conquered the known world, Alexander created an extraordinary cultural vacuum in his wake. All of the Gods on whom all of the nations depended proved totally inadequate for protecting them against Alexander. As a result there developed a spiritual and cultural vacuum in the Middle and Near East. A large number of competing religions rushed in to fill the void. Any religion that wanted to be taken seriously at that stage had to have four basic elements. The first one is that it had to be able to trace its origin to antiquity, preferably to Antediluvian antiquity. It had to have proven that it existed before the great flood. Secondly, the founder of this religion had to have received his vocation in some kind of a theophany or a divine oracle. Thirdly, this founder of the religion would have had to be a miracle worker and then fourthly, this miracle worker founder had to be able to confer the possibility of immortality on his devotees. Up to now, immortality only existed in some cultures for the elect, the Pharaohs of Egypt, for example. And so, at this stage, for the first time ever you get the notion of the possibility of immortality for ordinary people. Thus Israel began to experiment with it as well. The very Alexander the Great who was responsible indirectly for this extraordinary persecution of the Jews, was also indirectly responsible for the hope they held out for life after death.

My second point then is to give you the context to the debate between Jesus and the Sadducees. The Sadducees were the priestly caste of Judaism. They were conservative and wealthy and the status quo suited them very well. So they were conservative possibly in their fiscal outlook. They were conservative in their theology and they were conservative in their understanding of life after death. The Hebrew Scriptures are divided into three parts. There is an acronym that Jews used for it called the Tanakh, T standing for Torah, which means law, N standing for Nebhiim, which means prophets, and K standing for Kethubhim, which means the books or the writings. So the Hebrew Scriptures are divided into the law, the prophets and the writings. Now the Pharisees accepted all three, plus the oral tradition. The Sadducees accepted only the Torah; they did not accept the prophets and they did not accept the writings. And because there is no mention in the Torah of life after death, or of resurrection, the Sadducees did not believe in resurrection, they did not believe in angels, and they did not believe in spirit. The Pharisees, on the other hand, did. And obviously, Jesus also did. And so, the Sadducees come to Jesus today with tongue in cheek, and they are going to trip him up. They are saying to him, "If you believe in life after death, solve this one for us." Now it is a double whammy when you think about it, because the scenario itself is a trap and the very fact that the law on which it is based had to be obeyed, is also a trap. Let me explain that to you. They create this scenario based on the levirate law. And the levirate law says, "If a man dies childless, his remaining brother has an obligation to marry the widow in order to raise up children to the dead brother." Now the reason for this was that they did not believe in life after death and therefore, the only kind of immortality a person could experience was through his children. So if a man died childless, there was nobody to remember his name and he vanished. Therefore, it was a mitzvah, a good deed for the brother to marry the widow, and the children of that union would be regarded as belonging to the first brother. They would honor their dead father and therefore, their dead father would have some kind of immortality for a few generations. That is the first trap. The Sadducees are saying to Jesus, "Why is there a need for such a law if there is life after death? If someone gets to live on in his own right, why is it necessary to have to raise children to remember them for a few generations?"

The second part of the trap is the actual scenario itself. And the scenario is this, there were seven brothers, one of them married a woman and he died childless so the second brother honored the levirate law and he married the widow. But, he died childless and all seven of the brothers took their duty very seriously. They all married this woman and they all died childless. Then finally, the woman also died. Now the second part of the trap, with tongue in cheek, smirking as you can imagine, and grinning from ear to ear they say, "Now tell us, if there is life after death and there is resurrection from the dead, who's wife is she going to be? She was married to all seven." It is interesting, Judaism agreed to polygamy or more accurately polygyny where a man could have many wives, but they did not agree with polyandry where a woman could have many husbands. So if the boot had been on the other foot, it would not have been a problem because presumably one man could have seven wives in heaven. In fact, Islam seems to indicate that that is what happens. For wives, it does not happen the other way around and it was unthinkable that a woman could have seven husbands in heaven. So there is the second part of the trap. Now it is interesting that Jesus does what he often does. He answers with a double disproving. He takes them on their own ground, but he shifts the argument to someplace totally different. He shifts the argument not by arguing the details of the case they propose, but taking it to a totally higher perception of it. He is saying to them, "You do not even understand what the teaching of life after death is about. You think that life after death is just a continuation of this life. That is the first mistake you make. Continuation of Earth-life is not what the afterlife is about. In heaven, there is neither marrying nor giving in marriage because we are in a totally different order of being; it is not just this flesh with all its needs and all its cravings and all its insecurities. We are in a totally different mindset where we really are children of God." So the first thing he does is he takes the argument out from under them by raising it out of a legal debate into a spiritual and a mystical debate. And then he offered a second proof. He said, "You talk about God and you talk about the God of Abraham and the God of Isaac and the God of Jacob and you talk about the great stories which you accept in the second book of the Torah where Moses wants to know who this God is who is sending him back into Egypt to rescue the children of Israel, and God reveals Himself as, 'I am the God of Abraham and the God of Isaac and the God of Jacob.'" Now Abraham had died six hundred years before Moses was born. Judaism had an extraordinary aversion to dead bodies; you would corrupt yourself with any contact with a dead body. So Jesus now in fact is saying to them, "Are you telling me that God is revealing Himself to Moses as a God of cadavers?

You're telling me that God is saying to Moses, six hundred years after Abraham has died, 'I am the God of Abraham.' Is that what you understand? That God is a God of cadavers and the dead and the corrupt life forms?" Then He goes on and says, "God is the God of the living, because everything is alive to God. There is no death for God."

So Jesus is giving His own teachings on life after death. And it consists of a few elements. The first one is that life after death is not merely a continuation of this life. It is a totally different order of being. And on that level true love is experienced. And this in some sense is really upsetting to us. Why would we be afraid of really total love? But, we are afraid of it. All of us are afraid of total love, because if we love totally, and we love globally, then there could be no special relationships in our lives or no special people. If I really learn to love as God loves, then my child and my brother or my wife could be no more important to me than Joseph Doe in Boise, Idaho. There should be no difference between them. And this is frightening, really frightening because our mentality around death and our mentality around love is that everything is limited. If I take love from my beloved and give it to someone else then I have less love available to my beloved, and if she were to divide her love with others there would be less of her love left for me. It is a poverty mentality when we think of love. Jesus is inviting us to go to a totally different order of being. And so I am saying, in heaven there is neither marriage nor giving in marriage. It is not that Jesus is denouncing relationships or the ability to love each other, he is saying, I am going to give it to you in spades. I am going to invite you into a state in which that kind of love is possible for everybody you encounter. Not special people but everyone you encounter. And most of us are absolutely scared of that possibility. We are really scared by love, by real love, by total love, eternal love and global love. Give it to us in small pieces for special people because we are so insecure. Most of us are very much afraid of love. And now the real message that Jesus was offering to the Sadducees today is, "Could you open yourselves to the possibility of a total, eternal, global kind of love?"

For my third point then I want to look at the great world religions and look at some theories of life after death. They basically follow three schools. There are schools that say there is nothing. There is nothing after this; what you see is what you get. It is a

221

WYSIWYG world. We live here and we die and we fade off into obscurity; there is nothing afterwards." Now there is a little wrinkle on this that should not in any way be frightening to us. If we really believe that, we could not be afraid of death anymore than we could be afraid of going to sleep. Because when we go to sleep, (I am not talking about dreaming, I am talking about dreamless sleep,) there is no content to our consciousness whatsoever. We cannot know we're asleep when we're asleep. We can know we are going to sleep, we feel drowsy, we can know we have been asleep as we wake up, but we cannot be aware of the fact that we are asleep while we are asleep. We can sometimes be aware of the fact that we are dreaming when we are dreaming, but we can never be aware of the fact that we are asleep while we are asleep. Now if death is that, how could we be afraid of that? The problem is we do not quite believe it is like that. Our fear around death is that it is not that there is nothing afterwards; but that consciousness survives in a void and that we are tumbling through all of eternity in this black sensory deprivation chamber with only consciousness remaining. That is what scares us. If we really believe there is nothing afterward, there would be absolutely nothing to fear because there would be nothing left to feel the fear. So that is the first group's school of thought; there is nothing after this life.

The second group's school of thought will teach us that there is life after death and it is a one shot deal. The monotheistic religions buy into this particularly. There is no preexistence, we did not exist before God created a new soul at the moment of conception and fused it into a zygote. So we had no previous existence, but we live on this planet for a period of time and then at the end there is some kind of a great judgment and we get the thumbs up or we get the thumbs down. We are going to wind up in heaven for all eternity or we are going to wind up in hell for all eternity. Now there are various wrinkles on this, but that is generally the school of thought there.

And then there is a third school of thought and it is the school of what I call the "come again" theology; the notion of reincarnation, that we come back again and again and again and again. I declared my own bias many, many times. I declare unabashedly that the third one makes most sense to me. I know that if I were God, and I could create either of two systems, in one of the systems, half of my children would wind up for all of eternity away from me and divorced from me and cursing me. Or, I could create a system in which I would offer to my children the possibility of doing life as often as they needed to do it until they got it, not just in their heads, but in their hearts that the only thing that works is love. I have no doubt which system I would create. So there are the three great schools.

The final point I want to make is this. In order to wrestle meaningfully with the notion of life after death, I first have to figure out what I believe by the notion of self. What does self mean? What is the identity with self? Because, if something is going to survive presumably it is self. So unless I understand what I mean by self, I cannot understand what I mean by the possibility of life after death or no life after death. Many great cultures and philosophies and religious systems have wrestled with this notion. I am going to take them just chronologically very briefly. Just let me mention the Hindu notion. The Hindus call the self, Atman. The belief system of Hinduism is that this Atman is like a core essence that migrates from lifetime to lifetime and just takes up residence in different spacesuits, but that there is an accumulated wisdom that is hard-wired into every subsequent incarnation. So as I stand today I, Seán ÓLaoire, in the Hindu model, have built-in and hard-wired into me all the learning and all the mistakes and all of the successes that I have achieved over all of my previous lifetimes. I am the sum total of this. This is basically emphasized in the teaching of Karma. I am the sum total of everything I have done and said and thought. That would be the Hindu notion. They call it Atman.

Buddhism, which was a reaction to Hinduism by Gautama Siddhartha who lived about 550 years before Jesus, taught the principle of Anatman, no soul. The Buddha did not believe that there was a core essence that moved from lifetime to lifetime. Rather the Buddha claimed that the human being is constituted of five basic elements. He called them the skandhas and those elements are: form, feelings, mental states, emotions, and perceptions. So those five skandhas are like five elements that come together to create the illusion of self. And the example I have used to illustrate this many times is a Lego set. You buy a Lego set for your child that comes in five basic colors, and there are four or five hundred pieces. You give it to your child with a manual and the child looks at the manual and builds, for example, a supertanker. Then three weeks later he gets tired of it, breaks it up into four hundred pieces, and looks back at his book and sees that he wants to create a high-rise building. He creates a high-rise building. The question the Buddha would ask, if he knew about Lego, would be, "What happened to the super-tanker-hood of the supertanker when it got disassembled?" Of course, his answer would be that it never existed in the first place since it was an illusion created by the conjunction of parts. Those parts have now been disassembled and they are now part of something else. So, strictly speaking, the Buddha did not believe in reincarnation or in rebirth, but in what he called re-manifestation. The five basic elements are reconstituted in different configurations in different places. That was his answer.

A contemporary of the Buddha, who lived some hundreds of miles to the East, Kung Fu-tzu or Confucius, also agreed with the Buddha in some sense although they obviously never met. He believed that the self is the illusion created by the sum of its social roles. Every one of us is in five constant relationships; there is the relationship of husband to wife, parent to child, elder son to younger siblings, mentor to mentee and ruler to the governed. Every human finds himself in those five constant relationships. How I disport myself in those relationships creates the illusion of a personal self. So the self, in some sense, is the illusion created by the sum of my social roles. The best example I can think of this is to look at a cobweb with its concentric circles of silk and the spokes pointing towards the middle and I ask you where the center of the cobweb is and you point to someplace. If I strip away the concentric circles and I strip away the spokes and I say to you, "Now where is the center of the cobweb?" You cannot point to it, of course, because the center of the cobweb was an illusion created by the sum of the spokes and the concentric circles. That would have been the Confucian teaching.

The great monotheistic religions had a different take. They believed a little like the Hindus, except they did not believe in preexistence or in reincarnation. But they believed that there was a core essence inside us, that we are animated bodies or we are enlivened flesh or we are incarnated divinities. You can use any phrase you want for it. There is a core essence inside, which is the soul, which did not have a preexistence, but was created by God at the moment of our conception and then continues to exist forever and ever.

So these were all the theories. In order to deal meaningfully with a discussion of "Is there life after death?" you first have to ask yourself the question "What do I mean by the self that survives?" I will leave you with a conundrum, a paradox, which I have just come across. It is a story from the Jewish Talmud. Four people entered paradise, Ben Azzai, Ben Zoma, Akher, and Rabbi Akiba. Ben Azzai gazed and died from the fright. Ben Zoma gazed and went mad. Akher gazed and became an apostate. Rabbi Akiba went into paradise in peace and came back out of paradise in peace. And the reason that Rabbi Akiba alone was able to come back out in peace was because he came to the realization that even the absence of God is God.

29
Meeting the Buddha

Last Wednesday morning, I saw the Buddha in a bubble floating down on the surface of Pena Creek a half-hour beyond Healdsburg, California.

Let me back up and put it into context. At the end of last Sunday's homily, I left you with a little story from the Talmud, the Jewish book of wisdom, a Jewish reflection on the scriptures. Several people have asked me about that story during the week. My story of the Buddha, or the Buddha that I saw on last Wednesday, had to do directly with my own meditation on the story from the Talmud. The story again was this: Four people entered paradise; Ben Azzai, Ben Zoma, Akher and Rabbi Akiba. Ben Azzai entered heaven and he gazed and he died from the fright. Ben Zoma entered heaven and he gazed and he went mad as a result of what he saw. Akher entered heaven and he gazed and because of what he saw he became an apostate, an infidel, he lost his faith in God. Only Rabbi Akiba entered heaven and gazed and came back out in peace and the Talmud said that the reason he was able to enter and come back out in peace, was because Rabbi Akiba understood that even the absence of God is God.

So here I am on the banks of this little river on Wednesday morning in the middle of the forest and there are two little creeks that come together. The main one is called Pena Creek and there's another little tributary that comes at right angles and it is called Chapman Creek. I sat down thinking about this Talmudic story and wrestling with it. I was watching the water, and in the turbulence created by the confluence of the two creeks I suddenly became aware that the water was generating some really interesting phenomena. There were a whole lot of little bubbles, semispherical bubbles, floating on top of the water having been generated by the turbulence. They would float along about a minute and a half and then go pop. Then there were also vortices being generated, little funnel-shaped indentations on the surface of the water, also being generated by the turbulence, and after a while, I noticed a very strange thing. It was a beautiful morning; there was a very bright sun shining and I could see that the sun was shining through both the vortices and the bubbles and it was creating images of them on the pebbly floor of the creek. I began to watch what was happening to these images. I suddenly realized that the image of the sun shining through the semispherical bubble dome was a perfect cross. You can check it out for yourselves. Fill your bathtub, create turbulence and shine a flashlight through it, and you can see the same thing.

It was a perfect cross except it wasn't just a straight vertical arm with a straight horizontal arm. It was a star shaped cross. The configuration at the top of it was very, very narrow and then it widened out in a kind of very, very gradual curve to the wings and then came back in again and got thinner and thinner down to the end. It was a perfect star-shaped cross, a beautiful cross of light in a little circle. I would watch them float down stream for about two minutes and then go pop. The extraordinary thing was that even the ripples created by the pop themselves created an image on the pebble-strewn floor, little concentric shadows of gray that would bend, even out and disappear. The turbulence was generating these by the hundreds. I watched as each one came down and I saw the image on the floor and I'd see this perfect cross and then it would disappear. Then I watched the little vortices and they created a totally different image. They created a complete circle of dense blackness on the pebbled floor of the creek. After a while as it went down stream, the little vortex would resolve itself and suddenly the shadow on the floor would just dissolve very gradually until again, it was only the sunlight shining through. It felt to me like it was a living Koan. I felt as if I was a student in a Zendo with some kind of a Zen master and I'd been given a story. Someone had proposed a Koan to me, an impenetrable paradox wrapped inside a conundrum, and he was asking me to meditate on it.

I suddenly got it. There was the living proof of what the Talmud had been saying last Sunday. It said that even the absence of God is God, and that it was the same sun acting on the same water with the same turbulence that was creating the cross of light and the circle of darkness both of which dissolved in little ripples and left just the sun in their wake. This happened hundreds and hundreds of times as I watched over the course of an hour. That's what I want to talk about. This morning's readings are full of doom, gloom and darkness, the end of the world and apocalyptic kinds of visions. I want to make three main points. I want to talk about the notion of the Second Coming of Jesus. Secondly, I want to talk about using fear as a religious tool. And then thirdly, I want to talk about images of the reign of God.

So let me start with the notion of the Second Coming of Jesus. Part of the problem for us when we read the Gospel of Luke, Chapter 21, and we hear of this gloom and doom and apocalyptic catastrophe is to figure out what is happening here? The problem is that there are three totally different issues wrapped up in this imagery.

Sometimes Luke is talking about personal death. Every one of us will come to a stage in our lives when we will breathe our last. So part of what Luke is talking about is the death of the individual person and our preparation for that. Another part of what he is talking about is the destruction of the temple in Jerusalem and the fall of the city in the year 70 A.D. that happened about ten years before Luke wrote this passage. And a third part of it is talking about the notion of the end of the world when presumably there is going to be this global catastrophe that wipes out all life forms. These three sets of theological issues are all wrapped up in the imagery. It is very hard to extricate and to know which issue is being addressed. They are all wrapped up together. The church has very powerfully used this over the ages to induce all kinds of fear in us. So that is the origin of it; that is how all these things are wrapped up together. Paul is the first Christian writer and begins writing about twenty-one years after Jesus dies. Paul tells the Thessalonian community, "Jesus' return is imminent." They wait for Jesus and many people begin to think; well, if Jesus is coming on Tuesday at 3:30, what's the point of going to work on Monday morning? And so they did not go to work any more and they started creating problems for people who were going to work.

So Paul, several years later, has to write his second letter to the Thessalonians in which he said; "Here is my new rule; anyone who does not work should not be allowed to eat." In other words, Jesus is not coming back right yet. And so the notion that Jesus' return was imminent began to be delayed. Years were passing and he was not coming back. Now in Judaism, particularly, the year 40 is a very significant number. Forty is the number for completeness. Jesus died about 30 A.D., so by the year 70 Jesus should have returned. That was the year when Jerusalem fell and the Romans flattened it and they destroyed the temple and people said; "Yes, this is it, he is here, he is just about to come back." But the year 70 drew

228

to a close and 71 happened and 72 happened and 80 happened and Jesus still had not come back. People really began to lose faith in it. Jesus, who was going to return imminently, was now 50 years late and there was no sign of his coming. And so the change sets in and they began to rethink and reconstitute their theology. Now I tell you my own personal opinion of this. When the church begins to write down that the Second Coming of Jesus will coincide with the end of the world, and it will be an apocalyptic Armageddon in which Jesus will sit on clouds separating the sheep from the goats and giving the thumbs up to one crowd and the thumbs down to the other, I do not believe in the that kind of Second Coming of Jesus. I do not for a moment believe that there will come a day in the history of the planet when Jesus will come back as a judge to separate the sheep from the goats and leave the sheep slavishly following after him to someplace where they learn to play harps for all eternity and the other guys go down to have pitchforks stuck into them in the fire. I do not believe that for a moment.

As far as I am concerned the Second Coming of Jesus happens idiosyncratically. Whenever an individual person awakens to the notion of love, that person has already experienced the Second Coming of Jesus. Whenever a community of people acts in a fashion in which they manifest love in their relationships within the group and without the group, the Kingdom of God has already happened for such a group. Jesus' Second Coming is not about an apocalyptic event. It happens in the quietness of the human soul. It is the vision of Elijah on Mount Horeb where God does not appear in a thunderstorm. He does not appear in the earthquake. He does not appear in the fire. He appears as a small still voice. The Second Coming of Jesus happens so silently that most of us will never notice it because we have not taken time out to listen. That is the first point I want to make.

Secondly, I want to look at the notion of using fear as a tool in religion, and religion certainly has used this very, very powerfully. The initial numinous experience of God was experienced as an awesome event. Unfortunately, the awesomeness of the encounter with God has become the awfulness of the encounters with religion. Religion has turned awesomeness into awfulness. It has turned the numinous awe in the presence of God into the fear of the retribution that will happen when God revisits us. There is an interesting history as to how this happened. We have constantly moved from the notion of awesomeness to awfulness of God and it happens in all traditions. It certainly happened within the Christian tradition. Slowly by slowly people began to really fear God rather than to be in awe of God. During the time before humans began to believe in life after death, the fear of God was that God would visit us in this world with all manners of punishment, and so sickness and poverty were seen as indicative of God's displeasure with us as individuals or as communities.

Slowly, particularly after the year 313 A.D., Christianity became the state religion of Rome and now had the imperial backing for its positions. Heresy and treason were the same thing. To hold an unorthodox view and therefore to be guilty of apostasy or heresy meant that you could also be killed on a charge of treason, because to not believe what the state religion proposed was treason to the political setup and to the military establishment. And so slowly by slowly the awesomeness of God began to be visited upon Christian people as the awfulness of the system. And slowly by slowly any heterodoxy or any kind of strange thinking resulted in inquisitions, persecutions and death. The ultimate arrogance came when the Christian churches began to claim the right not just to punish us in this life, which they could do, because they had the full power of the state behind them, but they could predict what our eternal fate would be. Not only did they hold in their hands the right to punish us in this life for the views we held, but also they could punish us for all eternity for the views we held in this life, and then hell really came into its own. At this stage, we are talking about the Dark Ages in Europe, the eighth, ninth, tenth, and the eleventh centuries when even Jesus who had been the compassionate, loving, healing face of the distant demanding deity of the early old testament, is turned into the monster and the ogre who will come back to separate the sheep from the goats.

Is it any wonder then, in twelfth century Europe and in twelfth century Ireland, in a last desperate attempt to attain some measure of sanity, love and hope that people began to turn not to Jesus anymore but to Mary, the feminine face of God? This is the time of the great burgeoning of devotion to Mary in Europe. The great cathedrals of Europe are now built in the twelfth, thirteenth, and fourteenth centuries. This is when the great hymnologies of Mary, great songs in praise of Mary, and devotions like the rosary, were coming into their own. And finally, in one futile attempt to try to preserve themselves from the viciousness of this unpredictable God and the viciousness of the Jesus-turned-monster, they begin to appeal to the mother of Jesus to bring some semblance of sanity and some semblance of love back into the religious equation.

We have this notion that only Mary can save us, that even the prophets are not enough, that even Jesus is not enough, that God is not enough, because, in the course of the evolution of human religious thinking, even the prophets are a problem for us. There are three kinds of prophets in my experience that we encounter throughout the scriptural traditions and throughout human history. The prophet is the person who sees clearly what is. There are prophets who see clearly what is and they are filled with fear and they are worse than useless to us, because all they do is make us afraid. There are prophets who see clearly what is and they are filled with anger at the social inequalities of what they see and they are useless to us because all they do is inculcate more anger into the system. And then there are prophets who see what is and they are filled with a deep, abiding compassion for the entire human condition. And these are the only people worth listening to, and these are the only people worth following. This is what they were attempting to make of Mary in the twelfth, thirteenth, and fourteenth centuries, because Jesus, the prophet of compassion and love, had become the prophet of doom, anger and fear.

The last point I want to make is this. I want to talk then about images of the reign of God. As human beings have tried to wrestle with this notion of our relationship to God, what are some of the images and metaphors that we came up with? I want to trace chronologically just very briefly in the Judeo/Christian system, beginning about 1850 B.C., the time of Abraham, the notion that the reign of God was coterminous or equal with the notion of progeny. The kingdom of God was about having children and the great blessing of God to Abraham was that the barrenness of his wife and sterility of his own advanced old age could be turned into the fertility of child making. So the early human thinking was that the reign of God equals progeny, the ability to be fertile. That was our first notion. Six hundred years later you have a movement where in the time of Moses, in 1250 B.C., the notion of the reign of God is about a Promised Land, or homeland, someplace where we can be secure and govern ourselves. That became the notion of the reign of God. One hundred and fifty years later in the reign of Saul, the first king of Israel, and subsequently of David, the notion of the reign of God became the notion of a royal dynasty, and would set up a house for God, and the progeny of David would create a royal dynasty that would rule over the house of Israel forever. That was the third movement. Some 100 years later, during the reign of King Solomon, who built the first Jewish temple about 950 B.C., you get the notion for the first time that the reign of God is about God's living presence actually in a physical building where you can go and encounter the living ineffable God.

Three hundred and fifty years later came Jeremiah and Ezekiel, the great prophets who both came to the conclusion that the reign of God is about the interiorization of law. It is not about progeny, it is not about a land, it is not about a dynasty, and it is not about a building. It is internalizing the law of God. And so Jeremiah would say in a very famous passage in Chapter 31 of his book; "In the days to come I will write my law upon their hearts, not on stones, not on a covenant written so as to be seen by the eyes, but on a covenant deeply recessed into the human heart." Then 600 years after Ezekiel and Jeremiah came Jesus, with perhaps the most beautiful articulation of all. Jesus will say: "The reign of God is totally within, it is not a law, it is not a building, it is not progeny, it is not a land, it is not a dynasty. It is the realization of God ever-dwelling, lovingly inhabiting the human heart and the human soul." Then he goes on and talks about the destruction of the temple because we have to break all the preexisting paradigms in order to capture or to understand the final one. And so Jesus says, "This temple that you are in awe of, where you think God's presence dwells, I tell you not a stone will be left upon a stone. Everything will be flattened." It is an invitation from Jesus, it seems to me, to constantly have the openness of mind, the openness of heart, and the openness of soul to break the old paradigms that try to capture God anthropomorphically in any one system. And so 1300 years after Jesus, the great Christian mystic, Meister Eckhart will say; "I pray daily to God to rid me of God." I pray daily to God to rid me of God because any notion we have of God is made up. All the theologies we create are anthropomorphic efforts to localize and pigeonhole God. They must all go. One thousand, nine hundred years before Miester Eckhart said that, the Buddha said it, he said; "If you meet the Buddha on the road, kill him." If you think you

232

have understood God and you have personally pigeonholed God, kill it before it kills you.

30
Seasons

Dennis McCarthy was an alcoholic. In Ireland we grade alcoholics very subtly. In the technical language of Ireland, Dennis McCarthy was at the extreme end of alcoholism, what we call, in psychological language in Ireland, a red-roaring alcoholic. Dennis McCarthy died in his early 40's of cirrhosis of the liver. As was the custom of Ireland, he was waked for two days at home. The system of the wake in Ireland was this. The person stayed in his own home for two days and on the evening of the second day he would be taken to the church. This was called the removal. The next day there would be a funeral mass and he would be buried. For those two days, when he was being waked at home, the system was that he would be lying out on the kitchen table and people would come in to visit the wife who would sit at the head of the table receiving all of her guests like a queen sitting on her throne. As you would come in you had a choice, you could either make the sign of the cross with your thumb on the corpse's forehead or if you were really plucky, you could kiss the forehead. Then when you kissed the forehead you went up and you condoned with the wife and the bereaved and then you had lots of food and lots of drink. There was porter for the men and port wine for the women and lemonade and biscuits for the children. Everyone got a clay pipe and you smoked in memory of the dead. You also had the choice of taking snuff. If you took snuff, you took a pinch of snuff onto the back of your hand and closing one nostril you snuffed and said, "God bless the dead." That was the ritual part of it. After that, there were stories and dancing for the next two days.

Dennis McCarthy was lying on the table for the first night of his wake and one of his neighbors came in and she kissed him on the forehead. She looked startled and she said to the bereaved wife, "Julia, he's still warm." Julia didn't bat an eye and said, "I don't give a damn, warm or cold, he's going out that door tomorrow night." Julia McCarthy was very relieved that she did not believe in reincarnation. She did not want this guy recycled. She had had a terrible life with him.

Michael Lydon lived in a remote part of Ireland where there are little rocky fields and narrow roadways lined with stone walls.

Michael Lydon was married to Kate for nearly 30 years. Kate was the bane of Michael's life. She terrorized the poor man. When Kate died, she was waked for two days and the evening of the second day they were bringing her coffin down one of these narrow roads and when they came to a corner on the road there was a large boulder sticking out of the sidewall. The lead man carrying the coffin hit the boulder with his shoulder, stumbled, fell and the coffin crashed to the ground and Kate rolled out. To everyone's surprise, she blinked and sat up. For five more years she lived to terrorize Michael.

After five years, Kate died again and they waked her a second time. When they put her in the coffin and were carrying her down the road, Michael suddenly yelled, "Stop." He snuck around the side of the coffin to check if there were any boulders sticking out, and after checking, yelled, "Okay, but for God's sakes, lads, watch for boulders." Michael Lyden was very relieved that he did not believe in reincarnation. He was really happy that Kate was not going to get recycled.

Today, I want to talk about nature and recycling; fall, autumn, winter, and death. What do all these things have to do with spirituality and what do they have to do with liturgy? Firstly, I want to talk about this notion of nature; nature as a teacher. Secondly, I want to speak about hi-jacking paganism. Thirdly, I will give a brief history of life after death in the Judeo/Christian model and the Eastern models. Fourthly, I will talk about conscious evolution.

What have we got to do with nature? Why at this stage of the year does the church, in its wisdom, bring all these dire, dark readings about the end times and wintry kinds of occasions. Jesus said, "Look at this fig tree. When it begins to put out its tender little shoots, you know that summer is near. Why can't you learn to read the signs of the times like you read nature?" In actual fact, Jesus was not such a hot shot himself at reading nature. This story that we just read is from the Gospel of Mark Chapter 13. In this chapter, Jesus is saying that we should be able to learn from the fig tree. When the fig tree does A, you know such a thing is going to happen. When it does B, something else is going to happen. He has a very short memory. Only two chapters before in Chapter 11 Jesus got it wrong. There is the story of Jesus coming from Bethany to Jerusalem a short distance and he is very hungry and he sees this fig tree and he goes over to get some fruit and Mark says, "There is nothing on it because it isn't the season for figs." What did Jesus do? He got absolutely irate and he cursed the fig tree and it withered and died. So he was not such a hotshot when it came to recognizing fig trees. Maybe he was a quick learner. Maybe between Chapter 11 and Chapter 13 he got his act together. Because he had learned it recently himself, it was fresh in his mind and he was able to teach it to other people.

What does it mean to be tuned into nature? What is the whole idea of being tuned into nature, particularly for a technological, urbanized culture like our own? Is it a relic of passages totally meaningless? Why should we be doing liturgy? Why should we be organizing the church year according to the cycle of nature, we who live in technologically based, urbanized society? What is the whole point of it? The whole point is that it is very foolish for us to differentiate between nature and us. For us to think that there is nature and then there is humanity, is absolutely ridiculous. We are as much a part of nature as the dinosaur was or as earwigs are or as daffodils are.

It is an inescapable fact of our DNA that we are locked into nature. In fact, we all know that every single human baby ontogenetically recapitulates the entire phylogenetic history of the human race. Every human baby goes through all of the phases that the entire world has gone through. In the course of this little planet, 4.5 billion years of age, it took one billion years for any life forms to evolve on this planet. For the first billion years, there was no life form, just iron oxide and a lot of gas. About 3.3 billion years ago, the first single celled organism came into life; then very quickly we had multi-celled organisms coming together as organs and organisms.

We lived in the sea all during this period. It was only seven hundred million years ago that sea animals developed, real recognizable animals in the sea, and it took another 3 hundred million years for those first intrepid creatures to venture on to dry land. The first land creatures came and they crawled on their bellies, the reptiles. It took us millions of more years to learn to stand upright. It took us thousands of more years to learn how to vocalize. It was a long time before we could speak. It took longer still to learn how to think. Finally, less than two hundred thousand years ago, we learned to self reflect. That is the phylogenetic history of the evolution of this little planet. Every baby does it in a few short years.

236

Every baby is conceived in the ocean. The saline content of human blood is 3.4 percent, exactly the same saline content as seawater. Every baby is conceived in the water of the womb; the ocean that the females bring out of the ocean with them. That is where we begin our journey. We begin like it began, as single celled creatures. We continue to divide and to replicate exactly as it happened originally. We develop into fish and we swim around in the amniotic fluid. Then at some stage, we break out of the water or the water breaks and we come onto dry land. These creatures that have never breathed have to learn how to breathe. They do exactly what the first creatures did that crawled out onto the dry land on their bellies. Babies crawl on their bellies just as the reptiles do and at some stage just like the first primates they pull themselves upright and they stand erect. Just as these humanoids began to do they learn to vocalize and after a while they learn to speak and about the age of six or seven they develop the hardwiring that is necessary to walk in someone else's moccasins and to develop a social conscience. A little bit later, they developed the ability to self reflect. Here you have a child in the course of about three years recapitulating the entire 3.8 billion years of the evolution of life on this planet. Why are we locked into nature? Because it is in our DNA.

We can no more escape from nature through our technology and our organization than the earwig can or the daffodil can or the dinosaur did. We are totally locked into it. Therefore, any effort on our part to be aware of that is not going against our evolutionary thrust, but it is being totally in contact with it. Nature is a primary teacher. We can no more stand apart from nature than waves can stand apart from the ocean. It is where we come from, it is who we are, and it is our destiny for our future. That is my first point.

My second point is this: how about hi-jacking paganism? When you look at the evolution of religious thinking and you look at the evolution of religious belief systems and spirituality on this planet, you find that the earliest systems, the shamanistic religions, the pagan religions and the goddess religions are keenly attuned to the cycles of nature. There is a tribe in Kenya where every year the women of the tribe build from mud a giant vulva on the ground. The men then dance around it with spears prodding it in a ritualistic enactment of how life happens, how the female principle and the male principle meet in a dance that creates life. This is a dance symbolizing how babies get generated, and a dance symbolizing how all seeded life forms get generated. There was absolutely no embarrassment in anyone about any part of this ritual.

The Native American people on this continent had their rain dances, their nature dances that were so finely attuned to the cycles of nature, which were built into their DNA that they could bring into consciousness, and participate in and make that part of their ritual. However, when the more "intelligent" religions began to form we were a little embarrassed about a lot of this stuff. We had real hang-ups about sexuality and our closeness to nature, so we wanted to dominate nature in particular. We used other pretexts, like misunderstanding the serpent in the Book of Genesis to give ourselves the power to control nature or exploit nature or be responsible for nature. We chose to see this text as conferring on us the right to despoil or to dominate when, in fact, it was an invitation to be totally responsible for nature. We have dominated nature and despoiled nature and cut ourselves off from nature. In the course of the evolution of our religious thinking we have tried to go consciously further away from nature while we carry the thing in our DNA. What happens is that we try to abandon it, we try to forget it and we try to suppress it. But, of course, you cannot suppress nature; it is bound to come out. So it leaks through. And what happens when it leaks through is that we then begin to hi-jack pagan practice and we begin to project Christian motif on to it and pretend that we invented it.

One example of this would be Easter, the most important feast in the Christian calendar, the feast of Jesus' rising from the dead. What is it? It is a thinly disguised projected image on to the Easter bunny. The word Easter and the word estrogen come from the same old English word. The Easter bunny was the sign of fertility. Easter and springtime were a time when new life gushed into being with all the prodigality of the creativity of God. We captured that. Here was Jesus who was the new gushing forth of life and we plaster and project this new image onto the old ritual. There is nothing wrong with the old ritual whatsoever. What is wrong is that we do not recognize it, and we think that we have invented it.

Another example would be that the first and second day of November in the Christian dispensation is about All Souls and All Saints. We think we invented it. There is an ancient Celtic feast that was the first day of winter; October 31 and November 1 are the first days of winter. It is the beginning of nature resting so as to prepare its fecundity for the coming spring. It was not a time of death or mourning or giving up the ghost; it was a question of garnering our resources, resting so as to give nature the opportunity to do what nature does best, revitalize itself. Christian churches took that away and they overlaid it with two big feasts: All Saints and All Souls.

Another example, Christmas, the second biggest feast in the Christian calendar; what is it? It is the winter solstice of the pagan and shamanistic religions. It is a time in the Northern Hemisphere when the sun is at its lowest. When there is the least amount of light left for human beings. The darkest hour always comes before the dawn. It was recognition of the fact that in this extraordinary dance of nature, this very darkest day was the beginning of the resurrection. We take this and we plaster the birth of Jesus as new life for the world. There is nothing wrong with that as long as we recognize what we are doing. The danger is that when we try suppressing nature, of which we are an integral part, when we try to forbid it or abandon it or forget it or actively downgrade it, it has to leak out. It is far better to recognize that we are a part of this 13 billion-year experiment in the entire universe and that we are a part of nature. We are built into the cycle of nature and we need to take cognizance of that for our liturgies and our ceremonies, rituals, theology and mysticism.

What about the notion of life after death in the Judeo/Christian and Eastern models? In the Book of Daniel we had the story of Daniel making a promise to the Jewish people at a time of great persecution when the Greek-speaking emperors of the time were trying to foist Greek culture and language and religion upon them. Daniel is saying, "God is going to reward us." What is going to happen? Up to 300 years before the birth of Jesus, Judaism did not believe in life after death. There was no notion of life after death until the time of Alexander the Great. Between 333 B.C. and 323 B.C., Alexander the Great conquered the then known world creating an enormous vacuum in which all of the Gods that people had depended on for many years obviously proved ineffective against the God of Alexander. Finally, in the shakedown process, there were four criteria that were applied. In order to be recognized as a bonafide religion, first you had to show that your religion had ancient roots, before the flood. That was the first criterion. Secondly, you had to demonstrate that the founder of this religion received his mandate in an oracle from God. Thirdly, the founder had to demonstrate the origin of his mission by his ability to perform miracles. Fourthly, this religion had to be able to bestow immortality on its devotees. This is the first time when immortality becomes an issue. Subsequently, this will come into Judaism, and at the time of Daniel about 165 years before Jesus, Judaism is beginning to wrestle for the first time ever with the notion of life after death.

How did they do it? Daniel had a very definite model. Only the good people rise from the dead. So in his model the wicked ones are dead forever. There is no spirit; they are annihilated. Not like there is a hell and they are suffering forever and only the good rise. The afterlife consists only of good souls. That was their first stab at it. The second stab was this: it was not bad enough that evil people just ceased to exist, they had to be punished eternally as well. Then we created the notion of a heaven and a hell. One group would get in to rejoice forever and the other group got in to suffer forever. The Catholic Church in its infinite wisdom and its extraordinary compassion had a teaching that part of the joy of heaven was that people in heaven actually got ringside seats to look down at the suffering of the damned. It was not bad enough that they ceased to exist; they had to be punished for eternity.

We are trying to look to nature again for evidence to back up all of these positions. Early in Christian thinking Saint Paul would say, at a time when people expected Jesus to come back imminently, "I have a message for you. We are not all going to die. Jesus is going to come back very quickly. But there will be no distinction between those who have fallen asleep and those who are still awake. Here is what will happen. When the Lord comes back, those who have fallen asleep will rise up and go to meet him in heaven and then we who are still awake will rise up as well." That was Paul's cosmology of a life after death.

I want to take all these symbols about the sun being darkened and the moon losing its light and the stars falling from heaven. For me, it is not evidence of the end of the world. It is not evidence of personal death. I do not believe in personal death. I do not believe in death whatsoever. There is no death in my cosmology. There is only life in its various aspects. There is an incarnational aspect of life when we take on these space suits and there is a disincarnate form of life where we shed these spacesuits, but it is all life. It is the life of the tree in spring with its buds. It is the life of the tree in summer with its blossoms. It is the life of the

240

tree in the fall when it sheds its leaves and it is the life of the tree in winter when it is bare. Life continues through all of those stages. At no stage is the tree dead. There is no such thing as death in my belief system.

With that model, I can interpret what these images mean when I read that the sun will be darkened and the moon will lose its light and the stars will fall from the heaven. For me, it has to do with being awake or being asleep. The sun is the archetype of male intelligence. It is the ability to think logically and mathematically. But when that is divorced from wisdom it leads to a technology without morality. It leads to the possibility of the annihilation of the species and the destruction of our habitat. That is what it means for the sun to be darkened. It means to go further and further into the error of creating machinery without moral thinking, i.e., a technology without ethics. What does it mean when the moon loses its light? The moon is a symbol of the female intelligence. It is the intuitive way of knowing. When we abandon that, when we demonize that, and we cut ourselves off from what that has to offer us, then we fall asleep. Then we have really gone into what looks like death; the slumber of not being aware. The stars that fall from the heavens are the prophets that we constantly kill because it is nicer to be asleep than be awake. We drag them from the heavens and we trash them because they are inviting us to be awake.

However, the good news is that everything that nature does ultimately succeeds and we in this valley are sitting in the middle of the most extraordinary technology that planet Earth has ever created. Is that a bad thing? It is an extraordinarily good thing. When this valley wakes up and the sun begins to shine again, when male intelligence is not cut off from female intelligence, when our intuition and our reason are allied to our cycles of nature, the technology that we are creating will be part of the evolution toward enlightenment for all the people on this planet.

I read an extraordinary interview a few days ago from Tom Mahon, a high-powered executive in this valley who gave an interview in the San Jose Mercury News. He was asked about technology and its place in spirituality. He gave a great answer. "For 40 thousand years technology has been leveraging human muscle. All the technology for the first 40 thousand years has been a way of amplifying human muscle. We have created pulley systems, or we created oars and boats so that technology was literally assisting human muscle. Since the 1500's for the next 400 years technology has been leveraging our senses. We have developed microscopes and telescopes, ways of extending our senses out into the universe and down into the microscopic world. For the last 40 years, technology has been leveraging our minds with the microprocessor and semi-conductors and computer technology. Modern technology is leveraging our minds."

Where are we headed? I am predicting that technology will be leveraging our souls, not our muscles, our senses or minds but our very souls. There will be a technology of consciousness. There will be a technology that will allow us to make an extraordinary breakthrough into the realization that we are part of nature and that everything God creates is beautiful. Everyone, whatever color, socioeconomic status, ethnicity, sexual orientation, or religious affiliation is nature doing an extraordinary thing. When we get to that place, war will be unthinkable and violence will be unthinkable because it will be God visiting God once more.

In the spirit of the old posters that pointed fingers at you and said, "Your country needs you; join the revolution, "my invitation to each one of us today is to point the finger and to say, "Your planet needs you; join the evolution!"

31
The Messiah

On two different occasions in my life I had the extraordinary privilege of seeing a magic tree. The first time it happened was 1958. The second time it happened was 1978. In 1958, I was a small boy in Ireland and at that time Ireland was in the throes of a rural electrification scheme in which they were running electric poles across the country in order to bring electricity into the remoter parts. They were cutting down trees in the remaining forest and they were chopping them up in about 25-foot lengths, taking off the bark, treating them with black creosote and setting them in the fields in order to string wires. We lived in the middle of the country and they were running poles across the land around us. I remember coming home from school, some six or seven months after these poles had been erected, and I couldn't believe my eyes. In spite of the fact that it had been cut down, truncated, stripped of bark and treated with creosote, one of the poles had sprouted a little branch and there was a leaf on it and it continued to flourish many years later. I don't know what the explanation was. Obviously some little piece of the root was left and there was this one little branch that produced a few leaves. That was the first miracle tree that I ever came across.

Twenty years later, I was in a little mission in Kenya called Roret. We used to get very bad electrical storms and one night this huge tree that was quite near the mission got knocked down by lightning. It had fallen to the ground, was imbedded in the wet earth, and the roots were still a little bit connected. And so as people will do, they began coming and chopping pieces off of it for fire wood for the next three or four months. Then one day, an old lady who was gathering firewood came with a small hatchet and began chopping at it. Suddenly the tree rose up and stood erect and she fled! She absolutely scattered! What had happened, obviously, was that this old lady's chopping reached the critical mass and she chopped some more and the tree resurrected itself. People came from all over Kenya to look at this resurrected tree. And I finally got it. The second time around I got it. The first time, I didn't get it. I'm kind of slow. The second time I got it. I finally understood this extraordinary passage from Isaiah, Chapter 11, where he talks about this stump of Jesse, the line of Jesse. This stump, which is all that is left, suddenly produces a shoot that will flower into the Messiah. That's what I want to talk about today.

I want to make four main points. I want to talk firstly about the romanticism of Isaiah. Then secondly, I want to talk about the evolution of the notion of Messiahship. Then thirdly, I want to talk about the romanticism of John the Baptist. Then fourthly, I want to talk about the notion of the evolution of Jesus. Let me start first with Isaiah.

Isaiah, as you remember, was a prince of the tribe of Judah. He was advisor to three different kings. The second king to whom he was advisor was a very young man called Ahaz. Ahaz ruled the kingdom of Judea between 735 B.C. and 715 B.C. but he was really a pawn in the hands of others, a very weak character. Isaiah was constantly challenging him to put the faith of the nation in God and not go into military alliances particularly with Assyria, which had destroyed the Northern Kingdom of Israel. It was a very trying time. So, in final exasperation, Isaiah is looking at this little wimp who is sitting on the throne and he thinks about the great King David. He thinks about Solomon and he thinks about the glory of Israel and their military conquests and he sits down and he says; "Holy God, is this what it has come to? We are reduced to a stump." And God said; "Okay, it is only a stump, but I guarantee you I am going to make wonderful things happen from this stump. This stump is going to break into branches and shoots and create leaves and flowers for all of Israel." Now, at this point, Isaiah is thinking back to the great days of King David, the archetypal King of Israel, this extraordinary character, and I want to laugh when I hear Isaiah talk about this. Because when you go back and actually read the story of David, David was an adulterer and a murderer and he was a warmonger. But this David, somehow in the popular imagination, is the archetypal Son of God from whom the Messiah is finally going to emerge. It reminds me of this regular tendency in the human heart to want to romanticize historical figures. Somehow it creates enough distance between us that we can admire them, but we do not have to emulate them. We can put them up on pedestals, which has nothing to do with the actual historicity of these people. Then somehow this glorious King David, adulterer, murderer, warmonger, suddenly is going to be the best vessel that will produce the Lord Jesus, the Messiah. Jesus is going to be descended from David, and again I want to laugh. If you know the history of Israel, ten of the twelve tribes were destroyed, leaving only two tribes, the tribe of David that is called Benjamin and the tribe of Judah. Who in Israel at the time of Jesus was not descended from David? David was a polygamist who had many concubines. His son, who succeeded him, Solomon, who came through the lineage, had 300 wives and 1,000 concubines. So who was not descended from David at the time of Jesus?

This extraordinary claim that somehow Jesus would be the special descendent, reminds me of a famous Irish character, Daniel O'Connell, the great liberator. He was the person who brought Catholic emancipation to Ireland in 1829, an extraordinary orator/politician. They say down in Kerry, where Daniel O'Connell was from, that if you were to walk any of the roads of Kerry and take a stone and throw it over the hedge you would hit a child of his on the head. He was that prolific. David was a little bit like that. So everybody, in some sense, in Israel is descended from David. There is this tendency in us to want to romanticize so we can create distance that does not challenge us to imitate great deeds but merely to admire great deeds.

My second point is this. I want to look then at what happened to this notion of Messiahship first articulated so poetically by Isaiah. What happened to it? Here is a very brief history of it. Isaiah first talked about the notion of a Messiah about the year 742 B.C. In the year 721 B.C., there was an extraordinary event in the history of this country and in the history of Palestine where the great Assyrian Empire deports the ten northern tribes of Israel and they are never heard of again. At this stage it becomes imperative that God send a Messiah to rescue the remnant of Israel. There are only two tribes left. Within 130 years, the two southern tribes are overwhelmed by the next great empire of the day, the empire of Babylon. They are taken into exile in Babylon between 587 B.C. and 529 B.C. If ever Israel needed the Messiah, this was the time. This was the time of the writings about the Messiah who when he came would be a suffering servant whose own sacrifice would redeem Israel and remake the covenant with Yahweh. So the year 529 B.C. came and the Persian Empire that had overcome the Babylonian Empire released the Jews and they went back into the land of Israel. Because the first temple, the temple of Solomon, had been destroyed in 587 B.C., they built a new temple completing it about 515 B.C. Now, obviously, it was the time for God to send the Messiah. Now they were back in their own country. Now they once more had a temple. This was the time for the Messiah to visit. Unfortunately, it did not happen.

They waited and waited and finally the great Greek juggernaut, Alexander the Great, steam-rolled the Middle East right across to the gates of India until, finally, poor Alexander wept because there was no more world left to conquer. And Israel was flattened once more. Alexander had left no progeny; his empire was divided up among three generals. One of them took control of the Middle East, Syria and Palestine. In the year 167 B.C., the Jews revolted against this and they won their freedom again and now there was this extraordinary jubilation and now surely, God is going to send the Messiah. Once more we are ruling ourselves. We have thrown off the shackles of colonialism. We are a free people. Did the Messiah come? Very, very quickly, the leadership of Israel, their own kings, became every bit as despotic as the colonists who had preceded them. In the year 105 B.C., one of the Maccabean descendents, the King called Alexander Janeus, crucified 800 of his own people who were in a revolt against him. To increase the suffering of these 800 men as they hung on their crosses dying, he paraded their wives and children in front of them. Then he slit the throats of the women and children as the crucified men watched. This was the great Messiah?

We leap forward to the year 66 A.D. and there was the next huge revolt that lasted for four years and culminated in the destruction of the second temple in the year 70 A.D. If we ever needed a Messiah, this was the time for him to come. It did not happen. In the year 132 A.D., there was the next extraordinary revolt led by a character that many regarded as the Messiah, a man called Bar Kochba. Bar Kochba held off the might of Rome between 132 A.D. and 135 A.D. and then finally, he was killed. His prophetic mentor, the great Rabbi Akiba, was literally skinned and roasted in the desert of Judea. That was the end of the Messianic dream for almost 1,500 years. Then an extraordinary individual hit the scene in the year 1666. Mostly, Jewish people do not even know about him or do not want to talk about him. He was the great Shabbetai Tzvi and he believed that he was the Messiah and he rallied all of European Jewry to follow him. He finally declared that the reign of the Messiah had come and he was the Messiah. The sultan at the time summoned Shabbetai to Istanbul and gave him a choice. He said, "Either convert to Islam or die," and the Shabbetai, "the Messiah," converted to Islam.

In our own time, the 1990's, there was another false Messiah for Israel. Many of you know about him, the great Menachem Shneerson the Lubavitcher Rebbe from Crown Heights, New York. Many people believe that this man was the Messiah. He died unfortunately, in his 90's and nothing has happened since. As Christians, of course, we know the answer. The reason that all of these were false Messiahs was because the real Messiah was Jesus, right? So they were wasting their time beforehand and they were wasting their time afterwards, because Jesus was the Messiah. We all know that the scriptures say that when the Messiah comes he will usher in an era of world peace. So, obviously, Jesus was the Messiah, right?

On today, December 6, 1998, it is obvious that the Messiah has come because world peace is the order of the day. Justice and peace is the order of the day. Well, maybe things have disintegrated. Let us go back a little bit. Maybe nearer to the time of Jesus, was there world peace and justice? Let us look at the 1500s when the conquistadors came to this country and ravaged and pillaged and destroyed with the bible in one hand and the sword in the other. Obviously, the Messiah was not very much in evidence at that stage. Let us go back one hundred years to the 1400s to the great inquisitions where people were killed and pulled limb from limb because they would not subscribe to some made-up creedal formulation of the Gospel. The Messiah did not seem to be in evidence then. Let us go back a little bit further to the 1100s and the great Crusades when the warriors of Europe went across pillaging and destroying and murdering Greek Orthodox, Muslim and Jew indiscriminately. Where was Jesus and where was the Messiah in all of this. Has the Messiah ever come? Was Jesus the Messiah? We need to totally revamp our notion of the Messiah. The Messiah is the interior phenomenon. The Messiah has almost nothing to do with the coming of some archetypal, political-religious figure who is going to suddenly create this extraordinary global paradigm that will usher in a reign of peace.

For my third point, I want then to look at the romanticism of John the Baptist, a charismatic figure who suddenly appeared in the Judean desert, dressed in camel hair and a leather belt and eating locust and wild honey. Again I snicker because I remember during

247

my time in Kenya living in the desert next to a tribe of people called the Turkana. The Turkana were great camel people and if they wore anything at all it was camel cloth. I remember reading this Gospel passage to a group of Turkana. We were talking about John the Baptist, dressed in camel hair with a leather belt and eating grasshoppers and wild honey, and the audience groaned. They could not believe how lucky this John the Baptist was. It would be the equivalent of me standing here in Silicon Valley and saying, "I want to describe to you the great charismatic figure who was dressed in an Armani suit with Gucci shoes who dined on caviar and champagne. That was the equivalent for the Turkana. So the romanticism of John the Baptist very quickly collapses, depending upon your audience.

But who was this extraordinary character, John the Baptist? And what was he about? He was baptizing people at the river Jordan. Now there is a great significance here. The Israelites crossed the River Jordan in the year 1210 B.C. having come out of 450 years of slavery in Egypt and 40 years wandering in the desert and they crossed near the city of Jericho and they took the city of Jericho in the year 1210 B.C. Then for the next 210 years they set about conquering the entire land of Israel until finally Jerusalem itself fell in the year 1000 B.C. So this crossing of the Jordan became an archetype of God leading the Israelite people into military victories. Subsequently, anytime there was a revolt in Israel, they brought their forces east across the River Jordan and then came back west into the land of Israel to symbolically reenact what Joshua had done. Between the years 167 B.C. and 132 A.D., a 300-year period, there were 62 armed revolts in Israel against foreign occupation and 61 of these 62 revolts started in the Galilee of Jesus. The life expectancy of a Galilean male during this period was 29 years. Group after group went east across the Jordan, marshaled their troops and then symbolically came back across the Jordan in order to throw out the occupiers.

John was symbolizing the same thing. John took his troops, except now they were spiritual troops who were to go back in to conquer the land, not in the same sense of a military defeat of a colonialist empire, but in the sense of a spiritual defeat of egocentric agendas. John took them down to the Jordan and they were baptized one by one and then they went back into the land of Israel

248

as the shock troops of the kingdom, the New Kingdom of God. So that was the context.

The last point I want to make is this. What, then, was the evolution of Jesus coming out of the romantic notion that John was preparing the way for him? The very first statement that John makes in today's Gospel is, "Reform your lives." Now reform is one of those words that paradoxically has been fossilized by overuse rather than under use. The word reform is almost meaningless now because we have heard it in so many different contexts. What it really means, obviously, is to re-form or re-fashion. John is asking us to re-fashion our lives. Unfortunately, what has tended to get re-fashioned mainly throughout Christian history has been the image of Jesus himself. We have re-fashioned and re-tooled Jesus from era to era according to our own agenda. Albert Schweitzer wrote a famous book at the beginning of this century. Albert Schweitzer, who most of us remember as the great medical missionary to Africa, was in fact regarded as possibly the greatest scripture scholar of the 20th century and was also an accomplished musician and brilliant historian. He wrote a book called, "The Search for the Historical Jesus," in which he showed very powerfully that every generation of Christians has refashioned Jesus to its own political, social and economic agenda. Jesus, in the words of the status quo, has been a king and he has been a judge. In the time of the great thinkers of the enlightenment, he has been this extraordinary rational character. At the time when morality was central stage in religion, he was the great moral leader. He is the liberation theologian of the current times. Every single era has tried to refashion Jesus to its own image.

Every generation has had its own use for Jesus. We have mangled this man's reputation, his image and his mission. Nowhere more traumatically, in my opinion, than in the fourth century, when, to quote an Irish poet, "A terrible beauty was born." The Greek fathers of the fourth century took the vibrant, organic, Semitic metaphors, similes and idioms of a Galilean carpenter and force-fed them through the abstract, sterile templates of Greek rational philosophy and then insisted that we give blind submission to man-made dogmas and let go of the invitation to dance joyfully in the celebration of our individual encounters with the numinosity of the ineffable God. A terrible beauty was born.

249

32
Historical Context of the Virgin Birth

There is a big difference between the wisdom of the countryside and the wisdom that you find in books. The wisdom that you find in books tends to be dry and pedantic and to depend on dictionary definitions. The wisdom of the countryside tends to be much more earthy, subtler, more sensitive and maybe most importantly of all, more humorous. I will give you one example. In my childhood I was a voracious reader and once I came across the words "spinster" and "old maid." They seemed to me to mean the same things so I asked someone in my village, "What's the difference between a spinster and an old maid?" He looked at me with a twinkle in his eye and said, "Well, a spinster is a woman who never got married and an old maid is a woman who never got married or anything." I want to talk about that. It is the kind of subtle humorous distinction that really makes sense of one of the most famous prophecies of all time, Isaiah, Chapter 7:14. This is a very famous passage where Isaiah allegedly says: "The virgin shall be with child and she shall bring forth a son and you shall call his name Emanuel."

I want to make four main points. Firstly, I want to give you some historical background to this story out of which this prophecy came. Secondly, I want to talk about the prophecy itself because the prophecy is never quoted in full. Only one of three parts of the prophecy is ever quoted and I want to fill in the other two parts for you. Thirdly, I want to look at the problem that Matthew had and how very creatively he dealt with his problem. And fourthly, I want to talk about what I believe true lineage from God involves.

I will begin with some historical background. About the year 930 B.C., Solomon died and the kingdom of the Israelites was divided between a son of his, Rehoboam, and a pretender to the throne, Jeroboam, causing a civil war in the land. The ten northern tribes broke away and founded the New Kingdom called, "Israel" with its headquarters in a town called Samaria. The two southern tribes, Benjamin and Judah, with their headquarters in Jerusalem formed the southern kingdom of Judah. This story takes place about 200 years later in the year 735 B.C. By now, the great world power is the Empire of Assyria, which today would be located northeast of Syria.

It was a huge empire gobbling up the Middle East and the Near East at the time. Two local kings became very frightened. The king of Damascus, Rezin, and the king of Israel (the Northern Kingdom), Pekah, decided that they needed to go into an alliance in order to stave off this mighty juggernaut of Assyria. They invited the King of Judah, Ahaz, to take part in their alliance.

Ahaz had just acceded to the throne on the death of his father and he was very young and very impressionable. Ahaz and his many advisors decided against joining the alliance, so the king of Israel and the king of Damascus attacked Jerusalem. But the Assyrians intervened and repelled them. So, Ahaz, the king of Judah, decided to go into an alliance with the Assyrians. Then you have the young king of Judah with the Assyrians against the King of Israel and the King of Damascus. At this stage, Isaiah comes to advise the young king.

Isaiah is very upset that the young king is depending upon military might and political alliances instead of depending upon God. He said to Ahaz; "Do not do it. Do not go into alliance with the Assyrians. Depend upon God. I am God's prophet. Ask anything of God. Ask God for a sign that he really is with you and I guarantee you will get it." And very self-righteously and very hypocritically Ahaz says, "I will not put my God to the test. I will not ask him for a sign." However, he has already determined he will go into alliance with the Assyrians, but he is not going to put his God to the test. So Isaiah volunteers a sign and he says; "Look, if you need any verification from God, that God is really with you, here is the sign you will get. The virgin will be with child and she will bring forth a son." There was the guarantee from God.

Ahaz went ahead anyway and went into alliance with the Assyrians. Damascus was destroyed as well as the Northern Kingdom of Israel and the ten northern tribes were deported and were never heard of again. They are sometimes referred to as the "lost tribes" of Israel. That happened in the year 721 B.C. That is my first point, the historical background in which Isaiah is pressing this young king.

My second point then is this. What was the nature of the prophecy that Isaiah uttered in the year 735 B.C.? As I previously mentioned, there were actually three parts to it but only one is quoted every year in the gospel reading. The first part of the prophecy was this: Isaiah said, "I guarantee you that within 65 years the Northern Kingdom of Israel will be no more." Now he was right, but he was not accurate because within 14 years, not 65 years, the Northern Kingdom of Israel was destroyed and never heard of again.

The second part of the prophecy was, "The virgin shall be with child and she shall bring forth her son and you shall call his name Emanuel which means God is with us. Do not depend on the Assyrians; do not depend on military might; and do not depend on political alliances because God is with us." Now there is a problem with this, unfortunately. In the Hebrew Scriptures the word that Isaiah uses is "almah." He says, "Almah will be with child." Now almah does not mean a virgin. It does not mean, to use physiological language, "virgo intacta"; it does not mean a woman whose hymen is not broken. It simply means a young woman or an unmarried woman. What Isaiah was really saying was the young woman whom you are about to marry (and he was betrothed to a girl called Abby), will conceive and give you a son. She did actually birth their son Hezekiah. Hezekiah became one of the very famous rulers of the land of Judah. So Isaiah is saying, I guarantee you God will be with you. Your throne is not going to be overturned. Your son will occupy your own throne eventually and he will be a great king. And so it was.

Isaiah was very definite. He was not talking about a "virgo intacta." If he were choosing to talk about a "virgo intacta" he would have used another Hebrew word, "betulah," which means exactly a physiologically intact virgin. He did not use that word; he used "almah" which simply means either an unmarried woman or a young woman. So Isaiah very definitely has nothing in mind about some kind of an extraordinary conception against all the laws of physiology. He is saying, "Hang in there; this young woman to whom you are betrothed, I guarantee you she will give you a son and I'm going to call his name Emanuel."

Now the child was actually called Hezekiah and he became a very famous king. He is talking symbolically when he says he will be called Emanuel. The word Emanuel means, "God is with us." So the message is: "Depend on God, do not depend on military might or political alliances. Your throne will stand." Now that was the context in which this was being offered.

When the writers of the New Testament approached this text, they picked up on the word "almah" and mistranslated it in the

Greek as "parthenos" which is really the translation of the word "betulah."

The third part of the prophecy in Isaiah that is never mentioned is, "This young child who shall be called Emanuel, he will eat curds and honey until he is old enough to distinguish right from wrong, and good from evil." Now for some reason the church always leaves out the first and the third part of the prophecies and emphasizes the second part of the prophecy which it also mistranslates. So the full prophecy is: firstly, about the fall of Israel; secondly, about the birth of a child who would guarantee the lineage; and thirdly, about what the nature of this child will be. This child will have to learn how to discriminate the good from the bad and the right from the wrong.

For my third point, I'm going to spring forward another 820 years to the time when Matthew is writing his gospel. Matthew is writing his gospel about the year 80 A.D. that would be about 50 years after Jesus had died. Matthew has a big problem and it is this: Jesus, who Matthew knows to be the messiah, is regarded in the land of Israel as a bastard, an illegitimate child. This is obvious even in the gospel itself. In the gospel of Mark, which is the first of the gospels written, there is a very tough story where Jesus goes back to his own village as an adult for the very first time to preach in the synagogue. The response of the people was: "Who is this guy to talk to us? Isn't this the son of Mary?" Now in the Hebrew dispensation, a boy or a man is never called after his mother. To call a son after his mother meant that the child did not have a father, he was illegitimate. Instead of saying; "Who is this guy, son of Joseph, to talk to us," they said, "Who is this guy, son of Mary, to talk to us?" So Mark is very clearly indicating that Jesus is being regarded as illegitimate. The title has been given by his own town's folk who knew him as illegitimate. So they ask, indignantly; "Who is this illegitimate guy telling us about the kingdom of God?" So Matthew, writing ten years after the gospel of Mark was written, has a big problem. The man whom he believed to be the Son of God, the Messiah, and a whole community of people believed was the Son of God and Messiah, is regarded in his own village and among his own people as illegitimate.

There are actually apocryphal writings dating from this time that claimed to know the real father of Jesus. According to these writings, it was a Roman soldier and they even name him in some of the apocryphal writings. So Matthew has to contend with this problem and he does it very creatively. He does it in a one-two stroke.

The first thing he does is to create a genealogy of 42 generations for Jesus stretching from Jesus back beyond the Babylonian captivity, back beyond King David and back, ultimately, to Abraham. In that genealogy of 42, he only includes the names of four women. Out of 42 generations all of the men are mentioned while only four women are mentioned. Every one of these four women had some kind of sexual peccadillo.

The first one mentioned is a woman called Tamar who lived about the year 1700 B.C. She was the daughter-in-law of Judah after whom the Southern Kingdom of Judah would subsequently be called. Tamar was married to the son of Judah but the son died within a few weeks of marrying her. As Hebrew law dictated, his brother then took her as his wife. And the younger brother died within a few months. At this stage, Tamar wanted the third brother to marry her but the third brother was still very young and the father, Judah, said; "No, let's hold it for a while. You go back to your father's house and when my son is old enough to get married, I'll call you and you can marry him," not, however, intending to do it. He was afraid that this woman was some kind of a black widow. She was going to kill all his sons.

The youngest boy grew up and was of marriageable age but Judah did not invite Tamar back to marry him. This angered Tamar and she decided upon a ruse. Disguised as a prostitute, she stood at a famous crossroads where she knew her father-in-law would be passing on his way to the market. She seduced him and lay with him. Then because he did not have any money in his pouch, she insisted he give her a guarantee of payment in the form of his signet ring and his staff. Then she disappeared, in spite of his best efforts to find her and redeem his ring and staff with the appropriate fee.

Nine months later, the story is brought to him that his daughter-in-law is pregnant and Judah is outraged. "How could she do this to me? How could she destroy my good name, she needs to be taken out and stoned." So they took the young girl out to be stoned and she said, "Okay I agree to be stoned except I want to return these to the person who impregnated me." She handed the ring and staff and it immediately became apparent to whom they belonged.

And so Judah realized he was the father of her child. In fact, Tamar had twins, Perez and Zerah who are the direct ancestors of King David and direct ancestors of Jesus. That is the first story. So the first woman mentioned in Jesus' genealogy committed incest and adultery and acted as a prostitute. Not a great start.

Five hundred years later the next woman who is mentioned is Rahab, a professional prostitute in the city of Jericho. When the Israelites were about to cross into the land of Israel in the year 1210 B.C., they sent scouts ahead to reconnoiter the terrain. When they came to Jericho, Rahab gave them refuge. She knew they were going to be a very strong force and take over her city. So she exacted a promise from them that when they destroyed Jericho they would save her and her household. They told her to hang a scarlet scarf out of the window of her house so that when they attacked, they would be able to identify where she lived.

That is exactly what happened. The Israelite hordes crossed the Jordan River, captured and destroyed Jericho but spared the house with the scarlet scarf. She was saved. Not only was she saved, she married one of the Israelites and she became one of the progenitors of King David and of Jesus. That is the second woman, a professional prostitute who betrayed her own people in order to accommodate the foreigners.

The third woman mentioned in Matthew's genealogy was a very famous woman, named Ruth, about 100 years later, about the year 1100 B.C. Ruth was married to an Israelite who died within a few years of the wedding. Ruth, who was very loyal to her mother-in-law, said to her; "Wherever you go I will go, wherever you die, I will die, your God will be my God and your people will be my people." And so she came back into the land of Israel with her mother-in-law. Now impoverished, with no husband to look after her, she was a woman without any kind of support. Her mother-in-law gave her some sage advice, saying, "I want you to go down to where the men are harvesting and there's a rich man called Boaz who owns the vineyard and when they are harvesting the wine, he drinks and he gets drunk. He sleeps in the field with just his cloak over him. I want you to go down and lift the corner of his robe." Ruth went down to the field and this guy's been harvesting all day drinking the produce and he is drunk as a skunk. So she "lifted the corner of his robe." Lo and behold, nine months later, she gives birth to a child. Ruth is the great-grandmother of King David. That is the third woman in Matthew's genealogy.

The fourth woman mentioned is Bathsheba. Bathsheba was married to Uriah who was a Hititte and a soldier in King David's army. David fell in love with her, seduced her, impregnated her and then murdered her husband. She became the mother of King Solomon who is the progenitor of Jesus. So as Matthew points out, these four women all have some kind of sexual peccadillo. Moreover, and here's the crunch, none of the four of them was Jewish. So here might have been Matthew's reasoning: "If you're going to tell me that Jesus is illegitimate and that his father wasn't Jewish, let me tell you something. Look at Tamar, Rahab, Ruth and Bathsheba. Look at what they did. None of them was Jewish. And moreover, since in the Hebrew dispensation the lineage flows through the mother, if all of these women were not Jewish, King David was not Jewish. So why are you worried about Jesus' father being Roman? Lineage does not come through the father; it comes through the mother."

That was the first of Matthew's punches. Then the second, the crossover punches. Matthew would argue that Jesus is not the son of a Roman soldier. Jesus is not illegitimate. Jesus was begotten in this extraordinary way. He then goes on to construct the story of Jesus' miraculous conception by the Holy Spirit. Matthew is trying to demolish all of the arguments against Jesus' right to be king of Israel. It is a very clever way of doing it. Now is it true or is it a myth? In some sense, that is not the point.

The final point is this, I want to discuss true lineage. It doesn't matter what linear descent may or not mean. I will mention three great world religions and tie the story to them: Judaism, Christianity and Islam.

According to Judaism, the chosen-ness was passed on through physical descent. God chose Abraham and it was through physical descent from Abraham that the covenant promise continues. It goes through Abraham through his son Isaac, through Isaac's son, Jacob, and so on down the line. Christianity, when it came to usurp Judaism said, you guys got it wrong. It is not physical descent from Abraham that makes us the chosen race of the covenanted people. What makes us the chosen race of the covenanted people is that we demonstrate the same kind of faith that Abraham had. It was not physical descent from Abraham that created the covenanted people: it is demonstrating the same kind of faith that Abraham had. So Christianity is trying to usurp Judaism.

Finally, six hundred years after Christianity, we come to Islam. The Muslims will say that if the Jews claim descent through physical means and the Christians claim it through faith, they, the Muslims, have both bases covered because they rightly point out that Isaac was not the first child of Abraham. Abraham had a child before Isaac who was called Ishmael. He was born of an Egyptian slave woman and he was several years older than Isaac. If you are going to speak about linear descent and first- born, we Muslims have the right because we are descended from the first-born child of Abraham. And if you Christians claim that it is faith that makes the covenanted people, then our very name is faith. The word Islam comes from the notion of total submission to God. And they say, in effect, Abraham was the first Muslim. Abraham was the first faith-filled person, demonstrably, within the scriptural traditions of the peoples of the book, Judaism, Christianity, and Islam. He is the first person to totally prostrate himself and to submit to God. So Abraham was the first Muslim.

Now I think, in some sense, the Muslims have it right. It is perhaps the best articulation of the three because what they are pointing out is that it is an attitude of submission to God that puts us in the lineage and makes us people of the covenant. It is not about miracles, it is not about extraordinary births or extraordinary conceptions, it is not about the miracles attendant upon the signs and wonders of my coming or my going; it is about being in alignment with the law of God and the love of God.

And so the story of Jesus and the story of Christmas are not primarily about shepherds. It is not primarily about angels; it is not about miraculous signs. It is not about demonstrating that Jesus was or was not illegitimate or Jesus was or was not the Son of God in any fashion. It is about demonstrating the same kind of absolute trust and submission. It is about alignment with is-ness, alignment with the God who plays no favorites.

If we think God looks down on this vast universe of ours with its one hundred billion galaxies and picks the Milky Way as his favorite, and if we think that he further chooses within that galaxy our sun with its nine planets, and if we think he then chooses our planet as his favorite and from our planet he picks out one special group of people to love, if we think that is who God is, we do not know God. God is the God of all. God is the God who is neither Christian nor Jew nor Muslim. God is the God who favors neither daffodils above dinosaurs nor earwigs above elephants nor humans above fruit flies.

God is a God whose creation is a delightful dance and when we are in alignment with that, then the Christmas story is primarily about standing in the lineage of alignment with God.

33
Independence

He was born on the 10th of September in the year 1882. His father's name was Timothy Murphy and his mother's maiden name was Margaret Riordan. They called him James. When I got to know him, I had a different name for him. I called him Daddy Jim. Daddy Jim was my maternal grandfather. He was the youngest of seven children. When Daddy Jim was a young man, there wasn't a lot to do by way of employment except to join the British army. Three of his elder brothers joined the British army. But Daddy Jim decided to fight for Irish independence and so he was ousted from his own home and he had to go to another city, Galway, where he joined the IRA and took part in the freedom fight for Ireland that finally finished in the year 1922.

For four years he was what we called, "on the run," no place to call home, because the British troops and the Black and Tans were looking for the freedom fighters. Ireland got its freedom in 1922 and my grandfather married the year after, November 5, 1923. He was a most amiable man. He was a great dancer and a great musician and I rarely saw him get annoyed.

There was only one topic that annoyed him on a regular basis. That was the idea that people should be given pensions for having fought for Irish independence. When the Irish government instituted the IRA pension to reward all those who had fought for Irish independence it really annoyed him. He refused to apply for it. What really annoyed him was that two men from his village of Blarney applied for the IRA pension and he used to tell a story about them. He claimed that the only thing these two guys did in the struggle for Irish independence was one night they hijacked the train from Dublin to Cork that was carrying casks of Guinness. They stopped the train at gunpoint and while one guy was holding up the train driver, the other guy took a few barrels of Guinness, and rolled them off the train. They let the train go on and they hid the casks of Guinness in a ditch with the spout sticking out and, according to my grandfather, every night they'd go and lie on their backs with the faucet over their mouths and turn the faucets on. And that's how they spent the fight for Irish independence, getting drunk on a nightly basis on Guinness hijacked from a train. Then they had the chutzpah to apply for an IRA pension for having fought for Irish independence and that really annoyed my grandfather.

I want to talk about the difference between the fight for independence and the exercising of independence. I want to make three main points. The first one is this: I want to talk about the promise and the disappointments. Then I want to talk about the notion of chosen-ness. Then finally, I want to talk about what is really the word of God for us.

So first let me talk about the notion of promise and disappointment. This first reading today is from the Prophet Isaiah. There were three prophet Isaiahs actually. The book of Isaiah is one of the longest books in scripture: 66 chapters long. It is written at three different times in Jewish history. The prophet Isaiah who was a prince of Judah and flourished around 750 years before Jesus wrote the first 39 chapters. The second section of the book, Chapters 40 through 55, was written during the Babylonian exile when the two remaining tribes of Israel were taken into exile by Babylon. The third section of the book, Chapters 56 through 66, was written after the exile.

The piece we hear this morning is written after the exile. The remaining Israelites, who survived 70 years in captivity, were freed by the Persian Empire that had overthrown the Babylonian Empire. Of those who had survived, however, only a small minority actually chose to go back to the land of Israel. After 70 years, when they returned and found their country in chaos, their city in ruins, the temple gone, and the fields over-grown, they were disheartened. So this prophet, Isaiah, the third Isaiah, tried to appeal to them that God was still with them and that God would deliver on his promises and not to lose heart. But they began to see that the promise was very different from the realization. The fight for independence looked very different from the exercise of independence.

We all know that it is much easier to fight against an enemy and to want to be independent than to actually exercise the responsibility of being independent. We have seen this again and again in human freedom struggles. In the first elections after a fight for independence, there will be a 98 percent voter turn out. After 20 years, you are lucky if you get 40 percent of the people voting because it is a much more difficult thing to exercise independence than it is to fight for independence. Isaiah is faced with this problem. The people who have longed for independence, their own country and their own patrimony, their own city and their own temple, now have the opportunity of recreating all of this. But the truth and the reality are much tougher than the dream and the promise.

In actual fact, if we take the promise as literal, it never really happened. I went through the entire scope of Jewish history for myself and did a very quick analysis of it. I looked at what God's promise seemed to have been. I looked at the entire breadth from Abraham who flourished about 1850 years before Jesus, right through to the founding of the modern state of Israel in 1948: 3800 years. I looked at the promise that God seemed to be making and this promise was honored more in the breach than in the observance. In that entire scope of 3800 years, I found that for longer periods and more frequently, God seemed to dishonor this covenant with his people than he honored.

Let me just very briefly show you what I mean. God allegedly chose the 12 tribes of Israel. Within 1000 years, God had lost, permanently, 83 percent of his patrimony. Ten of the 12 tribes of Israel were destroyed in the year 721 B.C. when the Assyrians occupied the Northern Kingdom of Israel and they were never heard of again. So a quarter way into the history, God failed so badly to deliver that 83 percent of the people are lost forever; not a great record. What happened to the other 17 percent that remained? I went through it empire-by-empire and colonialization-by-colonialization and pogrom-by-pogrom and I estimated that for every year that God's people experienced self-government and freedom they experienced three years of exile and slavery. Not a very impressive record for God if this is what God is about: giving promises about political chosen-ness.

I looked at the Catholic Church and its 2000-year history. I looked at the scriptural foundation allegedly where Jesus says to Peter, "Thou art Peter and upon this rock I will build my church and the gates of hell shall not prevail against it. I will be with you all days even unto the consummation of the world." I saw that for every saint and every sage there have been sinners in high positions, that for every good work and every great mitzvah there have been crucifixions, persecutions, crusades, inquisitions, excommunications, intolerance and the inability to speak the truth. Not a very impressive record if this is what God means by being with us all days.

261

I came to the realization that the promise of God has nothing to do with institutions, ethnicity, or socio-theological covenants. The promise of God is a promise written deeply within the human heart. And it comes true for everyone who awakens to Christ-consciousness or Buddha-nature or whatever words you want to give it. It comes true for every single one of us when we open up our hearts to what God is trying to do for us.

That is what Christmas is about. Christmas is about the realization that God dwells deeply in the human heart and doesn't play favorites. God is not about covenants with groups of people. God is not about blessing institutions. God is not about having special relationships with particular organizations. God is the God who resides uniquely in the human heart: the image of God within each one of us of which the baby Jesus is a symbol. God is asking each one of us to be in covenant with her. God is not asking us to be superior to any other group of people.

The second point I want to make is this. I want to look at the notion of chosen-ness. Can we really believe that the ineffable God who is beyond all human categories, even the category of being or non-being, is peering down into the cosmos, looking at one hundred billion galaxies, choosing one galaxy and deciding to have a particular special relationship with the galaxy which we call the Milky Way? Can we really believe that God is looking down through this Milky Way of one hundred billion stars and is deciding that there is one particular star that she particularly loves which we call the sun?

Or can we really believe that God looks at the nine planets that dance around the sun perennially and decides there is one of these planets particularly loved and then picks out a spinning little orb and picks out a special nation, or a special religion or a special organization and says, "Yes, this is my special patrimony?"

It reminds me of a story of my two sisters, Eithne and Deirdre. Deirdre was a real domesticated little girl good at housework and knitting. Eithne was a tomboy who liked to play with boys. My mother, in one final but futile effort to domesticate Eithne, decided to hold a knitting competition between Deirdre and Eithne. She bought both of them yarn and knitting needles and a pattern for a sweater. She promised that whoever finished the sweater first would get a prize, hoping that Eithne would finally learn to be a little girl rather than be a little boy.

262

They slept in the same room and so the first day Deirdre knit furiously and she had about 18 lines of the back of her sweater done. Eithne only had about four lines done because she spent the whole day playing football with us. So Eithne woke up in the middle of the night and ripped Deirdre's knitting back until it was even with hers. The next morning they woke up and Deirdre looked at her knitting and said, "What's wrong with this picture? I thought I had a lot more done." She worked furiously the second day and she had about 25 lines done the second day. Eithne had done nothing the second day. The second night Eithne woke up and ripped it right back down to where it was and then Deirdre got the message.

It reminds me that so often it seems to us as if we can only feel special by destroying the work of other people, or that we can only puff ourselves up by somehow deflating the opposition: that we can't stand in our own right and realize that we are children of God, beloved of God: that we do not have to destroy each other or tear each other down or even compare ourselves with each other in order to be beautiful in God's eyes.

I have 18 nieces and nephews. I have a niece called little Deirdre and one called Martina and these two are sisters and there is only 11 months between them: Irish twins. Every three years when I came home from Africa, I would see these little nieces and one particular time they were about eight and nine years old. I had one sitting on one knee and the other sitting on the other knee. There is fierce competition between them. Deirdre said to me, "Uncle Seán, who is your favorite, Martina or me?" What am I going to say? And so I say, "I prefer you, but I'd rather Martina." She is still trying to figure it out.

Why do we constantly try to force God to decide among us? Do you prefer them or us, the black or the white, the Jew or the Christian, the Muslim or the Hindu, who do you prefer? What a question to be asking God. Our insecurity constantly wants to push God into choosing sides. Of course, there are no sides.

The third point I want to make is this. When we talk about the word of God, what is the word of God talking about in these passages from John's gospel? Perhaps the most famous text in the entire New Testament is this extraordinary poem where John says; "In the beginning was the word and the word was with God and the word was God. All things were created through him and without him was made nothing that was made. In him was life and this life was the life of humans. And the word became flesh and dwelt among us." I've heard many erudite explanations by Christian theologians and by scriptural exegetes telling me the meaning of this. The best talk I ever heard on it, however, was by an Indian guru in London in 1987. He was talking to a Christian audience and said, "You guys never got it. You think that the word of God is some kind of extraordinarily complex logos. I will tell you what it is. It is simply what it says. It is the sound of God creating. The word of God is the sound of God creating. All creation is through sound."

I began to think about how creation really sounds: the words we make, the noises we make and the words we speak to each other. How creative are they? In some sense, you could believe that all creation happens through the spoken word or through the sounds we make. There was an extraordinary festival in a city in Belgium about 15 years ago. They were celebrating 1000 years as a chartered city. As part of the celebration they commissioned a very famous musician to write a piece of music for the occasion. Instead of writing a piece of music he opted to do some musical experiments. One of the experiments he did was clamp a sheet of thick plate glass eight feet long and four feet high in an upright position. He poured soapy water across the spine so it flowed down both sides. Then he got musicians to play instruments in front of it. Of course, because of the vibrations in the glass, the most extraordinary patterns were created on the filmy water. Each instrument created a different pattern. Each note and each pitch created a different pattern. The Hindus say that sound is the beginning of it all. In fact, the special sound, "Om," they claim is the dial tone of the universe: that this is how God creates.

A second experiment that this famous musician did was to get people baking bread. One group was asked to sing and to pray as they were baking the bread and the other group was just asked to bake bread. Then at the end of this, he offered bread to people who were just coming in and didn't know the origin of the bread and he asked them which bread they preferred. He claims that with statistical significance, people preferred the bread that was sung over. Somehow there is an energy that comes from the spoken word and there is an energy that comes from music that builds love, compassion and concern into the fruit of its labor.

I think there is a significant difference between a Christmas dinner lovingly prepared by your mother and going to McDonalds's and being rushed through a line as someone barks an order into a microphone to some dude in the back whom you are never going to see. What is the quality of the food difference? Is it just about the fact that it is fast food? Or is there something about speaking words of love over the stuff that we are presenting and eating. I think of all the words we speak to our children, words that build our children or words that destroy our children. I think of the feast of Christmas, that the feast of Christmas is one more word of God. God continually speaks through every little baby; every single one of us is the word of God. At the creation of each one of us, God did something extraordinary. I have a personal theory that the big bang is the sound of God laughing ecstatically as she peers at the tiny universe that she has just created. That is the sound of the big bang and it reverberates in the birth of every baby and it doesn't matter what the baby looks like, what color the baby is or what gender the baby is.

Finally, I do not believe that the word of God is about most favored nation status. I do not believe that the word of God is about the one true church. I do not believe that the word of God is about a chosen nation. I do not believe that the word of God is about exclusive covenants with particular groups. I believe that the word of God is the sound of God's laughter reverberating through Jew and gentile, through male and female, through black and white. I would like to offer as my Christmas blessing for us almost the last words that Jesus spoke at the Last Supper and the very last words that John XXIII spoke when he was dying. For the last three days of his life, as this old man was slipping away from life, he kept repeating one phrase again and again and no matter what questions they asked him his only response was this phrase, "That all might be one." Little babies are as much the gift of God as was Jesus or Moses or David or Gautama Siddhartha, the Buddha, or any one of us. Every baby deserves to be conceived in love, carried in love, birthed in love, raised in love and related to in love. Every one of us is a gift of God, a prophet over whom God laughed ecstatically. We deserve to be treated with love.

ISBN 155395505-6